Facilitati

Palgrave Teaching and Learning

Series Editor: **Sally Brown**

Facilitating Work-based Learning
Facilitating Workshops
For the Love of Learning
Fostering Self-efficacy in Higher Education Students
Leading Dynamic Seminars
Learning, Teaching and Assessment in Higher Education
Live Online Learning
Masters Level Teaching, Learning and Assessment
Further titles are in preparation

Universities into the 21st Century

Series Editors: **Noel Entwistle and Roger King**

Becoming an Academic
Cultures and Change in Higher Education
Global Inequalities and Higher Education
Learning Development in Higher Education
Managing Your Academic Career
Managing Your Career in Higher Education Administration
Research and Teaching
Teaching Academic Writing in UK Higher Education
Teaching for Understanding at University
Understanding the International Student Experience
The University in the Global Age
Writing in the Disciplines

Palgrave Research Skills

Authoring a PhD
The Foundations of Research (2nd edn)
Getting to Grips with Doctoral Research
Getting Published
The Good Supervisor (2nd edn)
PhD by Published Work
The PhD Viva
Planning Your Postgraduate Research
The Postgraduate Research Handbook (2nd edn)
The Professional Doctorate
Structuring Your Research Thesis

You may also be interested in:

Teaching Study Skills and Supporting Learning

For a complete listing of all our titles in this area please visit
www.palgrave.com/studyskills

Facilitating Work-based Learning

A Handbook for Tutors

Edited by Ruth Helyer

 macmillan education   palgrave

First published 2016 by
PALGRAVE

Palgrave in the UK is an imprint of Macmillan Publishers Limited,
registered in England, company number 785998, of 4 Crinan Street,
London, N1 9XW.

Palgrave Macmillan in the US is a division of St Martin's Press LLC,
175 Fifth Avenue, New York, NY 10010.

Palgrave is a global imprint of the above companies and is represented
throughout the world.

Palgrave® and Macmillan® are registered trademarks in the United States,
the United Kingdom, Europe and other countries.

ISBN 978–1–137–40324–7 paperback

This book is printed on paper suitable for recycling and made from fully
managed and sustained forest sources. Logging, pulping and manufacturing
processes are expected to conform to the environmental regulations of the
country of origin.

A catalogue record for this book is available from the British Library.

A catalog record for this book is available from the Library of Congress.

Printed in China

I dedicate this book to Mary Allen.

Contents

List of tables and figures

Tables

Figures

Contributors

Pauline Armsby is the Director of Higher Education Research, University of Westminster, UK. Over the last 20 years she has developed and managed a range of WBL programmes from undergraduate to doctorate level for distance provision internationally, for higher education practitioners, and with collaborative partners. Her recent research and publications focus on professional doctorates and the accreditation of prior experiential learning.

Mark Atlay is the Director of Teaching and Learning at the University of Bedfordshire, UK, and has a long-standing interest in the use of credit to support student learning. Mark is a trustee of SEEC, a regional credit consortium, and of the UK's Centre for Recording Achievement (CRA). He has worked for the UK's Quality Assurance Agency since 1999, reviewing institutional approaches to quality assurance and enhancement.

Stephen Billett is the Professor of Adult and Vocational Education at Griffith University, Brisbane, Australia, and also an Australian Research Council Future Fellow. He has worked as a vocational educator, educational administrator, teacher educator, professional development practitioner and policy developer in the Australian vocational education system and as a teacher and researcher at Griffith University.

Darryll Bravenboer is the Head of Academic Development at the Institute for Work-based Learning, Middlesex University, UK. He is a principal fellow of the Higher Education Academy and has extensive experience of developing vocational and work-based higher education provision in response to the needs of a wide range of employment sectors in diverse professional contexts. His research interests include the philosophy and sociology of education, higher education policy, fair access, widening participation, lifelong learning and vocational, professional, work-based and employer-responsive higher education.

Helen Corkill is the Partnership Development Coordinator in the Centre for Academic Partnerships at the University of Bedfordshire, UK. She has written and presented on work-based learning within the UK and internationally. Helen works for the UK's Quality Assurance Agency and has also worked with other European organisations involved with quality assurance and enhancement.

Carol Costley is the Professor in Work-based Learning and Director of the Institute for Work-based Learning at Middlesex University, UK. She works with organisations in the private, public, community and voluntary sectors internationally in the learning and teaching of work-based, taught and research degrees. She has published widely on work-based learning and on professional doctorates, and chairs the International Conference on Professional Doctorates.

Jenny Fleming is a senior lecturer at Auckland University of Technology, New Zealand. She leads the cooperative education programme in the Bachelor of Sport and Recreation. She has a PhD from Deakin University, Australia, and a master's of science from the University of Auckland. Her recent research interests, including her PhD, have focused on work-integrated learning.

Jonathan Garnett is a senior research adviser at the Australian Institute of Business and Director of the Global Centre for Work-applied Learning. Previously he was the Director of the Institute for Work-based Learning and Professor of Work-based Knowledge at Middlesex University, UK. Jonathan has over 20 years' experience in the development and operation of work-based learning partnerships at higher education level in the UK and internationally.

Ruth Helyer is the Head of Workforce Development (Research & Policy) at Teesside University, UK, and a National Teaching Fellow of the Higher Education Academy. Actively developing the work-based learning agenda since the early 2000s, she has become an internationally acknowledged expert in this area and is involved in the development of numerous working students and their companies. Ruth is also the editor of the popular Palgrave book *The Work-based Learning Student Handbook*, 2nd edn (2015), and the editor in chief of the Emerald peer-reviewed journal *Higher Education, Skills and Work-based Learning* (HESWBL), the official journal of the University Vocational Awards Council (UVAC).

Mary Karpel is an educational consultant for Learn4Work and a part-time work-based tutor for Birkbeck College, University of London, UK. Following a successful business career in recruitment and training, Mary moved into the world of higher education and specialised in work-based learning and the accreditation of prior experiential learning. This included 18 years of lecturing at the University of East London, where she became Head of Work-based Learning, responsible for creating innovative undergraduate programmes that combined work activities with academic study.

Mike Laycock is an international higher education consultant who has spoken at national and international conferences, published widely, carried out much consultancy for UK HEIs and undertaken many national and international staff development workshops. While employed by the University of East London, UK (1972–2007), he developed and led an MA/MSc by Work-based Learning.

Ann Minton is the Principal Tutor in Work-based Learning at the University of Derby, UK, experienced in working in a variety of sectors to design and implement professional development requirements. She supports learners and tutors to articulate 'real world learning' into recognisable academic studies and developed the university's approach to accreditation of in-company training.

Andy Price is the Head of Enterprise Development and Education at Teesside University, UK, where he leads the university student entrepreneurship strategy. He has been involved in work-based learning for a number of years including leading the development of the ground-breaking BA in Multimedia Journalism degree course, facilitating numerous CPD courses for the news industry and working with Creative Skillset.

Ly Tran is a senior lecturer in curriculum and pedagogy at Deakin University, Australia. Her research focuses on teaching and learning in international education. Her book *Teaching International Students in Vocational Education: New Pedagogical Approaches*, published by the Australian Council for Educational Research, won the 2014 International Education Association of Australia Excellence Award for Best Practice/Innovation in International Education.

Tony Wall is a senior lecturer and Director of the Professional Doctorate at the University of Chester's Centre for Work-related Studies, UK. His facilitation of work-based learning and research with professionals across the globe forms a key strand of the research he presents in Europe, the US and Australia, and he has attracted multiple outstanding teaching nominations from students.

Anita Walsh is the Assistant Dean (Learning and Teaching) for the School of Business, Economics and Informatics at Birkbeck, University of London, UK, an institution that specialises in higher education for mature students. Her interest in terms of both research and practice focuses on the academic recognition of experiential work-based learning.

Barbara Workman is a freelance higher education consultant with a background in nursing and teaching. Based in the UK, she is also a National Teaching Fellow and Principal Fellow of the Higher Education Academy, with expertise in educational development, coaching, accreditation and facilitation of work-based learning across all higher education levels.

Series Editor's Preface

The Palgrave Teaching and Learning series for all who care about teaching and learning in higher education is designed with the express aim of providing useful, relevant, current and helpful guidance on key issues in learning and teaching in the tertiary/post-compulsory education sector. This is an area of sometimes rapid and unpredictable change, with universities and colleges reviewing and often implementing significant alterations in the ways they design, deliver and assess the curriculum, taking into account not just innovations in how content is being delivered and supported, particularly through technological means, but also the changing relationships between academics and their students. The role of the teacher in higher education needs to be reconsidered when students can freely access content worldwide and seek accreditation and recognition of learning by local, national or international providers (and may indeed prefer to do so). Students internationally are becoming progressively more liable for the payment of fees, as higher education is seen as less of a public good and more of a private one, and this too changes the nature of the transaction.

Texts in this series address these and other emergent imperatives, with a deliberately international focus. The particular issues addressed in this book around work-based learning are both current and important, and I am delighted to see this book in the series. Ruth Helyer is to be congratulated on bringing together a group of excellent authors who together help all of us working in higher education to better understand how we can help make learning happen for students in these contexts.

Sally Brown

Foreword

This unique publication provides a wide-ranging and practical guide to the field of work-based learning (WBL) in higher education. Ruth Helyer has brought together an edition that includes authors from a range of universities that have a long tradition of WBL programmes, modules and courses at their universities. This collective expertise has proven an invaluable asset to explaining the key concepts of WBL and also gives the reader a fuller understanding of its intricacies. Helpful case studies usefully provide concrete examples to demonstrate the complexities of WBL pedagogies.

The key curriculum structures are all addressed. The way learning from experience is inextricably linked to WBL is fully acknowledged and explained in detail. Reflection and reflexivity of the learner are integral to learning from experience and to all WBL modules; the theme of reflective learning runs through the book and is adopted in different ways by different authors. The frequently negotiated nature of the WBL curriculum is taken up with the inclusion of planning modules and learning agreements or contracts between university, student and employer or professional field. Finally, research methods or similar modules that introduce students to the processes of practitioner-enquiry are addressed, and this leads to the work-based project that equips work-based learners with an awareness of how developments at work can be moved forward using rigorous approaches to insider-researcher projects. The significant feature of the work-based project having a specific, useful outcome in the form of products that can make an impact in work situations gives the reader an important insight into the value of the work-based project.

Learning in, through and from work is explained as learning from real experiences. Working in teams, networking and connections with others are inevitable aspects of WBL. Facilitation skills to guide work-based learners are advocated rather than the teacher acting as expert conveyor of subject knowledge. Work-based learners are advised rather than supervised, and expertise in WBL pedagogy usually involves the use of technological tools and ideas such as virtual communities of practice. These flexible programmes of study are demonstrated to be rigorously quality assured.

The book addresses the multi and transdisciplinary nature of many of the approaches used in WBL. Creativity and innovation are now necessary to answer the questions of complex societies, and the WBL approach to programmes of study developed from perspectives of work, independent and experiential learning does not arise from single subject disciplines. WBL usually uses generic assessment criteria and focuses upon practice that has a particular work context and enables the use of existing expertise and self-directed learning.

WBL in higher education is responsive to societal needs and has expanded from a predominantly UK phenomenon to a more internationally known field. This book demonstrates its flexibility, its facilitative approaches and its capacity to generate knowledge production in practice situations. Other areas of higher education are now following the techniques and processes demonstrated in this book, and the growing awareness that all students can potentially benefit from the learning that happens in the workplace is addressed. The book includes information about placements and work-integrated learning as well as a detailed global terminology, which usefully recognises the overlaps and differing meanings around these terms. This is therefore a timely and relevant text for all higher education tutors.

Carol Costley
Director, Institute for Work-based Learning
Middlesex University

Acknowledgements

Acknowledgements and thanks are due to the chapter authors for sharing their knowledge and expertise and also to the case study contributors for supplying such engaging examples.

I also thank Teesside University for providing an environment where creating such a book is possible.

The manuscript would never have been finished without the amazing support of Neil, Max, Megan, Frankie, David and Dionne – so a heartfelt thank you to them.

Ruth Helyer, 2015

The author and publishers wish to thank SEEC, the HEA and SEDA for permission to reproduce copyright material.

Introduction

Ruth Helyer

▶ What is work-based learning?

It is common for learning and working to be considered separately, as distinct entities that are undertaken away from each other. Traditionally, education and training often take place independently of the workplace, with individuals not embarking on workplace activity until they have finished the required learning for that particular work role. In reality we continue to learn for our whole lives, and as much of our lives are spent at work, a good deal of learning takes place there. This means, of course, that learning isn't always official or prescribed; often it is informal, ongoing and unacknowledged, but lifelong.

The term 'work-based learning' (WBL) is used in UK higher education (HE) to describe the learning arising from real-life activity within the workplace – that is, what individuals and teams learn from undertaking their work tasks and interrogating workplace concerns, and it doesn't have to be paid work. WBL has gradually gained recognition within HE as it is increasingly acknowledged as a way in which to support both personal and professional development:

> Work-based learning is what is 'learned' by working – not reading about work, or observing work, but actually undertaking work activities. Interactions with others are often crucial ... this is learning from *real* work and *real* life and accepting how inextricably linked those activities are.
>
> (Helyer, 2015, p. 2)

There is immediacy to emergent learning, and WBL certainly helps workers to be capable and competent. However, at higher levels it also goes beyond this to encourage future progression and developments, and a genuine interrogation of practice, with the potential for new theories to be created in action (see, for example, the work of Chris Argyris). General and transferable skills, knowledge and expertise are created together with the specific and technical. Furthermore, evolving knowledge and capabilities are harnessed where they are most needed in terms of location and time-scale; responding to the challenges of what is actually occurring at work makes learning happen.

This book is about WBL at HE level (4–8). This kind of WBL can be facilitated and enhanced through higher education institutions, or HEIs as they are commonly known. HEIs include universities, further education colleges (FECs) and various other colleges and training providers, both public and private, which provide HE opportunities and have degree-awarding powers. The list of providers validated to provide HE will very likely increase in the future to reflect market need and commercial opportunity. However, these various venues still mostly have buildings and facilities that are typically educational. Work-based learners may use these facilities as a base to which they can bring their learning, but the practice of work-based learning itself generates knowledge from many different locations and situations, other than just the class and lecture room. WBL therefore questions the more traditional idea that knowledge is held by a privileged few who then pass it on through formal situations and in pre-determined ways. More detailed discussion about the features of WBL practice, and some work-based learners' experiences, can be found in Chapter 1, 'How does work-based learning fit into higher education?'

▶ Who is this book for?

This book has been written to assist tutors, mentors, trainers, lecturers and others who facilitate WBL, which can occur in many guises. With some of your students it will be very apparent that they are work-based learners who are learning through their jobs and then bringing this learning to their new HE course. When they attend an HEI they will require help in articulating what they have learnt already and advice and guidance about how to build on, use and progress their learning. In addition to this, many students also undertake formal training at work, which might already be professionally accredited, and they further supplement this learning and development, whether accredited or not, by simply carrying out their job roles and other roles in life.

Most people's jobs require them to solve real problems, sometimes problems that nobody else has ever had to solve in quite the same way; this requires ongoing but also instantaneous learning from the student/worker. This growing skill set firmly connects workers with HE-level learning, where graduates are expected to include 'problem solving' in their list of personal attributes upon graduation from their HEI (Helyer and Lee, 2014). Problem solving within a traditional degree might be accessed by the use of created scenarios; however, work-based learners are able to amass learning from solving authentic problems through their job, and furthermore bringing this learning and expertise to their HE course. During this process you actually learn a lot yourself as teacher, because learning in the workplace is 'situated, participatory and socially mediated' (Eames and Bell, 2005) and these elements have the potential to make HE more multi-faceted and realistic. Learning becomes reciprocal as your students' levels of expertise can mean that genuine knowledge exchange takes place.

▶ **What will you find in this book?**

This edited collection comprises chapter contributions from some of work-based learning's trailblazers and experts. The chapters have been put together with the aim of being clear and helpful; you will therefore find plentiful examples of innovative practice, case studies giving context from both the UK and internationally, exercises, activities, ideas and lists of teaching tips for you to use as and when they are helpful within your own practice. Some of this content might just be useful or interesting material for you, especially if it is an area new to you. You will also find that some of this information and advice also has resonance in your dealings with more traditional students as the employability and work experience of graduates is now strongly emphasised by the Government, by employers and by students themselves. Examining the way in which 'learning by doing' enhances WBL students' practices and profiles offers ideas, theories and useful context for working with *all* students (Helyer and Corkill, 2015).

Each chapter of the book tackles an interconnecting but different area or theme around WBL, with the aim of helping the reader to move their practice forward and enhance their learner's experiences. There are certain styles of learning, teaching and assessment which are particularly useful and appropriate for WBL, and these are discussed in Chapter 2, 'Learning, teaching and assessment in work-based learning', which reflects upon the influences of learning and teaching on work-based learners and interrogates different assessment strategies that might suit them and their organisations. Learning happens experientially due to the learner's engagement with what they are doing, and this engagement results in changes beyond merely acquiring new facts or data. Therefore assessments need to be capable of demonstrating deep learning and change. Chapter 2 discusses possible tools for this, including action and business plans, producing products, critical commentaries, group projects and more. The idea of collaboration, often frowned upon in HE, is viewed far more positively in the world of work, as is the idea that the carrying out of practice is itself proof of continuous learning, meaning that separate assessments are not always necessary.

One of the issues with this style of learning is that often the learner does not realise or acknowledge that it is taking place; it has become such a deeply embedded, and accepted, way of operating. Upon first contact with an higher education institution (HEI) employed learners are often surprised to find that what they have been learning (and more importantly using) at work is comparable in terms of difficulty to HE-level learning – and this can be demonstrated to them using level descriptors and learning outcomes from HE programmes. This process will make implicit learning become explicit. Using level descriptors creatively in your practice enables work-based learners to enjoy individualised programmes of study, which remain academically rigorous and transparent. Chapter 3, 'Flexible frameworks and building blocks', demonstrates how flexible frameworks are the key to designing and constructing a work-based curriculum by using work-based level descriptors alongside your HEI's quality policies and procedures.

▶ How can WBL be 'taught'?

WBL programmes acknowledge that learning also happens away from formal educational settings – outside the classroom – but that the learning requires facilitation of articulation and recognition at HE level. It is this facilitation process that falls to you as WBL tutor; you cannot 'teach' WBL in any traditional way; there is no pre-determined, content-based curriculum. Instead, you help and enable students to progress and build upon what they have already learnt using skills of negotiation (yours and theirs) and tools such as learning contracts, and personal and professional development planning. See Chapter 4, 'Negotiation and work-based learning', where the negotiation of WBL programmes is examined, explained and illustrated. This chapter discusses the elements of a WBL programme that may be negotiable within an HEI and the pedagogical theories underpinning such negotiation. Furthermore it details the logistics of documenting and approving WBL, and the significance of this for both you as a tutor and your students, and perhaps their employer. This process of negotiation is developmental in itself, requiring responsibility, self-management and autonomy in the learner, which is perhaps not so apparent when the process is pre-timetabled and bounded by modularity and semesterisation.

▶ What might it be called?

HE programmes devised specifically for work-based learners usually have titles like 'Work-Based Studies', 'Professional Studies' or 'Negotiated Learning'. The students attracted to these programmes have already learnt through their experience of work, and they bring this prior experiential learning to the HEI. The majority of learning from the workplace is not formally accredited with an HEI although much of it has the potential to be, due to its level of complexity and its originality and innovation; as the sophistication and level of the work increases, so too does the inclusion of research and theory. Often, work-based learners have their prior experiential learning – learning from actually doing – recognised as being at HE level using processes like the Recognition of Prior Learning (RPL), also widely referred to as APL (the Accreditation of Prior Learning). Chapter 5, 'Recognising and accrediting prior experiential learning', examines the importance of RPL/APL in WBL programmes through an overview of current pedagogic practices and theories of learning, including accreditation of company programmes and the use of technology to streamline the process. This chapter demystifies a challenging topic that regularly causes unnecessary worry amongst teaching colleagues but need not. It is often the case that all that is needed is a little more information, explication and some context, which hopefully we provide here. RPL above all supports the notion that practitioners learn from their practice. To gain academic credit for this learning, they may choose to retrospectively undergo the APL process, but the learning has already taken place.

▶ Experiential learning – it's the learning that counts, not the experience

The use of experiential learning in accredited HE programmes is sometimes unfairly criticised, as it is mistakenly believed that credit is awarded for experience. This is not the case; students do not gain any credit for experiencing the workplace passively. Learning requires active engagement: 'learning is the product of students' efforts to interpret, and translate what they experience in order to make meaning of it' (Cooper et al., 2010, p. 62). Students who claim credit for experiential learning must evidence this learning and the process for this is scrupulously overseen and examined (see Chapter 5). In order to successfully claim credit for experiential learning, students need to be adept in skills of reflective analysis. Often work-based learners are taking their knowledge, expertise and skills for granted; helping to make them aware of what they know and can do already is an important part of a WBL tutor's role. Effective reflection is long established in WBL practice, and it is vital in the process of articulating not only what is already known, but also where work-based learners can make useful connections and where they need to develop and progress. Research confirms that reflection on their WBL causes practitioners to review the values underpinning their practice (Siebert and Costley, 2013). Chapter 11, 'Learning to learn', explores this further.

▶ Core modules

As with other HE-level courses, WBL programmes usually contain some core elements, modules that are compulsory for your students. Chapters 3, 4 and 5 discuss this. Some HEIs have a mandatory RPL module that acts as a self-audit for work-based learners and guides them through the process of claiming credit for experiential learning. Learning to use research methods, sometimes called something like 'Practitioner Inquiry', is almost always a compulsory module, and this is definitely an area where WBL students appreciate some formalised input from a tutor. Although many work-based learners will have conducted practitioner research in their own work environment or within their life activities, they often feel that they do not have the skills required and that research is an alien concept. Work-based learners who are new to HE tend to associate research with traditional ideas of what they presume takes place within an HEI – an established part of a tradition that has the potential to make them feel like they do not belong. Chapter 6, 'Turning practitioners into practitioner-researchers', offers pedagogical scaffolding for work-based learners, ideas about research activities designed to value practical change and outcomes relevant to their own context. It is important to help these working students see the potentials and pitfalls of being an insider researcher and also to realise the value and new dimensions they can bring to a research scenario as an experienced practitioner.

▶ Student support – on campus and at a distance

Although experienced working practitioners, WBL students, like all students, require support from their HEI, their tutors and often their peers and employers. Chapter 7, 'Supporting work-based learners', examines the pedagogical differences in WBL that make specific support mechanisms key to its success and offers ideas for support that can be student centred and student led, with mechanisms to maintain impetus. Part of supporting work-based learners is ensuring that the flexible programmes of study they engage with are rigorously quality assured, in line with all other HE provision, as well as subjecting this provision to continuous quality enhancement. This process is not straightforward, involving as it does a learning experience that relies on several key stakeholders, including the educational institution, the students and their workplace. Continuous improvement can therefore be more difficult to instigate than in traditional educational settings. Chapter 8, 'Quality enhancement and work-based learning', identifies the key themes of quality enhancement important to WBL and is illustrated with some inspiring examples.

WBL students are not expected to frequently attend the campus, and social media technologies can help them to cope with learning at a distance. Although work-based learners might find themselves unable to be physically present at their HEI, due to work and other commitments, they do still need the contact and support of, and interactions with, others; after all, WBL occurs due to actually undertaking work tasks and this is often experienced with others. Technological tools, and ideas such as virtual communities of practice, can be useful, and Chapter 9, 'Using social media to enhance work-based learning', introduces the most popular social media learning tools and platforms together with suggestions for how you and your students might use and enjoy them for work-based learning. All students now rely on these technological developments to aid their learning, and the difference between WBL students and traditional students is beginning to be eroded; using technology is a good example of this as all learners can benefit from innovation.

WBL students are often distant from the campus, working at branches of their companies in many different areas of the globe, in real time. It is important to make sure that if these learners can use a computer, tablet, smartphone or similar and have access to the internet they are able to progress in their studies, build their networks and complete their assignments (and perhaps also submit them). Of course, this should also apply to all of our students, as they all need to operate in a fast-moving technological world, where being intuitive, connected and collaborative is increasingly presumed. Chapter 9 discusses how the technology now available as part of teaching toolkits can assist in the facilitation of this, in particular for those who are not digital natives. The contemporary multimedia assignments now encouraged by many forward-looking teachers are very familiar to work-based learners who have been compiling portfolios of evidence to back up their claims of learning for many years; it has just become easier to do this now (and perhaps do it more creatively) with picture, video and sound files.

▶ What are the students like?

The classic work-based learner is seen to be older, employed, only able to attend the campus 'out of hours', new to HE or in need of an HE qualification to remain employed/be promoted and so on (Helyer, 2015). These work-based learners will probably enrol individually on a 'work-based studies'-style programme or be required to attend an HEI by their employer, sometimes with a cohort of fellow employees. However, many of your existing students will be working as well as studying, so even if they might not be considered work-based learners in the pure sense of the term they will still undoubtedly be using what they learn at work to help with their studies, and vice versa; you only need to think of transferable skills like reflection, analysis, problem solving and so on. Chapter 11, 'Learning to learn', discusses these skills and points out the interesting overlaps between the diverse types of students who are experiencing the workplace in various ways and how they can therefore build up work experience, experiential learning and crucial skills. The meanings attributed to 'employability' are examined, together with the central role of analytical reflection. Reflection is key to self-analysis and metacognition, both crucial activities when conducting a self-audit of personal learning development and progression. Chapter 11 also introduces the idea of an entrepreneurial mindset, continuing professional development and individuals taking responsibility for their own skills development and lifelong learning, and suggests methods to help your students to demonstrate and articulate this learning.

▶ What can we learn from WBL? – cross fertilisation

Employed WBL students do not need to be sent on placements to experience the workplace, indeed they are invaluable in bringing information and knowledge based on real-life employability from their workplace into the HEI. Work-based students may require an HEI to formalise their learning into recognised qualifications but are often expert practitioners, sometimes more highly skilled in their precise area of expertise than their tutor (who operates as facilitator, rather than teacher). This can challenge the status quo and is a reminder of the learning happening in the workplace. The breadth and depth of knowledge and expertise demonstrated by work-based learners confirms the value of work experience and learning by doing: 'Students who just focus on their degree studies without spending time in the workplace are unlikely to develop the skills and interests that graduate employers are looking for' (Birchall, 2013); the experience of working with WBL students can therefore benefit *all* of our students.

There are many HE-level work-connected initiatives across the world, and Chapter 10, 'Learning in the workplace globally', offers some initial definitions in an attempt to not only provide some clarity amongst the growing terminology but also make apparent where the potential overlaps might occur, especially by offering examples. At the root of many of these initiatives is a belief in the value of the skills, knowledge and expertise that are gained from working. As overlaps can be confusing, we have taken this opportunity to spell out some of the similarities and differences between WBL, placements, cooperative learning and more. Chapter 12, 'A transcultural dance: Enriching work-based learning facilitation', investigates the multiple facets of being an international and culturally diverse work-based learner and reminds us of the exciting array of different perspectives international work-based learners can offer, which in turn can be viewed as empowering learning assets. The chapter also offers cross-cultural examples for evidence and inspiration.

▶ It is HE

The skills which work-based learners have accumulated in the workplace alongside their role, or sector-specific expertise and knowledge, are the very skills which HE claims to instil in its graduates, skills which have become ever more crucial as the world of work moves and develops at a growing speed and the employment market becomes increasingly constrained and competitive. Chapter 13, 'Promoting learning through work-based experience: Mimetic learning in action', brings the book to a close by sharing some of the findings of an Australian teaching fellowship in order to demonstrate how pedagogic practices and processes can support students, before, during and after participating in workplace experiences. The exponential rise of cooperative and work-integrated learning, especially in Australia and the US, using predominantly work experience placements, illustrates the usefulness of maximising the overlaps between learning at work and learning academically.

I hope the book provides a useful guide through this exciting, innovative and valuable area of higher-level learning by enabling you to make connections, grasp opportunities and progress your own practice.

Table 1.1 Key subjects and words

Headline chapter content	Chapter
Academic credit	Ch. 1, 3, 5, 7, 11
Accreditation	Ch. 1, 3, 4, 5
Accreditation of prior learning (APL)	Ch. 3, 5
Action learning	Ch. 4, 10, 11
Assessment	Ch. 2, 3, 4, 5, 7, 8, 9, 11, 12
Building blocks	Ch. 3
Certificated learning	Ch. 3, 5
Communities of practice (CoP)	Ch. 1, 3, 9
Cooperative learning	Ch. 8, 10
Credit accumulation	Ch. 3
Cross-cultural WBL	Ch. 12
CV and job description	Ch. 11
Degree apprenticeships	Ch. 10
Digital identity	Ch. 9
Employability skills	Ch. 11
Enterprise	Ch. 11
Entrepreneurial mindset	Ch. 11
Experiential learning	Ch. 1, 3, 4, 5, 11
Feedback	Ch. 2, 4, 5, 7, 8, 10, 12
Frameworks	Ch. 3, 4, 5, 6, 12
Generic/transferable skills	Ch. 11
Higher apprenticeships	Ch. 3, 10
International WBL	Ch. 12
Learning contract/agreement	Ch. 4, 7
Learning outcomes	Ch. 3, 4, 5, 8, 12
	continued overleaf

Table 1.1 Key subjects and words *continued*

Headline chapter content	Chapter
Learning styles	Ch. 1, 2, 5
Learning to learn	Ch. 2, 11
Levels and level descriptors	Ch. 1, 3, 4
Lifelong learning	Ch. 11
Mentors	Ch. 4, 7
Mimetic learning	Ch. 13
Modules	Ch. 3, 4, 5, 7
Multi-cultural WBL	Ch. 12
Negotiation	Ch. 1, 3, 4
Networking	Ch. 3, 7, 12
Online learning	Ch. 9
Peer support	Ch. 7, 13
Portfolios	Ch. 4, 5
Practitioner inquiry	Ch. 1
Practitioner-researchers	Ch. 6
Professional skills	Ch. 4, 11
Projects (WB)	Ch. 1, 2, 3, 4, 7, 8, 10
Recognition of Prior Learning (RPL)	Ch. 1, 3, 5, 12
Reflection/reflective skills	Ch. 1, 2, 4, 5, 7, 8, 9, 10, 11, 12
Research methods	Ch. 6
Social learning	Ch. 2
Social media	Ch. 9
STEPELO analysis	Ch. 2
Support	Ch. 7
Technological learning tools	Ch. 9
Terminologies	Ch. 10
Transcultural WBL	Ch. 12
Work-integrated learning	Ch. 10
Work placements	Ch. 4, 10, 12

▶ **References**

Birchall, M. (2013) in Coughlan, S. (2013) *Job Advantage for Graduates with Work Experience – Survey*, BBC News 13.6.13. Available at http://www.bbc.co.uk/news/education-22875717 accessed 14 June 2014.

Cooper, L. Orrell, J. and Bowden, M. (2010) *Work Integrated Learning – A Guide to Effective Practice*. Abingdon: Routledge.

Eames, C. and Bell, B. (2005) Using sociocultural views of learning to investigate the enculturation of students into the scientific community through work placements. *Canadian Journal of Science, Mathematics and Technology Education.* 5, pp. 153–169.

Helyer, R. (2015) Introduction, in Helyer, R. (Ed.), *The Work-based Learning Student Handbook,* 2nd Edn, pp. 1–12. London: Palgrave.

Helyer, R. and Corkill, H. (2015) Flipping the academy? How the recognition of learning from outside of the classroom is turning the university inside out. *Asia-Pacific Journal of Cooperative Education* (in press).

Helyer, R. and Lee, D. (2014) The role of work experience in the future employability of higher education graduates. *Higher Education Quarterly.* 68 (3), pp. 348–372.

Siebert, S. and Costley, C. (2013) Conflicting values in reflection on professional practice. *Higher Education, Skills and Work-based Learning.* 3 (3), pp. 156–167.

1 How does work-based learning fit into higher education?

Ruth Helyer and Jonathan Garnett

IN THIS CHAPTER YOU WILL:

▶ Look at the key characteristics of work-based learning
▶ Be introduced to the importance of experiential learning
▶ Be given an overview of some learning theories of particular significance for work-based learning
▶ Be introduced to Mode 2 knowledge and transdisciplinary learning
▶ See that both individual and organisational development arise from work-based learning
▶ Compare the similarities between work-based learning and other flexible pedagogies

▶ Work-based learning as an educational device

Work-based learning (WBL) is learning which takes place primarily at and through work and is for the purposes of work, although it is mediated through a higher education institution (HEI). Gibbs and Garnett define WBL as:

> A learning process which focuses university level critical thinking upon work (paid or unpaid), in order to facilitate the recognition, acquisition and application of individual and collective knowledge, skills and abilities, to achieve specific outcomes of significance to the learner, their work and the university.
>
> (Gibbs and Garnett, 2007, p. 411)

In the UK, WBL as an educational device is often associated with lower levels, but it can be at any level from 1 to 8 on the Qualifications and Credit Framework (QCF) (see Chapter 3). WBL at higher education (HE) level can range from a component of a course unit to entire qualifications at undergraduate, postgraduate and doctoral levels; it can be used to help young people integrate work and learning to help them enter employment, or it can be the vehicle that mature students choose to facilitate part of their continuing professional development (Garnett, 2012). WBL focuses on the benefits of real learning from real work.

A work-based learner can be in paid or significant unpaid (for example, voluntary) work. The key defining feature for work-based learners who are studying with an HEI is that the work they are engaged in requires the development and application of high-level learning (levels 4–8) in order for them to be effective in their work. Some of this learning requirement might come from formal learning, but, in most cases, the main source of learning will be the experience of work. Many work-based learners will already be well established in their professional area and are likely to be engaged with HE-level WBL for continuing professional development. Such learners are prone to having considerable knowledge and skills relevant to their work, and so a HEI work-based programme that allows for this pre-understanding to be formally recognised and become part of an integrated programme of personal and professional development is very attractive. This is demonstrated by the following Case study 1.1, where a work-based learner uses his existing expertise to make HE work for him:

Case study 1.1 Work-based learner profile (A): Andrew, a project manager

Andrew is in his mid-forties and has been a project manager for a multinational information technology company for the last 15 years. He chooses an HEI's work-based learning programme as it enables him to gain recognition for his project management and technical abilities and to plan a programme which focuses upon real-life projects of interest to him and of potential value to his employer and does not require large elements of formal classroom attendance.

Andrew does not have a first degree, but, on the basis of his extensive work history, it has been suggested to him that he could benefit from undertaking a university module designed to facilitate the development of a claim for RPL (recognition of prior experiential learning). The module takes Andrew through a process of guided reflection upon his experience and helps him identify his prior learning in the areas of project management and construction quality assurance. Andrew is required to articulate his learning achievement and supply evidence of it, drawing upon real-life documents and artefacts. The learning described is measured against HE learning outcomes and shows that he is already demonstrating learning achievement beyond that normally expected at undergraduate degree level. As a consequence of this evaluation Andrew is able to gain direct entry with advanced standing to a master's programme.

continued overleaf

Case study 1.1 Work-based learner profile (A): Andrew, a project manager *continued*

The next stage is Andrew to negotiate with the HEI and his employer a work-based programme of study that takes into account his own academic starting point and his personal and professional needs and aspirations. The programme is attractive to Andrew's employer as it does not require time away from work and provides HE-level support for Andrew to address a project of direct relevance to the company. The agreed focus of the programme is a review of the processes for project managers to report construction defects to the company. The aim of the project is to improve reporting so that the same mistakes can be avoided in the future.

This case study illustrates how RPL can provide the basis for a negotiated work-based programme that takes as its starting point the knowledge and capabilities of the individual learners and their employers, rather than being rooted in a rigid, prescribed programme of study.

Higher-level WBL in the UK developed from a range of initiatives funded by the Employment Department in the early 1990s (Brennan and Little, 1996) and benefited from a favourable policy context which valued graduate employability and sought to extend participation in HE (Mumford and Roodhouse, 2010). The employability and skills agendas have remained key to successive governments; their overlaps with WBL drivers are debated further in Chapter 10, 'Learning in the workplace globally', and Chapter 11, 'Learning to learn'. Although a small number of UK HEIs (notably Chester, Derby, Middlesex, Northumbria, Portsmouth and Teesside universities) have long-standing experience in delivering programmes created around work-based learners, it is still regarded as an innovative area of practice. Case study 1.2 illustrates the new and developing areas where WBL provides an ideal route for an innovative SME (small and medium-sized enterprises, with less than 250 employees) due to its flexibility, relevance and origin in the real-world workplace:

Case study 1.2 Innovative WBL routes: NAK Australia

NAK Australia is a wholesale distribution company that supplies hair care products. The company's mission is 'to supply hairdressers with an Australian-made range of hair care that exceeds the expectations of themselves, their staff and their clients in quality, value and service'.

The work environment is entrepreneurial, non-formal, non-bureaucratic and very fast. NAK management identified that their staff are a critical resource. The concept of learning to learn continuously and rapidly so as to keep abreast

continued overleaf

Case study 1.2 Innovative WBL routes: NAK Australia *continued*

of continual change in the sector is a key driver of the organisation. The most pressing problem was how and where did NAK Australia and its people acquire these ongoing skills without each member of staff undertaking many years of personal study within formal courses?

Over a number of years NAK staff had undertaken a range of vocational educational programmes, including a Diploma of Business and a Diploma of Management within a workplace environment. After completing these programmes some of their people decided to enrol on HEI business degrees; however, they found this more traditional education sometimes far too theoretical, removed from the workplace, irrelevant to NAK's needs and developed by academics not at the workface. They found methods of delivery inflexible in terms of learning styles and participants' previous skill levels.

They were introduced to the Middlesex University 'WBL' model by a consultant to the business; this programme was different, with learning focused on learning at work, learning through work and learning for the purpose of work. Through a Review of Learning module the programme recognised and awarded academic credit for previous learning and work-developed capabilities. Through NAK the Review of Learning module found recognition as a unique learning concept within the Australian HE system.

After taking part in the Review of Learning module, participants took part in further modules: Self-development Plan, Professional Practitioner Inquiry and the Work-Based Project.

The NAK students' success on the programme was related to several factors:

▶ The programme used 'WBL' methodology.
▶ The organisation was in support of developing its people.
▶ The HEI provided excellent resource materials to support the students.

The students were mentored and guided by a professional academic mentor who offered a combination of academic and practitioner credibility, together with a passion for developing people within a work-based environment.

The cohort all successfully completed the BA (Hons) (Professional Practice) and the general manager developed an Organisational Learning model with the following three strands:

▶ Accreditation and articulation
▶ WBL
▶ Mentorship

Dr Malcolm Cathcart, Middlesex University and Renee Ngaparu, NAK Australia

---

▶ Practitioners learning from their authentic practice

WBL derives from learning activities anchored in authentic practice and focused upon developing the practitioner's ability to solve the problems of their everyday professional job roles (for more about what it means to be a professional see Ions and Sutcliffe, 2015). Knowledge and skills developed whilst carrying out work-based activities are acquired in the situation and context in which they will be subsequently used, rather than in an abstract context (Collis and Margaryan, 2003, p. 726). Whilst this is not traditional classroom learning, it maximises learning wherever it occurs by combining the strengths of formal and informal learning opportunities and integrating work-based activities within formal courses. This can be seen to be a 'best of both worlds' scenario, which, if approached astutely by HEIs, can result in the creation of new, cutting-edge knowledge and an exceptionally appropriate and satisfying learning experience for the work-based learner, as well as the potential for learning and development for the HEI employees who get the opportunity to get closer to the workplace.

WBL cannot be 'taught' in a classroom sense; it arises from work practice and from actually doing rather than reading about it or only observing. Because of the nature of WBL, the tutor often acts as an architect, enabler and critical friend, rather than a subject expert. This change of role can cause difficulty for some academics, especially if they are accustomed to being the holder of knowledge that they filter out to their classes in a more traditional way. This method is not useful for work-based learners; with them the learning process becomes much more of a joint enterprise, where the tutor can potentially also learn a great deal about their student's jobs, industries and real-life work experiences. The most important role the tutor can take is that of learning facilitator, helping and advising their students about how to learn, how to gain credits and how to progress, building their confidence and demonstrating to them – using level descriptors, for example – that they are already operating in some areas at HE levels (see Chapter 2, 'Learning, teaching and assessment in work-based learning'). Often work-based learners do not realise or acknowledge how much they are learning at work, and WBL programmes can help them to make this implicit learning become explicit, as the following Case study 1.3 shows:

Case study 1.3 Making employees' WBL explicit: Articulating expertise in the construction industry

Ben was well known within his company as the expert on design and build contracting. The company was dependent upon him to such an extent that whenever they wanted to bid for design and build work, Ben had to be central to that process and whenever they had problems with a design and build project, Ben had to be on call. To expand their work in this area his employers realised they needed to understand more about the nature of Ben's expertise

continued overleaf

Case study 1.3 Making employees' WBL explicit: Articulating expertise in the construction industry *continued*

and how to share that within the organisation. They decided to facilitate this by sponsoring Ben's attendance at their local HEI, a university offering WBL programmes.

The programme commenced with an Initial Learning Review, which was designed to capture the learning from experience, at higher level, that Ben had acquired through doing his job and make it explicit. To achieve this Ben worked closely with a WBL adviser at the HEI to assemble a portfolio that evidenced his learning. This was made possible by actively reflecting on his experience and analysing this reflection in order to articulate what he had learnt. Ben provided real-life performance evidence of both his learning and the application of that learning within his portfolio. The WBL tutor supported and guided Ben through this process (see Chapter 5 for more on claiming credit).

The next stage was to use the supporting structure provided by a major work-based learning project module to produce 'A Guide to Design and Build', based upon Ben's learning from experience and to trial and refine this with feedback from a range of managers. The HEI provided support and scaffolding for this in the form of two modules.

The first focused upon the design of the project by considering the issues of practitioner inquiry and the second provided support for the actual implementation of the project – the creation of the guide. The role of the HEI's WBL tutor was critical at each stage in this process; as a critical friend during the Initial Learning Review the tutor was able to ask questions which helped draw out and make explicit the nature of Ben's knowledge and skills relevant to design and build contracting. The tutor was then able to facilitate the use of this information as the basis for the project work.

The resulting guide was not only academically rigorous but it was also exactly what Ben's organisation had hoped for.

▶ Distinctive features of HE-level WBL programmes

Boud and Solomon (2001, p. 1) identify a range of distinctive features of higher-level WBL:

▶ WBL is a partnership between an external organisation and an educational institution specifically established to foster learning.
▶ Learners are employees or have some contractual relationship with the external organisation and negotiate learning plans approved by the educational institution and the organisation.
▶ The learning plans are derived from the needs of the workplace and of the learner, rather than being predetermined by a subject disciplinary curriculum.

▶ The starting point and the level of the negotiated learning programme are established after a structured review and evaluation of the current learning of the individual.

▶ A significant element of the programme is WBL projects that meet the needs of the learner and the organisation.

▶ Assessment of the learning outcomes of the negotiated programme is carried out with reference to a transdisciplinary framework of standards and levels.

▶ Transdisciplinarity

The last point here mentions transdisciplinarity, a term increasingly used to describe the way in which work-based programmes at higher levels operate. Used in this context the term acknowledges that for work-based learners, research strategies and applications of theories will cross many disciplinary boundaries to create a universal, yet nuanced and hybrid approach, which is useful and appropriate for the context in which it is applied. As a term now increasingly used in academia and applied to scholarly activity, it recognises that much research focuses on problems that cut across disciplines and can refer to and utilise concepts, methods and theories originally developed by one discipline but which are now used much more widely. This has implications for the methods available to assess WBL and ensure that it is carried out within a quality-controlled framework of standards and levels.

A key feature of WBL-level descriptors is often the use of the word 'generic'; to reflect the transdisciplinarity of the work the descriptors integrate vocational, academic and professional aspects of learning, which can be applied to all learning contexts. WBL level descriptors therefore, usually have the benefit of general applicability to any specialist area of work/practice (Costley, 2015). (See also Chapter 3, 'Flexible frameworks and building blocks', and Chapter 8, 'Quality enhancement and work-based learning'.) However, the development of transdisciplinary approaches to work and learning is not merely a matter of WBL being applicable across differing work/practice contexts, but more importantly that transdisciplinary approaches support work/practice creativity and innovation.

▶ WBL methodologies

Along with a combination of research strategies and theory, WBL also utilises a variety of learning methodologies. Many of the learning approaches used in negotiated WBL have their origin in independent learning – a range of learning theories and approaches to learning such as 'experiential learning', an interdisciplinary approach based on the premise that experiences framed by reflection will lead to learning (Schön, 1983). One of the most well-known approaches to experiential learning is that of Kolb, who suggests that educational achievement depends on an individual's learning style as much as it depends on abilities and aptitudes (Kolb, 1984). Kolb views experiential learning as an active, self-motivated way of learning based upon a cycle that is propelled by action then reflection, and experience then abstraction. The learning theories of experiential learning build upon the research and beliefs of prominent 20th-century scholars of human learning and development, such as William James, John Dewey, Kurt Lewin, Jean Piaget, Lev Vygotsky, Carl Jung, Paulo Freire, Carl Rogers and more. Combining the work of these founding scholars, Kolb proposed six features of experiential learning and cited learning styles as the consistent way in which a learner responds to, or interacts with, stimuli in a learning environment (Kolb, 1984; Loo, 2002, p. 252). Kolb and Kolb (2008) devised an experiential learning model based on the original six propositions, suggesting that experiential learning is:

- best conceived as a process
- not defined in terms of outcomes
- about re-learning
- best facilitated by drawing out the learner's beliefs and ideas so that they can be examined, tested, and integrated with new, more refined ideas
- driven by conflict, differences and disagreement
- a holistic process of adaptation to the world

Theories of andragogy are germane when working with work-based learners, as they highlight the importance of treating adults as capable of self-direction in the learning process, and taking seriously their life experiences, not only as a potentially rich source of learning but also as a potential source of bias and presuppositions (Knowles et al., 2005). Adult learners need to understand why they need to learn something. WBL draws upon the principles of andragogy by valuing (for example by accreditation of prior experiential learning (APEL)) the learning from the experience of the individual learner and making them key stakeholders in a negotiated programme of study which also typically needs to take into account the interests of their employer or other interested group (for example clients if the learner is self-employed). The performative nature of andragogy complements work-based learners as WBL explicitly addresses the knowledge and skill requirements of work (see also Chapters 4 and 7).

WBL is situated and constructed at work; it therefore generally has an impact that goes beyond the learner and their academic facilitator. Often work based learners will be part of a community of practice (CoP), which is defined as 'groups of people who share a concern or a passion for something they do and learn how to do it better as they interact regularly' (Lave and Wenger, 1991). This often means that the work based learner is part of several communities of practice – perhaps one in the workplace, which is work-based, and another based at the HEI, where studying is taking place. This second CoP may well be made up of peers undertaking the same WBL qualification, although they do not necessarily have to share the same sector or subject background. Work-based communities of practice can provide a fantastic key resource for learning, as much learning happens in social settings and/or within a social context (See Chapter 9, and Smith and Smith, 2015). In this case 'social' does not necessarily mean leisure activities; it literally means shared and collective behaviours and events; however, learning can and will also occur in communities of practice which emerge around hobby and leisure pursuits, as well as the more professionally focused ones.

▶ Mode 2 knowledge and transdisciplinarity

Dalrymple, Kemp and Smith suggest that the more interactive and stimulating the pedagogical conditions, the more realistic, relevant and meaningful to participants the learning environment will be. Learning outcomes become beneficial rather than an afterthought, and the extent of inquiry and discussion goes beyond the level of defined academic content when work-based participants apply ideas to their own workplaces (Dalrymple, Kemp and Smith, 2014, p. 77). According to Revans, work-based learners will more readily take the risk of questioning their knowledge and practice when they have:

▶ freedom of informed choice
▶ a degree of control over the learning process
▶ responsibility for the learning outcomes
▶ the security and challenges of a group of peers (Revans, 2011)

In WBL the context and purposes of work are directly related to use of knowledge, and thus the nature of the value attached to that knowledge. This contests the supremacy of the role of the HEI in curriculum design, delivery and validation of knowledge and suggests that higher-level WBL should seek alignment with thinking and practice relating to knowledge creation and use in the workplace (Garnett, 2009; Abraham, 2012). HEI-constructed paradigms of knowledge and the systematic (research) process by which new knowledge is created and judged are increasingly contested. Consideration of dominant research paradigms suggests that no one paradigm is adequate to frame work-based learning 'research'. Gummesson (1991, p. 15) defines a paradigm as 'peoples' value judgments, norms, standards, frames of reference, perspectives, theories ... that govern their thinking and action'. The empirical positivist paradigm associated with 'scientific inquiry' is deeply rooted in the accepted understanding of research and holds sway over much of the general research literature and assumptions and expectations of higher-level research. In this paradigm the researcher is a detached and objective observer of the object of study; the resultant research concentrates upon description and explanation and is conducted systematically and logically via well-defined studies, which are governed by explicitly stated theories and hypotheses (see Chapter 6 for more about the modes of practitioner research that work-based learners and their organisations find useful).

▶ Socially constructed knowledge

In contrast to the positivist paradigm, WBL is, by design and necessity, concerned with knowledge which is often unsystematic, socially constructed and action focused by the worker researcher in order to achieve specific outcomes of significance to others (Garnett et al., 2009). These characteristics appear to fit more comfortably within an interpretive paradigm in which the researcher is an actor involved in the partial creation (through assigning meaning and significance) of what is studied. Research concentrates on understanding and interpretation and is conducted recognising that the researcher will be influenced by pre-understanding (Gummesson, 1991). In the context of work the value of knowledge is performative; it thus follows that sufficiency and timeliness of information to inform or bring about action are key considerations for WBL. The following Case study 1.4 illustrates the kind of research a work-based learner might want to propose:

Case study 1.4 Linking the workplace and academia through WBL research: A proposal for a practitioner research project

Project aim

The aim of my research is to investigate the ongoing factors that affect the implementation of health and safety legislation within a complex market environment in light of the recent legislative changes.

continued overleaf

Case study 1.4 Linking the workplace and academia through WBL research: A proposal for a practitioner research project *continued*

Issues of practitioner research and making the most of being an insider

I believe that my experience in managing large staff teams, and particularly managing people within the Silchester Market environment, will help me in enlisting the cooperation of the research subjects, especially the Market Tenants' Association, who do not trust 'outsiders' easily. For this reason, I believe my inside knowledge as a participant researcher will act as a clear advantage whilst carrying out this research, although I also acknowledge the disadvantages of participant observation, which I will look at in more detail later within this proposal. Equally, my knowledge of strategic and financial planning and managing operations will assist me in understanding and interpreting the qualitative data collected using a very simple pattern matching technique.

Research methodology

After discussing the practicalities of carrying out case study research with my line manager, including my positionality as a worker/researcher (which would allow me to make observations at liaison meetings, engage in email interaction and facilitate relatively easy access to both staff and tenants to collect the necessary data), I resolved that a single case study approach would be the best method to answer my research questions. I will gather data using the following techniques:

Direct observation: I intend to carry this out by impromptu site inspections and by attending market committee and liaison meetings.

Focus groups: I intend to hold two focus groups with frontline staff to obtain their views on the research questions.

Interviews: I will be arranging six semi-structured interviews with senior staff and a further six semi-structured interviews with prominent market members to obtain their views on both subject areas. I am aware that these two groups may have very different views, which will need to be analysed and recorded.

Analysis of work documents: I intend to review documentation such as Markets Committee reports, annual performance plans for the Markets Department and Food Standard Agency legislative guidelines.

Outcome

A report on the implementation of health and safety legislation in the market, which includes recommendations to improve future practice.

The work-based learner in Case study 1.4 has clearly focused on solving a defined problem. Nowotny et al. (2001) argue that since the latter half of the 20th century new forms of knowledge production have emerged which are context driven and focused upon real-life problem solving. Such knowledge is labelled 'Mode 2' as in contrast to 'Mode 1'; it does not fit neatly in traditional subject disciplines. Mode 2 knowledge recognises a diversity of knowledge production sites (such as the workplace) and is argued to be transdisciplinary in nature (Gibbs, 2015) as it is rooted in the messy problems of real life and is thus primarily emergent, complex and embodied, involving a reflexive approach to 'actors' and 'subjects' where the status and value of knowledge are negotiated with 'producers', 'collaborators', 'disseminators', 'users' and so on (Nowotny et al., 2003). Nicolescu goes further to suggest that the development of transdisciplinary approaches to work and learning is also a key aspect of leadership. 'It is recommended to universities to make an appeal in the framework of a transdisciplinary approach ... with the goal of developing creativity and the meaning of responsibility in leaders of the future' (Nicolescu, 2008, p. 9). Transdisciplinarity, as suggested above, offers us new and multifaceted ways to understand the intricate modern world, which are particularly valuable for constructions of WBL as a field of study as well as a mode of study (Garnett et al., 2009). This means that rather than taking as a starting point for practitioner inquiry the knowledge contained in the literature of a traditional academic subject, it is the real-life needs of work and the student as practitioner which drive the aim and the conduct of the WBL and possibly an entire WBL programme.

WBL provides an approach to individual development which:

1. is learner-centred; it takes the work context and work priorities of the individual as its starting point and allows the negotiation of a customised programme
2. provides recognition and accreditation of existing knowledge and skills
3. is located in the workplace and, therefore, does not require large blocks of time away from work
4. is focused on learning through work, which is relevant to both the individual and the organisation
5. provides a coherent framework for individuals to review and establish the lasting value of learning from short courses and experience
6. encourages and enables individuals to take responsibility for their own continuing development
7. enables the individual to be a creator of work-based knowledge of relevance and potential value to others

The following Case study 1.5 exemplifies (and is cross-referenced to) the above seven points:

Case study 1.5 Work-based learner profile (B): Acknowledging experiential learning

Karen is a personal assistant to a member of the executive team of a large HEI. She has over 30 years of work experience and has participated in many in-house development courses (5) but has no qualifications beyond a secondary school leaving certificate.

Within the HEI Karen was well known as a highly effective and extremely knowledgeable professional, but she lacked confidence in her ability to undertake an HE programme and described herself as 'only a secretary'.

With support and encouragement from her line manager, and from a work-based learning academic as a facilitator, she successfully completed an APEL portfolio (2) that demonstrated that she not only had knowledge and skills at undergraduate level but also had expertise which most closely mapped across to the learning outcomes of postgraduate modules in a master's in HE management (5).

This formal recognition of learning had a transformative effect upon Karen's confidence (6); she went on to complete an individually negotiated (1) work-based master's programme in HE administration.

The programme included major projects that impacted positively upon the HEI she worked for (3) by enhancing the administrative information contained within templates for memoranda of cooperation between the HEI and external partners. Karen was able to draw upon her years of experience and insight to work with colleagues from across all the central services as well as the academic departments of the HEI together with a sample of key partners to identify information gaps in the standard template.

Revised documentation informed by the evidence from this research was produced and piloted. The outcome was increased efficiency for the HEI through greater collaboration with external partners who felt consulted and subsequently more involved (4 and 7).

As the above Case study 1.5 encapsulates, WBL is an approach that has the potential to combine individual and organisational development. It does this by:

i.   providing a framework for the individual and the organisation to agree on WBL activities which contribute to the goals of the organisation and the aspirations of the individual
ii. recognising and developing the workplace as a source of learning, for example, through the recognition of formal training courses and learning gained from experience, which in turn is gained through work
iii. developing the individual as an effective work-based learner able to undertake research and development activity of direct relevance to work

iv. developing in the individual key abilities such as action planning, analy-
     sis, synthesis, evaluation, communication and reflection on practice
v.   providing a structured approach to 'real' work-based projects, which
     enhances their potential to contribute to the development of the
     organisation at levels from local operational to strategic
vi. providing a means of facilitating and measuring the transfer of learning
     from formal training courses to application in the workplace
vii. aligning learning and development activity with the goals of the organi-
     sation through programmes of personal development, which are work-
     based and required to demonstrate added value to the organisation
viii. focusing on the importance of knowledge as a key resource of the
     organisation

▶ HEI and employer partnerships

WBL has proved to be an effective means of applying higher-level expertise to
meet the business objectives of employers (Boud and Solomon, 2001). Such
programmes require the development of a genuine partnership between the
HEI and employer based upon an understanding of the business imperatives
and the related knowledge and skill needs of the employer. The HEI must be
genuinely willing and able to work in partnership with the employer as a provider as well as a consumer of high-level learning. For HEIs this might involve
no longer seeing themselves as the monopoly provider of courses and other
educational initiatives to augment the learning of employees, and instead
recognising that the employer may also have high-level learning formalised in
their own training programmes and organisational competency frameworks.
    The following case studies (1.6 and 1.7) illustrate further how individual
and organisational development can come together. Case study 1.6 refers
to the bullets i–viii above:

**Case study 1.6 Work-based learner profile (C): Embedding
organisational change in the UK financial services sector**

Part of the response of a national UK bank to extreme turbulence in the UK
financial services sector was to introduce a major change initiative to increase the
effectiveness of bank branch management teams.

    The focus of the nationwide initiative was to improve local-level business
planning and customer service. The bank worked with private sales training
experts to design a national in-company training programme that was developed
in partnership with an HEI (vii and viii).

continued overleaf

Case study 1.6: Work-based learner profile (C): Embedding organisational change in the UK financial services sector *continued*

The HEI contribution was to design and support work-based projects to be undertaken by course participants, which reinforced the transfer of the sales and planning training to the real-life work situation of producing the business plan for individual bank branches. By making the real-life business plan the focus of work-based projects, the WBL programme brought to bear high-level skills of analysis, synthesis and evaluation upon real-life issues critical to the success of the business (i, ii, iv and v).

A major evaluation of the programme was carried out by the bank which showed that those branches whose senior teams had been through the programme were achieving higher performance, using the bank's standard financial and customer service indicators, than the branches that had not participated in the programme (vi and vii). The impact upon individual members of staff was also significant as they greatly valued the opportunity to achieve an HE qualification and appreciated the relevance and value of what they were doing for their work (iii and vii).

Many commented that the WBL programme gave them a chance to gain an HE qualification that they would otherwise not have had. Senior managers also recognised and commented very favourably upon changes in their staff and how the use of 'reflection' had suddenly become a key tool for managers in their work (iii and viii).

Such were the business and personal benefits of the programme that the bank has sponsored over 600 participants.

Case study 1.7 Work-based learner profile (D): Organisational development – a company cohort undertaking a WBL programme

A WBL partnership between an Australian university and a leading retail bank was established in order to support and incentivise the professional development of a group of high-performing managers. The WBL programme enabled individual participants to claim academic credit for the learning that they had acquired through the successful completion of an intensive 'in-house' leadership development programme. Following a detailed programme review by the university, individuals completing the in-house programme were able to claim academic credit equivalent to a graduate certificate if they self-selected into a WBL qualification programme at a higher award level.

The bank recognised the importance of providing ongoing professional development opportunities as a means of retaining its high-performing staff and recognised that offering a development programme linked to the award of a university qualification would provide a powerful incentive. However, they were also aware that the significant financial commitment of supporting learners though an HE programme would be under regular scrutiny. If the value of the investment was not evident, the sustainability of the programme could be jeopardised. The

continued overleaf

Case study 1.7 Work-based learner profile (D): Organisational Development – a company cohort undertaking a WBL programme *continued*

view of a number of the bank's senior executives was that sponsoring university qualifications delivered little in terms of measurable performance improvement for the organisation.

The WBL approach provided an ideal opportunity for the bank to leverage its investment in their in-house programme and support the individual's ongoing development as well as enhance the organisation's business performance.

Upon commencement of the WBL programme, the employer and programme participants held detailed discussions to review business plans, and individuals' workplace performance requirements and professional development aspirations. Based upon these discussions, they identified either individual or team-based research and development projects, which were tied directly to the organisation's business plans. The supervision of an academic adviser would bring rigour to the way that the employees conducted their work-based research and ensured that this was appropriate to the chosen level of qualification.

For the bank, a mandatory requirement of these project proposals was that the work-based learners were able to forecast a return on investment from their work as well as meet the programme's academic requirements. The return on investment could take a variety of forms including increased revenues, improved productivity or cost efficiencies, but the anticipated value must equate to at least three times the cost of the employer's sponsorship of the qualification.

This approach was seen as a means of 'future-proofing' the university partnership and ensuring that the programme delivered measurable benefits to both the employer and learner.

Nicholas Shipley, Monash University, Australia

▶ **WBL round the world**

A number of UK HEIs have experience of providing WBL programmes outside of the UK, often with individual distance learning students or with collaborative partners or through their own international centres. A small number of international HE providers (notably in Australia and New Zealand) have adopted and adapted a WBL approach, and the underpinning educational philosophy of WBL has contributed significantly to more sector-wide developments relating to work-integrated learning and graduate employability (Hunt and Chalmers, 2012).

The following Case study 1.8 from Australia illustrates that the learning issues discussed here are global ones:

Case study 1.8 WBL alters the dynamics between 'tutor' and 'learner': Experience from Australia

Whilst educational concepts such as andragogy, Mode 2 knowledge and transdisciplinarity are increasingly features of individual units within HE qualifications in Australia, they are far less well known or understood as a valid basis for the attainment of an entire HE qualification.

These concepts present challenges to educators because they shift the emphasis of their traditional role from that of 'discipline expert' to a 'facilitator of learning', challenging the established perceptions and values of employers and students who are trying to reconcile the relative merit and worth of WBL when compared to traditional academic learning.

Research conducted in Australia to gauge the propensity of employers and learners to engage with models of higher-level WBL produced some unexpected findings:

▶ Employers appreciated the attractiveness of WBL models in terms of academic study aligning to workplace issues, and the enhancement of staff performance in the workplace.

▶ Fewer employers understood the relative value and portability of qualifications earned in a specific employment context.

▶ Employers generally did not understand the idea of awarding qualifications on the basis of learning acquired from an individual's professional experience.

▶ There was a general lack of awareness about higher-level work-based qualifications as a distinctive category of HE – with typical responses being, 'What is being recognised?' and 'Is this a real academic qualification?'

Just as HE educators are challenged by shifting their 'expert' role in the learning partnership, learners can also find it challenging to understand and accept their position as an 'expert practitioner' in the context of their work and as a generator of work-based knowledge.

For tutors, employers and students alike, the disruption to roles, relationships and accepted notions of HE learning requires an explicit repositioning of the work-based learning 'brand' as an HE offering. The process of education with WBL often extends beyond the learning programme itself to include a raising of awareness and acceptance of its fit with academic learning amongst a broad range of stakeholders at all stages of the engagement the process.

Nicholas Shipley, Monash University, Australia

▶ Where does WBL sit in HE?

WBL is flexible and innovative; it brings a different kind of student to HE. Barnett (2014) offers four critical components of a flexible pedagogy, and WBL pedagogies include these:

▶ Immersion (in a professional field)
▶ Reflection (analysing what is already learnt)

▶ Criticality (serious evaluation of learning experience)
▶ Interaction (listen, engage, collaborate)

Discussions around flexible learning often focus on the logistical processes rather than the philosophical debate as to 'why' we are doing this. Initiatives like WBL must be about more than a commercial response to students' busier lives (they cannot attend during the day and so on). It is about the evolution of learning and the realisation that knowledge can come from anywhere; it is not just housed in the HEI. What work-based learners know already, and bring with them to the HEI, has the potential for great collaboration, reciprocal learning and authentic knowledge exchange. HE is about making connections and progressing, and WBL certainly offers plenty of opportunity to do both.

SUMMARY

▶ Much learning occurs away from classrooms and other formal settings; WBL happens at work.
▶ WBL occurs at many levels; we are looking at HE level (4–8).
▶ Through WBL, learning from experience is identified and often awarded credit; no credit can be awarded for simply having an experience.
▶ Both individuals and organisations benefit from WBL.
▶ HEIs can offer structured frameworks to assist WBL students in creating their own HE awards.
▶ WBL draws on existing learning theory and is aided by social networks like communities of practice, which may also be virtual.
▶ WBL is happening around the world.

▶ References

Abraham, S. (2012) *Work-applied Learning for Change*. Adelaide: Australian Institute of Business.
Barnett, R. (2014) *Conditions of Flexibility*. York: Higher Education Academy.
Boud, D. and Solomon, N. (Eds) (2001) *Work-based Learning: A New Higher Education*. Buckingham: SRHE and Oxford University Press.
Brennan, J. and Little, B. (1996) *A Review of Work-based Learning in Higher Education*. London: DFEE.
Collis, B. and Margaryan, A. (2003) *Work-based Activities and the Technologies that Support Them: A Bridge between Formal and Informal Learning in the Corporate*

Context. Presentation at the conference Learn IT: Information and Communication Technologies and the Transformation of Learning Practices, Gothenburg, Sweden.

Costley, C. (2015) Educational knowledge in professional practice: A transdisciplinary approach, in Gibbs, Paul (Ed.), *Transdisciplinary Professional Learning and Practice,* pp.121–133. Switzerland: Springer International Publishing.

Dalrymple, R., Kemp, C. and Smith, P. (2014) Characterising work-based learning as a triadic learning. *Journal of Further and Higher Education.* 38 (1), pp. 75–89.

Garnett, J. (2009) Contributing to the intellectual capital of organisations, in Garnett, J., Costley, C. and Workman, B. (Eds), *Work-based Learning: Journeys to the Core of Higher Education,* pp. 226–238. London: Middlesex University Press.

Garnett, J. (2012) Authentic work integrated learning, in Hunt, L. and Chalmers, D. (Eds.), *University Teaching in Focus: A Learning Centred Approach,* pp. 164–179. Melbourne: ACER Press.

Garnett, J., Costley, C. and Workman, B. (Eds) (2009) *Work-based Learning: Journeys to the Core of Higher Education.* London: Middlesex University Press.

Gibbs, P. (Ed.) (2015) *Transdisciplinary Professional Learning and Practice.* London: Springer.

Gibbs, P. and Garnett, J. (2007) Work-based learning as a field of study. *Journal of Research in Post-Compulsory Education.* 12 (6), pp. 409–421.

Gummesson, E. (1991) *Qualitative Methods in Management Research.* London: Sage.

Hunt, L. and Chalmers, D. (Eds) (2012) *University Teaching in Focus: A Learning Centred Approach.* Melbourne: ACER Press.

Ions, K. and Sutcliffe, N. (2015) Developing yourself, developing your organisation, in Helyer, Ruth (Ed.), *The Work-based Learning Student Handbook,* 2nd Edn, London: Palgrave.

Knowles, M., Holt, E. and Aswansu, R. (2005) *The Adult Learner,* 6th Edn, London: Butterworth Heinnemann.

Kolb, D. (1984) *Experiential Learning: Experience as the Source of Learning and Development.* London: Prentice Hall.

Kolb, A. and Kolb, D. (2008) Experiential learning theory: A dynamic, holistic approach to management learning, education and development, in Armstrong, S. and Fukami, C. (Eds), *Handbook of Management Learning, Education and Development.* London: Sage.

Lave, J. and Wenger, E. (1991) *Situated Learning: Legitimate Peripheral Participation.* Cambridge: Cambridge University Press.

Loo, R. (2002) A meta-analytic examination of Kolb's learning style preferences among business majors. *The Journal of Education for Business.* 77 (5), pp. 252–256.

Mumford, J. and Roodhouse, S. (Eds.) (2010) *Understanding Work-based Learning,* London: Gower.

Nicolescu, B. (Ed.) (2008) *Transdisciplinarity: Theory and Practice.* Cresskill, NJ: Hampton Press.

Nowotny, H., Scott, P. and Gibbons, M. (2001) *Re-thinking Science: Knowledge and the Public in an Age of Uncertainty.* Cambridge: Polity Press.

Nowotny, H., Scott, P. and Gibbons, M. (2003) Mode 2 Revisited: The New Production of Knowledge. *Minerva.* 41, pp. 179–194.

Revans, R. V. (2011) *The ABC of Action Learning.* Farnham: Gower.

Schön, D. A. (1983) *The Reflective Practitioner: How Professionals Think in Action.* New York: Basic Books.

Smith, S. and Smith, L. (2015) Social learning: Supporting yourself and your peers, in Helyer, R. (Ed.), The *Work-based Learning Student Handbook*, 2nd Edn, London: Palgrave.

▶ Recommended further reading

Engestrom, Y. (2004) New forms of learning in co-configuration work. *Journal of Workplace Learning.* 16 (1/2), pp. 11–21.

Garnett, J. (2012) Authentic work integrated learning, in Hunt, L. and Chalmers, D. (Eds.), *University Teaching in Focus: A Learning-Centred Approach,* pp. 164–179. Melbourne: ACER Press.

Hager, P., Lee, A. and Reich, A. (2012) Problematising practice, reconceptualising learning and imagining change, in Hager, P., Lee, A. and Reich, A. (Eds), *Practice, Learning and Change: Practice-Theory Perspectives on Professional Learning* (pp. 1–14). Dordrecht: Springer.

Helyer, R. (2011) Aligning higher education with the world of work, *Higher Education. Skills and Work-based Learning.* 1 (2), pp. 95–105.

Helyer, R. (Ed.) (2015) *The Work-based Learning Student Handbook*, 2nd Edn, London: Palgrave.

Helyer, R. and Lee, D. (2012) The twenty-first century multiple generation workforce: Overlaps and differences but also challenges and benefits. *Education and Training.* 54 (7), pp. 545–578.

Helyer, R. and Lee, D. (2014) The role of work experience in the future employability of higher education graduates. *Higher Education Quarterly.* 68 (3), pp. 348–372.

Kolb, A. and Kolb, D. (2008) Learning styles and learning spaces: Enhancing experiential learning in higher education. *The Academy of Management, Learning and Higher Education.* 4 (2), pp. 193–212.

Nicolescu, B. (2010) *Disciplinary Boundaries – What are They and How They Can Be Transgressed? Paper Prepared for the International Symposium on Research across Boundaries.* Luxembourg: University of Luxembourg. Available at http://basarab. nicolescu.perso.sfr.fr/Basarab/Docs_articles/Disciplinary_Boundaries.htm#_ftn1, accessed 24 June 2015.

Raelin, J. (1997) A model of work-based learning. *Organization Science.* 8 (6), pp. 563–578.

Raelin, J. (2008) *Work-based Learning: Bridging Knowledge and Action in the Workplace.* San Francisco: Jossey-Bass.

2 Learning, teaching and assessment in work-based learning

Barbara Workman and Ruth Helyer

IN THIS CHAPTER YOU WILL:

▶ Consider the influences of teaching, learning and assessment aimed at work-based learners: how it affects them, their organisation and their higher education institution

▶ Reflect on learning strategies that work-based learning involves

▶ Consider how to maximise learning opportunities from the workplace – for the learners, their organisation and their higher education institution

▶ Reflect on the change in role from 'teacher' to 'facilitator' in work-based learning and gain further understanding as to how to develop your own skills as a facilitator

▶ Develop awareness of different work-based assessments and how these might suit diverse purposes for learners

---

▶ Flexible pedagogies for work-based learners

Participants in higher education (HE) work-based learning (WBL) programmes are predominantly full-time adult workers who are studying alongside their work, so ideally these programmes should be delivered part time using pedagogical approaches that encompass flexible learning delivery as well as flexible programme access. The workplace is the primary site of learning, with a strong emphasis on experiential learning and practical application of knowledge and skills, often through work-based activities such as projects and problem solving (Nixon et al., 2006, Ball and Manwaring, 2010).

▶ Learning strategies

Modern workplaces are complex, challenging and changing rapidly, particularly in relation to technology skills and business demands. In a time of change it is often easier to focus on what you do know, rather than look outside of your comfort zone to stretch your knowledge and understanding of a complex environment. Facilitated WBL aims to:

▶ Build learners' capabilities to encounter and manage change
▶ Engage learners with new ideas and develop problem-solving and inquiry skills
▶ Develop confidence in what the learner already knows and can do

Significantly, work-based learners are adults and bring their own prior experiential learning with them. This will include their education journey, and both the good and bad experiences this may have provided, together with their work experiences, which may have been rigid, flexible, repetitive, creative or restrictive. Past experiences of learning have a profound influence on how learners engage with current and future academic work and how they are then motivated to develop professionally and personally. When working with work-based learners, you will need to appreciate their learning journey, the impact that it may have had on their readiness to learn and their internal and external motivations to learn. This becomes even more crucial when supporting students through challenging times in their programme, when they may be struggling with competing priorities for their time and attention and are therefore in need of strong motivational factors and support systems to keep them on track (see Chapter 7).

Brookfield (1986) emphasises that adult learners are not beginners but bring previous unique learning experiences and expectations to their new programmes. They will have their own set patterns of learning already in place, which may have to change as a result of new learning; this can be unsettling. Knowles et al. (2005) confirm the importance of prior experience for adult learners and the influence and assumptions that experience brings. They suggest some drivers for adults who are returning to formalised learning, including:

▶ The relevance of the learning
▶ The ability to be self-directing and self-determining in learning outcomes
▶ The motivation of application to real life

These factors are fundamental; the learners' 'need to know' encourages them to become self-directed in their pursuit of learning. It might help you relate to the demands upon your work-based students if you consider yourself as a work-based learner. The Case study 2.1 below illustrates how we learn from doing, from our work practices and from our colleagues, even if we often do not acknowledge it:

Case study 2.1 Making WBL explicit: Studying for a Postgraduate Certificate in Learning and Teaching in Higher Education

This Postgraduate Certificate in Learning and Teaching in Higher Education includes a module called 'Teaching Work-Based Learners'. WBL occurs in the workplace where the work activity, problem solving, discussions and developments are happening and therefore cannot be 'taught'. However, the lecturers and tutors who facilitate learning for these kinds of students can develop their teaching methods and expertise to fully encompass what is useful and appropriate and even innovative.

When trying to explain to a class of new lecturers what exactly it means to be a work-based learner, the module tutor used the class themselves as her example, saying, 'You are all work-based learners'. The lecturers looked horrified as if they had been insulted. They thought of themselves as aspiring to be 'lecturers' and 'academics', not workplace practitioners, but the truth was the following:

▶ They were at work (the sessions were all on the campus).
▶ They were learning more about their work (the sessions were all aimed at their workplace practice).
▶ They were studying for their job (they all wanted to be better at their jobs and 'get on').
▶ They were part of a discernible community of practice.
▶ They were bringing to the classes what they knew already.
▶ They were practitioners already started on careers, however fledgeling.
▶ Many also had collected vast experience from life and different employment sectors.

Although initially unhappy with the tutor's suggested identity, by the end of the module, when they knew a lot more about WBL, all of the students agreed with the tutor that they were indeed WBL. Furthermore, by then they were proud of the title, because they actually understood it and appreciated the complexity and expertise it suggested.

As the above Case study 2.1 suggests, work-based learners are multifaceted individuals. Designing learning activities and strategies to engage such complex experts requires an understanding of different learning styles. Undertaking your own learning style assessment such as VARK (Visual, Auditory, Reading, Kinasethetic Learning Styles, see http://www.vark-learn.com/english/page.asp?p=categories) or Honey and Mumford's (2006) learning styles inventory (Atherton, 2013) may help your teaching to move away from traditional HE methods and towards approaches that are student-centred and interactive and resonate with work-based learners. Developing your understanding of the sectors in which your learners work will also give you insights into their preferred learning approaches. For example, many engineers enjoy problems to solve which involve hands-on practical experience, whereas research shows that many nurses are activists and may be keen to leap into a learning activity before having all the information available.

▶ Purposeful reflection

Whatever the learners' preferred approach one of the most important skills for work-based learners to develop is purposeful reflection, as this helps them to consider their other skills (see Chapter 11, 'Learning to learn').

Teaching tips: Reflection	
Some commonly asked questions about reflection and learning approaches are detailed below:	
Question	**Answer**
How do I develop reflective learning approaches and give my WBL students the tools to capture their progression?	Introduce WBL students early to the use of reflective models and the different modes of reflection, such as keeping a learning journal (see Chapter 11).
How can I encourage a culture of continuing professional development (CPD) in my WBL students?	Encourage work-based learners to reflect on their CVs and job descriptions. If they analyse the content to highlight new skills and knowledge that has been learnt in each job role, this will evidence the knowledge and skills they have already.
How do I help my students evidence their learning for job and promotion interviews?	Encourage them to keep a record of learning approaches that work well for them.
How do I encourage my students to keep good records and to reflect on their learning?	Ask them to record challenges and solutions that helped them to develop autonomy in problem solving and overcoming study and work difficulties. They will reflect on the usefulness of these later.

Developing your own reflective skills will help you to help your students. Try the activity below:

ACTIVITY

In your tutor role try to consciously adopt reflective learning methods yourself; this will maximise reciprocal learning and help you to better understand your WBL students. Go through the stages outlined below:

▶ Reflect on what you have learnt from work in the last two to five years.
▶ Was this through 'formal' taught learning?
▶ Or 'informal' learning, in that you learnt through 'doing'?
▶ How could you use these insights in supporting your work-based learners and helping them to identify learning experiences?
▶ What is your preferred learning style?
▶ How does that influence your teaching style?
▶ How could you explore other approaches to teaching and learning in your own workplace/higher education institution (HEI)?
▶ What development opportunities are available to you to experience a range of alternative learning and teaching approaches?

▶ Context

A climate conducive to learning encourages students to engage in relevant learning activities, particularly if supported by a tutor who facilitates learning rather than teaching didactically. A facilitative style encourages the learner to become self-directed and involved in their own process of learning (Ball and Manwaring, 2010). For example, work-based learners are often less inclined to be academically orientated (focusing on theories and models) but more likely to be pragmatic and action-orientated, finding the application of theory to their own practice more engaging than studying theory in isolation or seemingly for its own sake. Understanding work-based learners' needs, and catering for their varying learning styles, is a good place to start when adapting your teaching methods to accommodate them. Developing your understanding of your learners' work context is core to offering relevant learning opportunities. You might find it helpful for your students to undertake the activity on page 38 (STEPELO analysis, Workman, 2007) in order to appreciate the range of factors that could influence them. Ask them to complete the grid with the factors which have an impact on their learning opportunities and activities:

ACTIVITY: STEPELO Analysis			
S	Sociological trends	*These affect business, location and career*	
T	Technical factors	*Influence business and learning strategies*	
E	Environmental	*Considerations that impact work, such as sustainability*	
P	Political	*Both internal and external political agendas and drivers*	
E	Ethical	*Values that inform business and relationships, ways of working and studying*	
L	Legal	*Legislation that constrains or enhances business opportunities or learning, such as intellectual property rights, data protection*	
O	Organisation	*Different types of public, private, voluntary sector organisations, profit making, service provision and resultant priorities and values*	

Rich information will hopefully be gathered from this STEPELO analysis that will help you to extend your understanding of your learners' work environment and the learning opportunities available to them. Are there opportunities for you to build relationships, for example, with the employer/professional body/sector skills council, who may enhance your understanding of your WBL students' employment sector?

The STEPELO information will also enhance your knowledge of what type of learning activities your learners are exposed to in the workplace, who supports these work activities and how this is physically done. Furthermore, what are the potential implications for yourself with regard to preparing such supporters? If your learners' understanding of their organisation needs to be enhanced to a more strategic level within it, how can you help them to do this? The following teaching tips offer more ideas in this area:

Teaching tips: Helping your WBL students understand their work environment and associated learning opportunities

▶ Use learning agreements/contracts to help to determine workplace resources, learning culture and support (see also Chapters 4 and 7).

continued overleaf

> **Teaching tips: Helping your WBL students understand their work environment and associated learning opportunities** *continued*
>
> ▶ Emphasise the power of professional networks and strategic business contacts; encourage networking by building it into the assessment process, for example, the creation of a professional blog.
> ▶ Use analytical tools such as SWOT and PEST to investigate the structures and strategies within their organisation.
> ▶ Use a self-audit module – often found at the commencement of a work-based studies course (see Chapter 5).
> ▶ Use work-based projects to help students adopt new models and theories to their own context, which can enhance the relevance of the learning.
> ▶ Use the learners' own real-work scenarios as case studies, examples and discussion opportunities to give authenticity to the learning process.

▶ Maximise learning opportunities

Talk to your students about their sectors and organisations; this will help you to orientate yourself to their world and the possible learning opportunities available to them. Learning in the workplace takes a number of forms, but four main routes are common:

▶ skills based (performative)
▶ problem based
▶ project based
▶ social learning (Hardacre and Workman, 2010)

Each of these requires a different approach from the tutor and learner, as well as having implications for colleagues. For example:

The **skills-based** approach commonly prepares individuals for technical skills such as professional competencies and involves a work-based assessor, but it might also offer the learning of soft skills such as management techniques, which would require a manager's cooperation.

Problem-based learning occurs frequently in the workplace, although it is rarely acknowledged as such. It tends to be multidimensional, potentially involving a cross section of people and departments, and can therefore be influential in changing work practices in order to solve the problem. Consequently it may include other stakeholders in a business and provide an ideal environment for learning strategic business skills and developing professional networks for the student worker.

Project-based learning may arise from a specific project allocated to the learner and his/her colleagues in the workplace as part of the 'day job'; however, the project may benefit considerably from academic input and support.

Such **problem-based** and **project-based** learning often contributes to any RPL (recognition of prior learning) claim an individual might have; they both represent significant sources of previous informal learning (see Chapter 5).

Social learning also occurs through work. It is used to instil professional behaviour and attitudes and to socialise individuals into ways of working that may promote entry into a profession through 'situated learning' (Lave and Wenger, 1991; Smith and Smith, 2015). It can develop the 'employ-ability' skills that employers desire from new graduates (Helyer and Lee, 2014 and Chapter 11), and they always need enhancing and developing in order to facilitate continued employment, oppurtunity for promotion and career change.

The following Case study 2.2 demonstrates an approach to **problem-based** learning as work-based learners engage with HE to update their skills in a fast-moving area of practice:

Case study 2.2 Engaging with real-life problem-based learning: Teaching body location and recovery in forensic contexts

A skills gap was identified by regional police forces when processing crime scenes involving human remains and requiring anthropological and archaeological skills.

A collaborative course devised between Durham and Teesside universities offered the best solution by amalgamating the forensic expertise at Teesside with the archaeological and osteological expertise and facilities at Durham.

The course offers scientific support managers and crime scene investigators cutting-edge knowledge and practical expertise in body recovery and analysis; it was created in consultation with Cleveland, Humberside and Durham police authorities.

'It was important to collaborate on the design to meet practical, financial and logistical requirements, whilst ensuring that the learning outcomes and mode of delivery were appropriate.'

The course interspersed lectures with practical laboratory sessions to ensure learning was 'hands on' for the range of practitioners. To discourage student passivity in learning, knowledge from the lectures was directly applied to a series of practical student tasks, involving observation, recording, and practising different techniques. Simulation exercises established a deeper understanding of the locating and excavating of graves.

> Multiple 'mock graves' were simulated containing cast skeletons and 'personal effects'. The students had to locate the graves using a variety of field survey and remote sensing techniques and then excavate the 'bodies' using appropriate methods. Real-life forensic case studies were also used; the students abstracted the knowledge that they learnt during the course to these different scenarios.

The course has:

▶ Run for six years
▶ Trained over 80 forensic practitioners from around the world
▶ Improved cost efficiency in the region

continued overleaf

Case study 2.2 Engaging with real-life problem-based learning: Teaching body location and recovery in forensic contexts *continued*

▶ Maximised evidence retrieval and interpretation at a range of crime scenes in the region
▶ Directly caused the application of academic research to acute 'real-life' situations
▶ Gained approval from The Chartered Society of Forensic Sciences

'Using real cases and students' actual practice has contributed to the success of the course, particularly by applying the latest scientific research to current practitioner practice. This has had immediate impacts; insights from the course have altered the evidential approach to ongoing police investigations.'

Knowledge transmission is a two-way process; practitioners also inform tutors of their current research imperatives. This has resulted in a research project with Durham police cadaver dog handlers to address key questions regarding decomposition, which will co-produce practice and research knowledge.

The course continues to evolve, currently extending to encompass national and international agencies recovering bodies from areas of conflict and mass violence.

R. Gowland, Durham University and T. Thompson, Teesside University

Within this case study the work-based learners' learning is scaffolded; despite the reduction in formal class teaching there is ample engagement with the appropriate theories and academic infrastructure. If using such an approach, what would you need to put in place to guide your own students through a successful learning process? (see Chapter 3 for more information on frameworks).

Teaching tips: Considering your students' practice

Before you devise learning activities for your students it is important to ask questions about their practice, for example:

▶ What does the learner need to 'know' and 'do'?
▶ Where, or who, are their sources of information and support?
▶ What does the learner need from you?
▶ What is their expertise?
▶ Who asks them for advice?
▶ What sorts of projects are they involved in?
▶ What does their manager or professional body expect/require from them?
▶ You need to understand future developments coming up in your students' profession causing imminent changes in their practice, and what they need to do to prepare for this?
▶ What are the expectations or development needs identified in their annual appraisal?

continued overleaf

Teaching tips: Considering your students' practice *continued*

▶ What products or outputs would be the evidence of significant learning for your learners?

ACTIVITY

▶ Discuss in depth with the work-based learner, and employer where possible, what learning activities are available in-house for their professional development. Consider: *study days, secondments, work shadowing, professional body courses, projects, new product orientation*

▶ Together identify a learning activity which stretches them academically but is also highly relevant to their daily work. Consider: *undertaking a management task under supervision, accessing, analysing and investigating organisational and national policies and procedures to inform their practice*

▶ Remember the employer's perspective – what needs to be factored in to meet their requirements? Consider: *time in or out of the work environment and consequent replacement costs, skills training and supervision, identification of appropriate workplace mentors*

▶ Facilitation

Because the work context takes precedence over the subject content work-based learning cannot be 'taught'. Instead the teacher becomes a facilitator of learning, offering tools, techniques and support for inquiring within a work environment. Even if you have experience in a professional sector, the learner will come from a different context and is the expert in their own workplace. You will find there are many similarities but some significant differences between workplaces, so, for example, management tools and approaches may be transferable, but organisational politics and personalities will vary considerably.

Facilitating means to ease, support, enable and assist; when applied to learning it means that rather than providing content, the tutor uses a constructive dialogue and their questioning and listening skills (Raelin, 2008). Previous experience in mentoring and coaching can be useful in developing facilitator skills as both practices aim to lead to positive changes in the learner's self-knowledge by encouraging autonomy in learning. Costley et al. (2010) make some useful suggestions regarding facilitating research within WBL and similarly emphasise the change of focus from 'supervisor' to 'facilitator'. The work-based tutor's role develops from that of 'sage on the stage' to more of 'guide on the side' (King, 1993). Supporting work-based learners has considerable overlaps with advising research students (see Boud and Costley, 2007).

The focus has to be on the learner's context and needs, not what the HEI has to offer; that may not be perceived by the employer as appropriate or relevant. Great tact may be required when dealing with students, their employers and their individual situations, and ingenuity may be necessary when developing problem-solving skills due to potential resistance to ideas external to the company. You will need to include the employer's perspective when organising learning activities and cater for a tripartite approach to negotiating learning requirements (see Chapters 4 and 7).

▷ Becoming a learning facilitator

In becoming a learning facilitator you should do everything you can to help your students to identify what they need to know and how they will go about it; this will help them to plan their learning journey (see Chapter 4). Try to enable your students to appreciate that by undertaking learning they change their knowledge, skills, and attitudes, which in turn affects their future life choices. As a WBL tutor you should do whatever you can to develop your own understanding of the learning theories, which can facilitate a variety of learning styles and approaches, therefore enabling learning that is 'fit for purpose'. Develop your students' ability to critique and question their own assumptions and values; they will need to evidence the validity of their knowledge and how it is substantiated. They will gain the confidence needed to do this when you emphasise their capability to 'do' their job; they can build upon what they already know and can do.

Teaching tips: How to facilitate learning for work-based learners

▶ Increase your own capacity for critical reflection (Chapter 11).
▶ Focus on the skills they will need in the future.
▶ Champion 'learning to learn'.
▶ Promote students' autonomy and self-directedness of their own learning.
▶ Learn to guide rather than direct learners.
▶ Practise letting go; let the learners work it out with prompts like: *'How? Why? What? When? Who? Where?'*
▶ Offer alternative perspectives.
▶ Ask about differing scenarios – 'What if...'
▶ Ask questions you don't have the answers to.
▶ Give, but also seek, constructive feedback; these are adult workers.
▶ Support students in becoming agents of change.
▶ Reflect on the whole learning process, not just solutions to problems.

continued overleaf

Teaching tips: How to facilitate learning for work-based learners *continued*

▶ When problems are solved, how might that be useful in the future?
▶ Balance the essential teaching content against the students' self-directed learning.
▶ Be aware that formal and informal learning emerges from the workplace.
▶ Be prepared to learn yourself; this is a partnership, and WBL are experts.
▶ Reflect on concrete actions you have engaged in with students – what works, what doesn't?
▶ What could a community of practice (Wenger, 2006) offer to your learning facilitation?
▶ Design authentic assessments which are capable of recognising relevant situated learning and which also meet HE and employer requirements

ACTIVITY	
What qualities do you think make the ideal WBL tutor?	
Are they a trainer or an educator?	
How much overlap is there between being a coach, mentor, academic and tutor?	
List the characteristics of work-based learning tutor.	
How could this role fit with your own teaching and learning skills and preferences?	
Reflecting on the facilitator skills required, what could you cultivate? How could you go about this?	
How could you increase your learners' ability to become more self-directing and autonomous in their learning?	

▶ Assessment

As part-time students and full-time workers, work-based learners tend to focus on the assessments they will be expected to undertake in order to balance their time across working, and personal and academic endeavours. Assessment can be therefore viewed as a problematic hurdle to be overcome, usually at the end of a module or teaching period. Assessment should instead be considered as an intrinsic part of the learning process. Work-based assessments that reflect real-work activities, within an academic framework, encourage deep and relevant learning and ensure that what is taught, and how it is assessed, enables students to construct their learning in a personal way based on both their previous experience and their exposure to new knowledge. Biggs (2003), an advocate of innovations in university teaching, quotes Tyler (1949): 'Learning takes place through the active behaviour of the student: it is what he does that he learns, not what the teacher does' (Biggs, 2003, p. 25). It is how the learner engages with the available learning opportunities that will make learning happen. This richer, more nuanced way of approaching learning results in conceptual changes that go well beyond that of just acquiring new information (Biggs, 2003). Assessments that facilitate deep learning and enable change to occur are the best kind of assessments. A qualitative dimension can still be assured by using criterion referencing as assessment criteria, hence ensuring consistency within the assessment process (Biggs, 2003) (Table 2.1).

Table 2.1 Examples of assessment methods and tools suitable for work-based learners

Type of assessment	Helps WBL by
Action plans	Identifying a topic for development and driving the articulation of a rationale for action and creation of the route through which it will be accomplished. Plans can be short with just key reference points of 'who, what, where, when, how and why?' Or longer, with a more narrative approach, where a reasoned argument, supported by research and evidence, is put together to support a case for action. For example, an action plan detailing the rationale for a training plan for staff, together with a project plan describing how and when it would be completed and details of the training.
Business plan	Allowing a learner to choose a topic relevant for their organisation and role and create a scenario for change, drawing on relevant research and organisational information, thereby combining several perspectives; this develops a learner's ability to compile a persuasive argument or cause for action. For example, a proposal for changing practice in mending road potholes for a borough council, delivered in a PowerPoint presentation (10 minutes), detailing a saving of £100K if the proposal was adopted (it was!).
Case study	Applying new knowledge to a common situation, for example, in management, the analysis and application of knowledge, and the evaluation of alternative outcomes and conclusions may be used in very differing contexts. Case studies have the added benefit of using 'real world' examples, usually the learner's own, and help to develop understanding of a current or strategic situation, such as managing change; they can be a concise way of giving a lot of context. For example, a case study analysis of a department preparing to change its management structure, identifying the current practice to be changed and presenting alternative change strategies that could be used to effect change.

continued overleaf

Table 2.1 Examples of assessment methods and tools suitable for work-based learners *continued*

Type of assessment	Helps WBL by
Critical commentary	Involving reflection on the process of compiling an academic piece of work, informed by reading and information from other sources, as applied to the learners' own contexts and experiences; developing critical analysis and evaluation skills.
Group projects	Supporting opportunities to develop team-working skills via real-work projects that involve multidisciplinary people and departments. Group projects can be challenging to coordinate and may not be perceived as being relevant to all participants unless they are all in the same profession or workplace. For example, a group created and managed a toy library and presented in a portfolio evidence of the stages of acquiring the location, preparing the environment, equipping it with toys, and the strategic networking and liaison activities required across all stakeholders to bring it about, together with advertising the new facility using social media tools (Chapter 9).
Learning contracts	Constructing contracts that can cover from one learning experience to the components of a whole programme – may be partly reflective and partly speculative in relation to learning intentions. Contracts allow learners to take ownership of their learning focus, subject content and time span (Chapter 4).
Online assessment	Giving the opportunity be assessed away from the campus (Chapter 9). Work-based learners are increasingly asked to produce, individually or in groups, blogs and wikis which demonstrate their learning.
Portfolios	Facilitating the gathering of a wide range of evidence on a related topic to show development of learning and understanding from alternative perspectives. Evidence can include a comprehensive range of forms, ranging from written work to images, videos or performances. Portfolios can be compiled online as well as in hard copy, making them easier to manage and transport.
Presentations	Professionally communicating the essence of a topic, in a set time, to a particular audience. This can be particularly helpful for emergent professionals and undergraduates who may not routinely be required to communicate their ideas to a critical audience. If an employer is sponsoring learners it can be beneficial for them to experience the presentation to gain understanding of the learners' accomplishments.
Production of a product	Encouraging work-based learners to use their real work activities within assessment. For example, development of a DVD with video clips of how to play an instrument, together with a critical commentary of the teaching techniques used and supporting rationale for the choice of teaching approaches.
Professional competencies	Valuing practical skills – particularly suitable for learners who have to acquire technical skills for professional practice.

continued overleaf

Table 2.1 Examples of assessment methods and tools suitable for work-based learners *continued*

Type of assessment	Helps WBL by
Project – individual	Engaging with a range of work-based projects, varying from deskwork and exploration of supporting literature or occupational and professional information, to fieldwork where a 'real time' work project is managed and undertaken. Projects can be tailored to an individual's learning level and need. For example, it can result in recommendations for action or in a product that is applicable to an individual's work role and context.
Reflective essay	Capturing learning from the process of experiencing a learning activity; the essay can be compiled using extracts from a reflective learning journal, thereby allowing some editing by the learner before submission; it can record development of thinking and understanding and occasionally moments of transformative learning. For example, an essay summarising personal and professional learning from the process of compiling a portfolio with evidence to make a claim of experiential learning.
Self-review	Developing personal and professional judgement skills which enables a review of progress so far – sometimes a starting point from which to build a learning plan or make an APEL/RPL claim.

▶ Who assesses work-based learners?

Tutors can assess WBL, but it is also good practice for students to develop the skills of self- and peer assessment as part of their learning process. Employers' contributions to assessment can lead to concerns regarding consistency and fairness if the process and criteria are not transparent. Involvement of mentors, senior staff and/or colleagues and learning peers in assessment may be daunting for the learner, but it enables feedback into an organisation regarding the work-based learner's achievements and develops skills of evaluation and judgement. Senior practitioner input is essential when professional competence or fitness to practice in a profession has to be mediated by practising professionals, and the design of assessment should cater for that. Should the type of WBL not include a practice element, then the employer and colleagues may make a contribution from an advisory perspective rather than an assessment judgement that affects the outcome for the learner, thereby reducing the potential conflict of interest between manager and assessor roles. The responsibilities of and reference points for assessors, from whatever perspective they are contributing from, should be clear. The HEI will have its own quality assurance processes, which the work-based tutor must adhere to. This means that the tutor has the final decision (see Chapter 8 for more on quality processes and enhancement).

Case study 2.3 shows how an HEI can devise an appropriate assessment for work-based learners:

Case study 2.3 Authentic assessment: A foundation degree in retail management

Work-based learners studying a foundation degree in retail management programme required module assessments that focused on real-work activities.

To ensure the assessment was authentic and appropriate, relevant discussions were held with a retail consultant, the sector skills council and employer representatives to gather information about the work roles, the expected competencies and knowledge and the varying contexts in which learners would be working.

The assessment challenge was to make this relevant but not over assessed. It was also designed to use activities that were used in the workplace and therefore build skills capacity for both practice and learning.

An assessment for a level five 15-credit module in 'Learning to Lead a Team' was fairly typical:

Part 1: A presentation (ten minutes) outlining your company's approach to leadership and the techniques used to improve team performance within specific contextual influences underpinned by relevant theory.

Presentations are useful in helping working students prepare their assessments. It requires initial theoretical exploration of the literature to find out underpinning theories and helps the students to structure their work with a beginning, middle and end. This helps them with their academic skills and to refine their topic. For work it is also helpful in developing their confidence in putting forward a case for their point of view, thus building skills of argumentation.

Part 2: Devise your own leadership capability action plan that is developed from feedback gathered from colleagues in the workplace, identifying leadership strengths and development areas (1,000 words). This action plan will be incorporated into your personal and professional development plan, which will be included as an appendix.

This assessment requires the student to interact with colleagues and to seek and act on feedback about performance. This is very challenging for some but helps to develop teamwork skills, being able to take and give criticism, and gives a structure for their personal and professional development, which they have had ownership of.

Part 3: A written reflective account outlining a critical incident where you adapted your leadership style to take account of the situational, contextual and environmental factors (1,000 words).

Reflection upon their own learning and practice experience is an essential tool for an emerging professional and one that is useful to incorporate into work-based programmes to help the development of critical self-reflection and learning.

The above case study demonstrates a successful assessment strategy, and there are elements of good practice evidenced here that can be adopted in your own practice.

▶ Presentations:
  - Are useful in helping working students to develop their confidence in putting forward a case for their point of view whilst building their oratory skills
  - Require theoretical exploration of published material and underpinning theories
  - Help the students to structure their work logically and subsequently help them develop their academic skills and refine their topic
▶ Personal and professional development plans:
  - Require the student to interact with colleagues by seeking and acting on feedback about performance, which can be challenging but is necessary
  - Develop useful skills, such as teamwork skills and taking and giving constructive criticism
  - Give a structure for personal and professional development
▶ Reflective accounts:
  - Offer an essential opportunity to reflect upon own learning
  - Allow emerging professionals to build on practice experience
  - Offer a useful tool for the facilitation of the development of critical self-reflection and learning when incorporated into work-based programmes

SUMMARY

▶ The tutor's role becomes one of facilitator when working with work-based learners.
▶ Remember these are workplace practitioners – often experts in their area of work activity.
▶ You need to adopt and create flexible pedagogies appropriate for students who are already learning through their job role.
▶ There are many significant others impacting on how and where work-based learners learn; familiarise yourself with this group.
▶ Investigate different approaches to work-based assessment and begin to extend your knowledge of and skills in them.
▶ Employers and workplace mentors are key to this assessment process and you should develop these individuals for their role in work-based assessment.

▶ **References**

Atherton, J. S. (2013) *Learning and Teaching; Experiential Learning* [On-line: UK]. Available at http://www.learningandteaching.info/learning/experience.htm accessed 25 September 2014.

Ball, I. and Manwaring, G. (2010) *Making It Work: A Guidebook Exploring Work-based Learning*. Gloucester: QAA.

Biggs, J. (2003) *Teaching for Quality Learning at University*, 2nd Edn, Maidenhead: The Society for Research into Higher Education and Open University Press.

Boud, D. and Costley, C. (2007) From project supervision to advising: New conceptions of the practice. *Innovations in Education and Teaching International*. 44 (2), pp. 119–130.

Brookfield, S. (1986) *Understanding and Facilitating Adult Learning: A Comprehensive Analysis of Principles and Effective Practice*. San Francisco: Jossey-Bass.

Costley, C., Elliot, G. and Gibbs, P. (2010) *Doing Work-based Research Approaches to Enquiry for Insider-Researcher*. London: Sage Publications Ltd.

Hardacre, K. and Workman, B. (2010) *Planning and Reviewing Work-based Learning: A Practical Guide*. Faringdon: Libri Publishing.

Helyer, R. and Lee, D. (2014) The Role of Work Experience in the Future Employability of Higher Education Graduates. *Higher Education Quarterly*. 68 (3), pp. 348–372.

Honey, P. and Mumford, A. (2006) *The Learning Styles Questionnaire*. Revised Edn, Maidenhead: Peter Honey Publications.

Lave, J. and Wenger, E. (1991) *Situated Learning: Legitimate Peripheral Participation*. Cambridge: University of Cambridge Press.

King, A. (1993) *From Sage on the Stage to Guide on the Side College Teaching*, vol. 41, pp. 30–35. Available at Instructure-uploads.s3.amazonaws.com, accessed 24 June 2015.

Knowles, M. S., Holton III, F. and Aswansu, R. (2005) *The Adult Learner*, 6th Edn, London: Butterworth Heinemann.

Nixon, I., Smith, K., Stafford, R. and Camm, S. (2006) *Work-based Learning: Illuminating the Higher Education Landscape*. York: HEA.

Raelin, J. A. (2008) *Work-based Learning: Bridging Knowledge and Action in the Workplace*, New and Revised Edn, San Francisco: Jossey-Bass.

Smith, S. and Smith, L. (2015) Social learning: Supporting yourself and your peers, in Helyer, R. (Ed.) *The Work-based Learning Student Handbook*, 2nd Edn, London: Palgrave, pp. 184–204.

Tyler, R. W. (1949) *Basic Principles of Curriculum and Instruction*. Chicago: University of Chicago Press.

Wenger, E. (2006) *Communities of Practice: A Brief Introduction*. Available at http://www.noetikos.org/sitebuildercontent/sitebuilderfiles/copandsituatedlearning.pdf accessed 8 August 2014.

Workman, B. (2007) 'Casing the joint': Explorations by the insider-researcher preparing for work-based projects. *Journal of Workplace Learning*. 19 (3), pp. 146–160.

▶ Recommended further reading

Barnett, R. (2014) *Conditions of Flexibility: Securing a More Responsive Higher Education System.* York: Higher Education Academy. Available at https://www .heacademy.ac.uk/sites/default/files/resources/FP_conditions_of_flexibility.pdf, accessed 24 June 2015.

Burke, L., Marks-Maran, D. J., Ooms, A., Webb, M. and Cooper, D. (2009) Towards a pedagogy of work-based learning: Perceptions of work-based learning in foundation degrees. *Journal of Vocational Education and Training.* 61 (1), pp. 15–33.

Burrill, J., Hussain, Z., Prescott, D. and Waywell, L. [no date] *An Introduction to Practice Education* Available at www.practicebas edlearning.org http://cw.routledge. com/textbooks/9780415537902/data/learn   ing/4_Developing%20New%20 Supervisors%20and%20Assessors%20of%20Practice%20Learning.pdf   accessed 26 August 2014.

Gordon, N. (2014) *Flexible Pedagogies: Technology-enhanced Learning.* York: Higher Education Academy. Available at http://www.heacademy.ac.uk/resources/detail/ flexible-learning/flexiblepedagogies/tech_enhanced_learning/main_report, accessed 24 June 2015.

Jones-Devitt, S. (2013) *Thinking Critically about Assessment Practices and Processes for Part-time Students in the Marketised University.* York: Higher Education Academy. Available at https://www.heacademy.ac.uk/node/4998, accessed 24 June 2015.

Kettle, J. (2013) *Flexible Pedagogies: Employer Engagement and Work-based Learning.* York: Higher Education Academy. Available at http://www.heacademy.ac.uk/ resources/details/flexible-learning/flexiblepedagogies/employerengagement/ report, accessed 24 June 2015.

NHS Education for Scotland (2011) *Train the Trainers Toolkit.* Available at http:// www.nes.scot.nhs.uk/media/2042600/trainthetrainers__final_.pdf accessed 28 August 2014.

Nottingham, P. and Akinleye, A. (2014) Professional artefacts: Embodying ideas in work-based learning. *Higher Education, Skills and Work-based Learning.* 4 (1), pp. 98–107.

Rowson, R. (2006) *Working Ethics: How to Be Fair in a Culturally Complex World.* London: Jessica Kingsley Publishers.

3 Flexible frameworks and building blocks

Barbara Workman and Darryll Bravenboer

IN THIS CHAPTER YOU WILL:

▶ Be introduced to the key components central to designing a work-based curriculum framework

▶ Consider what a framework could offer to your learners, your institution and your employer partners

▶ Consider how work-based frameworks incorporate flexible approaches to learning, teaching and assessment in response to a variety of professional contexts for higher-level learning

▶ See how flexible work-based frameworks can construct awards from short courses to full degrees, incorporating accreditation of in-company training, prior experiential and certificated learning, work-based projects and other learning activities

▶ Become familiar with the differences between programme approval and academic accreditation for organisations and individuals and how these contribute to the operation of a work-based framework

▶ Understand the academic infrastructure that is required to support a validated work-based curriculum framework, including QAA and professional body standards, the use of work-based level descriptors, institutional quality policies and procedures

---

▶ Frameworks to support a flexible response

Designing a flexible and responsive work-based programme that meets the needs of the learner, employers and higher education institutions (HEIs) can present a number of challenges to the design and development team. The use of a curriculum model within higher education (HE) is, surprisingly, unusual as traditional academic programmes tend to emerge from a subject specialism located within an HEI rather than a curriculum philosophy. Work-based learning (WBL) is predicated on the notion that people learn as they work and that this learning can be equivalent to that which takes place in HE. The study of this learning that emerges from work typically crosses traditional academic disciplinary boundaries; for example, 'management' is relevant to most areas of practice. This means that the starting place for thinking about how this learning can be recognised is not necessarily in terms of its academic subject content but rather those aspects of higher-level learning that are 'transdisciplinary' (McGregor and Volckmann, 2011; Bravenboer and Workman, 2015). Consequently, a work-based curriculum 'framework' is a means to construct a learning pathway that can be recognised by HEIs and lead to the award of HE qualifications. This chapter discusses the key components of a work-based curriculum framework, its benefits, and how you can create a framework that is adaptable and responsive to learning in the workplace.

▶ Curriculum philosophy

A work-based curriculum philosophy informs the teaching, learning and assessment strategies that are used to deliver the programme. The curriculum may be located within a process model (Sheehan, 1986) that promotes personal and professional development and learning with a focus on evidence and outcomes of the learning process. Many HEIs offering work-based studies style programmes build upon the ideas behind Kolb's (1984) experiential learning cycle to create modules appropriate for working students (Workman and Garnett, 2009; Bravenboer and Workman, 2015; Workman and White, 2015). A humanistic and andragogical learning and teaching approach is used to engage with adult work-based learners, enabling recognition and accreditation of prior knowledge and experience, responsive to your learners' own learning needs and personal motivations (see Chapter 2 and Workman, 2009). It builds upon your learners' own learning and working experience, enabling them to develop their understanding of knowledge that they have created in the workplace, thereby being socially constructed (Brown and Duguid, 2001) and promoting autonomous learning. It enhances and capitalises on experience from the workplace, peers, colleagues, tutors and other learners, thus introducing the concepts of professional networking (Uzzi and Dunlap, 2005) and communities of practice (Wenger, 2006). This promotes skills for lifelong learning and development, which will continue after the qualification has been completed.

The work-based curriculum framework therefore needs to:

▶ Specialise and localise your learners' own WBL as the subject of study through the development of reflective practice
▶ Situate your learners' WBL within wider practice contexts through negotiated engagement with communities of practitioners, employers,

co-workers, collaborators, stakeholders, clients, academic tutors and others implicated in a specific area of work/practice
▶ Develop transdisciplinary approaches to WBL that support and promote innovation and enhancement of work/practice

Designing a curriculum framework

An HE curriculum framework can be designed to lead to HE qualifications ranging from small awards such as a university certificate to larger awards such as bachelor's or master's degree. A curriculum framework also provides the guiding principles, academic architecture and rules of combination that set the parameters within which programmes of study can be constructed. For WBL, ensuring academic coherence is an essential component as programmes are usually designed around the needs of work-based learners who are working within a specific organisational, professional or industry sector. A curriculum framework must, therefore, be sufficiently flexible to reflect these diverse work contexts but also provide a means to establish coherent programmes of higher-level learning (Table 3.1).

A flexible curriculum framework can be used to:

▶ Promote and foster skills of learning to learn, such as information search and retrieval and critical reading, study skills and literature search
▶ Create opportunities for your students to review and reflect on previous experience and create claims for the accreditation of prior learning (APEL/RPL) (see Chapter 5)
▶ Facilitate the excavation of personal and professional learning through reflective models and exercises, leading to identification of future learning and development needs, and enable the discovery and critique of new information
▶ Foster creative approaches to generating innovative solutions and enhancing work practices through problem solving, critical thinking, project work, inquiry skills and networking

Table 3.1 Characteristics of work-based frameworks

Characteristics	**Purpose**
Customisation, negotiation and approval of programmes (and award titles without repeated validation – see also Chapter 7)	• Responsiveness to organisational/individual learning needs • Efficiency of programme approval process • Enables a 'roll-on/roll-off' approach to programme development *continued overleaf*

Table 3.1: Characteristics of work-based frameworks *continued*

Characteristics	Purpose
Work-based level descriptors, such as SEEC (2010), FHEQ (Quality Assurance Agency, 2008), institutional-level descriptors	• Provides benchmarking against WBL characteristics and FHEQ descriptors • Provides a reference point for learning outcomes and assessment criteria • Locates work-based study within the programme
'Negotiated', 'open' or 'shell' modules of a variety of sizes, adaptable for a range of work-based contexts	• Negotiated modules can be customised to reflect a specific area of work/practice • Can be used as benchmarking for APEL/RPL claims in terms of the volume and level of credit sought • Enables flexible adaptation to work-based contexts and professional development needs
Mechanisms to facilitate and incorporate accreditation of prior learning from experience, certification, or recognition of in-company training as equivalent to HE-level learning (see Chapter 5)	• Facilitates incorporation of prior learning through a process and/or modules to make an APEL/RPL claim • Organisations gain accreditation of in-company training through HEI procedures that are incorporated into an HE qualification • Specific amounts of accredited learning are recognised within awards by institutional regulations (normally between a half to two thirds of the award)
Work-based modules at varying levels and credit sizes, ready-validated, minimal barred combinations, providing a variety of WBL skills and topics	• Enables entry points at all academic levels (4–7) to work towards small and large awards, through a 'mix and match' approach to module combinations • Promotes learning from a starting point of reflection upon self-/personal learning progressing towards professional learning and development • Facilitates investigation, critical analysis and evaluation skills within a work-based context reflecting appropriate academic levels
Approval process for individual programme learning agreements/contracts (see Chapter 4) and organisational learning agreement pathways	• Demonstrates coherence of individual- or organisation-focused programme pathways through a formal quality process • Ensures qualification titles appropriately reflect the relevant area of work/practice and do not conflict with professional award titles or other HE programmes
Incorporation of subject-based modules from other HE programmes or disciplines, within specific credit and time constraints (see Chapter 5)	• Facilitates learners to pursue appropriate topics of specialist interest within their programme • Reduces duplication of learning time and effort if learning is still current (usually within five years) or still used in current role
Incorporates relevant content Reflective learning	• Topics are transdisciplinary and therefore transferable to a wide range of work contexts *continued overleaf*

Table 3.1 Characteristics of work-based frameworks *continued*

Characteristics	Purpose
'Learning to learn' techniques Negotiated learning and personal/ professional development Ethics of being a worker-learner Critical analysis and research skills Creative, problem-solving and project management skills Professional networking skills Authentic work-based assessment	• Subject knowledge is located within the workplace, enabling learners to maximise their learning opportunities through work-based activities/projects/inquiry and research • Develops key WBL skills, which support employment and progression
Quality processes and infrastructure Identify student learning support systems Tutor and work-based mentor roles Staff development requirements Organisational links through tutors Liaison with records department Finance department and quality processes Easy and distance access to learning resources	• Develops effective networks to support work- based learners who study (mainly) off campus • Ensures administration systems are in place, supports the 'non-traditional' work-based learner and keeps key personnel updated with programme developments • Ensures effective working and supportive relationships for learning between the HEI, the employer and the student • Ongoing staff development, for example, in use of APEL/RPL, facilitation skills, distance and open learning resources

Source: Adapted from Willis (2008)

▶ Initial considerations for creating a framework

When creating a new framework you need to check for flexibility, coherence and validity as well as the ethical implications of the proposed programme of study (see Appendix for further details). Answering the following key questions will provide a good starting point:

ACTIVITY	
In your tutor role try to consciously adopt reflective learning methods yourself; this will maximise reciprocal learning and help you to better understand your WBL students. Go through the stages outlined below:	
How much academic credit will the HE qualification carry?	
What level will the credit be at?	
How much credit gained from external sources and/or from prior learning can be recognised?	
How many modules or units of study are required to construct the proposed programme?	
	continued overleaf

ACTIVITY *continued*	
What do your institution's regulations and level descriptors state regarding the use and combination of modules and academic credit?	
Similarly, what do external reference points state, for example, QFQUAL, *QAA Framework for Higher Education Qualifications* (FHEQ), SEEC-level descriptors, QAA Subject Benchmarking Statements?	
What appropriate reference points have you used to inform taught components for a given academic level and qualification and area of professional practice?	

▷ Key components of a WBL framework

Many facets need to be considered when devising a framework, as well as the above characteristics a WBL framework needs to include certain key components (see Figure 3.1).

When designing a work-based curriculum framework, an essential component is 'building blocks', the inclusion of modules with different credit values (10, 15, 20, 30 and so on), at each academic level that can be combined to create various qualifications. This use of variable amounts of credit from different sources builds learning pathways, which then lead to the qualifications available within the framework. Traditional degree programmes do not tend to build in the recognition of external learning (although the majority of HEIs are able to do this via RPL processes). Table 3.2 (below) summarises the amount and levels of credit for qualifications used by most HEIs and includes the standard awards described within the *QAA Framework for Higher Education Qualifications (FHEQ)*.

Work-based learners bring their current and previous learning from work to their programme; this influences how programmes are planned and constructed, including the syllabus approach to learning, teaching and assessment. In addition, your work-based learners may or may not meet traditional HE entry requirements but will usually be able to demonstrate their potential to successfully complete a programme through other forms of evidence, such as:

▷ The level of responsibility within their work role, for example, leading or supervising others
▷ Professional or vocational qualifications
▷ Continuing professional development activity
▷ The number of years of experience in relevant work
▷ Reports or data from significant work projects

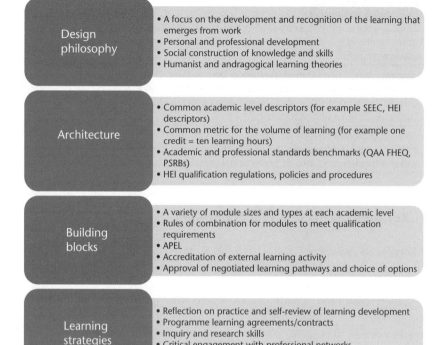

Figure 3.1 Key components of a work-based curriculum

Table 3.2 Credit distribution leading to HE qualifications

HE qualification	Academic level	Total credits required for award
University certificate	4	40
Certificate of higher education (Cert HE) Higher national certificate (HNC)	4	120
University diploma	5	40
Professional diploma	5	120
Diploma of higher education (Dip HE) Foundation degree (Fd) Higher national diploma (HND)	4 & 5	120 @ L4 120 @ L5 = 240
Graduate certificate (Grad Cert)	6	60
Graduate diploma (Grad Dip)	6	120

continued overleaf

Table 3.2 Credit distribution leading to HE qualifications *continued*

HE qualification	Academic level	Total credits required for award
Ordinary bachelor's degree (BA, BSc)	4, 5 & 6	120 @ L 4 120 @ L5 60 @ L6 = 300
Bachelor's degree with honours (BA (Hons), BSc (Hons))	4, 5 & 6	120 @ L4 120 @ L5 120 @ L6 = 360
Postgraduate certificate (PG Cert)	7	60
Postgraduate diploma (PG Dip)	7	120
Taught master's degrees (MA, MSc, MEng)	7	180
Professional doctorates (credit-based) (DProf, DPych)	7 & 8	180 @ L 7 360 @ L 8 = 540

This kind of evidence can highlight a significant degree of higher-level learning – so far not formally recognised. Work-based programmes are designed with entry criteria that recognise such prior learning to avoid duplication of learning. Figure 3.2 shows a work-based framework incorporating a combination of study from work through accreditation of prior

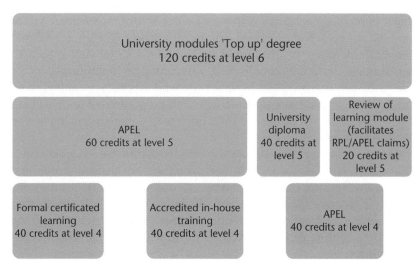

Figure 3.2 Using a framework to construct a personalised work-based degree programme

experiential and certificated learning (APEL/RPL) and accreditation of in-company training as small HE awards. This individual learner accessed a final year 'top up' programme to achieve an Honours degree.

The components of a work-based framework need to incorporate appropriate structures and processes to enable customisation of a learner's or organisation's work-based pathway, using the framework to combine modules and credits in variable sizes, transferable through the Credit Accumulation and Transfer Scheme (CATS). Transfer of academic credit is calculated using a common metric for establishing both academic level and volume of learning. The number of credits that form a module is based on notional hours of learning (ten learning hours per one credit) with achievement of the stated learning outcomes for each specific academic level of study. These learning outcomes may be subject specific or 'transdisciplinary'.

Recognising learning from outside of the classroom, in a credit-based approach, means that work-based programmes are designed to reflect your learners' needs and prior learning achievements, rather than being pre-determined by the academic subject curriculum. Workforce development programmes for organisations can also be created, focusing on identified specific learning aims (Willis, 2008; Bravenboer, 2011). The learning is located in the workplace, supported by a curriculum framework process to customise, negotiate and approve the specific programme's content, without involving an HE validation event for every new employer or learner. Specialist content is negotiated with your learner and/or organisation and/or professional body and integrated into the programme. The use of validated 'negotiated', 'open' or 'shell' modules also allows customisation so that, for example, the learning outcomes, which may be 'transdisciplinary' or 'generic', can be specialised to reflect the work or practice context of an organisation or professional sector. Identified proportions of prior learning from experience and certificates (APEL/RPL) or in-company training can be included (Chapter 5).

When planning the supporting infrastructure for a work-based framework it is key to include the means by which to approve and record the customised programme. Coordination with institutional quality processes (Chapter 8) and academic records will ensure that programmes and approval processes are recorded appropriately on the HEI's data capture systems; wherever possible use the conventional HEI procedures.

The following three Case studies 3.1, 3.2 and 3.3 offer some good illustrations of innovative use of a framework approach.

Case study 3.1 Using a framework approach (A): Developing an honours degree in combined sciences for Collision Investigation Officers (CIOs)

The Institute of Traffic Accident Investigators (ITAI) contacted the university to inquire about developing a WBL honours degree in combined sciences for Collision Investigation Officers (CIOs). CIOs analyse the causes of traffic accidents using scientific and mathematical skills and knowledge. Significant market demand for such a course was established in consultation across the UK.

▶ There are approximately 600 CIOs based in Collision Investigation Units (CIUs) throughout the UK.
▶ CIOs have a wide range of higher-level skills, experience and learning, presenting significant opportunities for claiming university credits through both accreditation of prior certificated learning (APL) and accreditation of prior experiential learning (APEL) (see Chapter 5).
▶ The role of a CIO is 'project based' around individual collision investigation cases, therefore work-based projects are utilised in the award.
▶ Most CIOs do not have degrees and many employers are unwilling to sponsor them to undertake degree-level courses.

The course cost was a major issue, but the university's work-based studies (WBS) framework offered a way of approving a suitable course quickly and cost-effectively (due to the use of APL). Although the new title required the university's approval, the WBS framework was already approved, and the requirements for adding a new title within the framework are not onerous and are indeed much faster than approving a new, non-WBS course.

The WBS framework therefore supported the development of a new WBS title (combined sciences) to enable CIOs to gain:

▶ 260 credits through experiential and/or certificated prior learning
▶ 60 credits through taught modules delivered in four regions across the UK
▶ 40 credits through a distance-supervised work-based project

The development timescale for the course was compressed into six months from inquiry to delivery of the first workshop. It involved:

▶ Consultation with CIOs and ITAI to establish market demand (January–March)
▶ Business case documentation completed and approved by university (March)
▶ Development of approval documentation for new title within the framework (programme specification and handbook) (March–April)
▶ Site visits to approve four proposed new delivery centres across the UK (March–April)
▶ Approval event (April)
▶ Response to panel's recommendations (May)
▶ New title final approval (June)
▶ Enrolment of 60 students (June)
▶ Course commenced in June, first graduates in November

continued overleaf

Case study 3.1 Using a framework approach (A): Developing an honours degree in combined sciences for Collision Investigation Officers (CIOs) *continued*

| Learning Recognition and Development Module (10 credits @ L6) | RPL and/or APEL (120 credits @ L4, 120 credits @ L5, and 20 credits @ L6) | Professional and Organisational Development Module (30 credits @ L6) | Research Proposal Module (20 credits @ L6) | Work-based Project Module (40 credits @ L6) |

BSc (Hons) Work-based studies (combined sciences) route

Kevin Ions, Programme Leader, Teesside University

Case study 3.2 Using a framework approach (B): University of West England (UWE) Shell Award Framework

The Shell Award Framework enables professional development awards (for example BSc Professional Development) to be cross faculty and cross discipline and they are available from foundation degree to master's level, offering learners a bespoke, flexible and work-based pathway. Supported by a programme leader from the relevant faculty, and often a workplace mentor, learners can use HE credit 'gathered' throughout their career and build this into an individual programme of study. Previous experience and learning that can count towards an award may comprise:

▶ WBL, for example, project work, reports, development of policy, presentations, initiatives, service evaluation, in-house study
▶ Accredited prior experiential learning (APEL), for example, study days, role development, project work, evidence of experience
▶ HE accredited learning, that is, modules from the University of the West of England (UWE) or other universities

All learners must complete a current, supervised 'Evidencing WBL' module, normally taken towards the end of their programme, as a compulsory element for all levels of the professional development programme, the size of which depends on the final award. This is part of ensuring that graduates' pathways meet the institution's regulations for obtaining a named UWE award.

The use of a negotiated learning plan provides the opportunity to formally recognise experience and learning as part of the learner's final award and to

continued overleaf

Case study 3.2 Using a framework approach: (B) University of West England (UWE) Shell Award Framework *continued*

design the focus of their award. It identifies their target award and contains a personal statement outlining aspirations and experiences. Of particular interest is that RPL claims are facilitated by an electronic APEL tool to help turn experience into credit using evidence and critical narrative, and previous marks can be transferred from previous HE accredited learning, including other HEIs or UWE modules, to count towards the final classification of the work-based award.

Example

Omar is a ward manager working in general medicine. Following registration as a nurse in the UK, he has previously gained credit alongside work experience and promotion. He wishes to consolidate his learning and gain a degree to enhance his career.

Omar enters the programme with 240 credits:

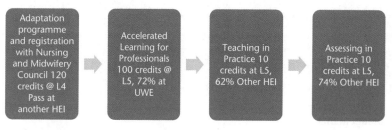

To complete his programme he undertakes:

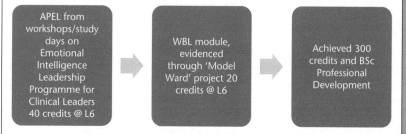

Clive Warn, Senior Lecturer in Nursing and Programme Lead Professional Development Awards

---

Case Study 3.3: Using a framework approach (C): Thomas's individually negotiated master's programme

Thomas was self-employed as a project manager working as a consultant in large engineering organisations. To promote his professional profile and develop his skills, he decided to undertake a work-based master's programme, which recognised his previous learning from experience and enabled him to investigate a project located in his practice.

continued overleaf

Case Study 3.3: Using a framework approach (C): Thomas's individually negotiated master's programme *continued*

He took a module that facilitated reflection on, and review of, his prior learning in order to make an accreditation of experiential learning (APEL) claim for 70 credits at master's level. This claim focused on his knowledge of commercial and financial planning and risk management that contributed towards the overall master's credits (180 credits).

Thomas then negotiated the focus of the rest of his programme by undertaking a planning module, where he identified topics for further professional learning and argued for his award to be entitled 'MSc Work-based Learning Studies (Project Management)'. He concurrently studied a practitioner research module, which introduced research and development methods, to design his final research project that investigated new models of project management appropriate for his work context.

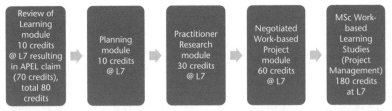

Thomas's pathway to an MSc Work-based Learning Studies (Project Management)

Academic level descriptors

In level descriptors the level and type of learning is described in a way that can be benchmarked against national (and possibly international) standards. Most HEIs have their own level descriptors to standardise the academic level of HE programmes and relate to the *QAA Framework for Higher Education Qualifications* (FHEQ) (Quality Assurance Agency, 2011) and/or the SEEC Credit Level Descriptors *for Higher Education* (2010).

WBL differs from traditional subject disciplines as the learning that emerges from work itself is the 'subject' of study. At undergraduate and increasingly at postgraduate level, the expectations for what people will know, understand and are able to do on successful completion of a degree programme are described in the QAA Subject Benchmark Statements (Quality Assurance Agency, 2014). Certain professions, such as nursing, have a strong practice focus and are required to fulfil specific professional standards, including a license to practice, which is reflected in HE programmes. However, work-based curriculum frameworks are not necessarily guided by professional regulations and can be used to construct HE programmes in a wide range of sectors that may or may not be aligned with traditional academic subject disciplines. For this reason, the academic standards of WBL frameworks are usually aligned to level descriptors, such as those produced by the SEEC (2010).

The learning from work/practice is often reflected in the qualification title of awards from WBL framework programmes, such as 'Professional Practice', 'Integrated Professional Studies', 'Work-based Learning', 'Work-based Studies', 'Professional Development Studies', 'Applied Professional Studies' or similar. Sometimes the specific area of work or professional practice is referenced, for example, 'Applied Professional Studies (Executive Coaching)' or 'Professional Practice in Arts Management'.

It is important with WBL to make sure that the level descriptors describe the type of learning at work and the types of knowledge, understanding and skills required to demonstrate professional levels of practice (Table 3.3).

These characteristics of learning are equivalent to those used in traditional academic subjects, in terms of difficulty and amount of study, because they align fully with UK HE requirements (see Quality Assurance Agency, 2011 for FHEQ). The FHEQ also aligns with the *Qualification and Credit Framework* (QCF) (http://www.ofqual.gov.uk, Office of Qualifications and Examination Regulation , 2013), demonstrating equivalence against other UK qualifications. The SEEC level descriptors have been mapped against European Standards to demonstrate parity and equivalence with European qualifications. If learning

Table 3.3 SEEC (2010) work-based level descriptor characteristics

Level descriptors	
Setting	Operational context
	Autonomy and responsibility for actions
Knowledge and understanding	The factual and/or conceptual base of the subject or field of study
Cognitive skills	Conceptualisation and critical thinking
	Problem solving, research and inquiry
	Synthesis and creativity
	Analysis and evaluation
Performance and practice	Adaptation to context
	Performance
	Team and organisational working
	Ethical awareness and application
Personal and enabling skills	Personal evaluation and development
	Interpersonal and communication skills

has been acquired outside the UK it may be possible to use it towards a UK qualification, if it carries currency and evidence of credit rating. The relationship between the FHEQ and European qualifications is provided by the QAA at http://www.qaa.ac.uk. Alternatively, programmes studied in the UK can be recognised abroad, provided they meet the European guidelines. The QAA academic skills are summarised on the website: http://www.qaa.ac.uk/Pages/default.aspx. At the time of writing they are under consultation for review, so check for any updated versions.

Professional bodies often use accredited programmes to maintain standards, and offer prestige, across their membership. These accredited academic courses can include work-based programmes, so it is worth tailoring any WBL framework to reflect identified professional competencies. Although specific to particular areas of professional practice, the ways that professional standards are described can be similar to the learning outcomes of HE programmes, particularly those that are work or practice based, making it easier to map across the two sets of benchmarks.

▶ Using accreditation within a framework

HE programmes comprise validated modules, with some modules being used by more than one programme. Usually a WBL framework facilitates the use of validated modules from other programmes, individually or in multiples, within the framework. The flexibility of WBL frameworks means that they can encompass external employer-based training or in-company learning, which has been 'accredited' (leading to the award of academic credit), along with the more usual learning from routes which have been 'validated' (leading to the award of an academic qualification). Formal recognition of expertise from within employer organisations offers further potential for future collaborative working between HEIs and employers (Bravenboer, 2011; Wilson, 2012).

The following Case studies 3.4 and 3.5 illustrate using a framework for accreditation and developing new qualifications.

Case Study 3.4 Using a framework for accreditation: MSc Professional Practice in Leading Sales Transformation

Consalia Ltd, a training company, specialising in training sales management executives, has significant experience of delivering professional sales education and training and wished to develop a validated MSc programme. As an established university partner, Consalia presented a suite of modules in an accreditation

continued overleaf

Case Study 3.4 Using a framework for accreditation: MSc Professional Practice in Leading Sales Transformation *continued*

proposal to the university's Accreditation Board. The proposal was approved after being assessed by the Accreditation Board and conditions had been met. Following scrutiny of assessed work by a university accreditation link tutor and external assessor, individuals could be awarded a certificate of credit to count towards a university qualification. Accrediting the programme confirmed it was at HE level and quality and allowed Consalia to test the market and see whether it attracted an appropriate audience.

The second stage built on this accreditation to enable progression to a full master's programme. The maximum credit that can be brought into a Middlesex University qualification is two-thirds of the total credit of the target qualification, so a master's programme allows up to 120 credits out of 180 credits at Level 7 to be recognised. To ensure that individuals progressing to the master's would be appropriately prepared, the programme also included a Practitioner Researcher module to design the compulsory final 60-credit Negotiated WBL Project module. Consequently, the programme was constructed from two elements: 90 credits of accredited Consalia modules and 90 credits from university WBL framework modules.

The programme has proved popular with some international companies who are using it to develop their business. Additionally, the success encouraged Consalia to progress to a fully validated programme, working in partnership with the HEI, thereby changing the business model with the HEI, but allowing for a sustainable collaboration.

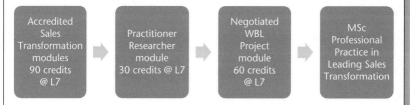

The Consalia pathway to an MSc Professional Practice in Leading Sales Transformation

Case Study 3.5 Using a framework to develop new qualifications: Higher Apprenticeship for care sector managers

Skills for Care, the Sector Skills Council for the care sector, identified that care sector managers needed professional development to meet the changing needs of their employers in the sector. An 80-credit Level 5 QCF Diploma in Leadership for Health and Social Care Services was core to the programme as part of a new Higher Apprenticeship. Skills for Care identified that care sector managers should develop specialisms and that, furthermore, both individuals and employers would value a university qualification.

continued overleaf

Case Study 3.5 Using a framework to develop new qualifications: Higher Apprenticeship for care sector managers *continued*

The university worked with Skills for Care to develop a suite of accredited external courses in professional specialisms. Using its WBL framework a 120-credit university Level 5 higher diploma was constructed. Building on the learning from the QCF diploma and after consulting their employer, learners chose module specialisms such as Dementia Care, Quality and Service Improvement, Mental Health or End of Life Care. These topics were determined by the Sector Skills Council and the care sector managers in consultation to reflect the needs of the care industry. Learners' progress to a final Negotiated Work-based Project module, which applies their specialism to a specific leadership and management context, aims to enhance practice (Skills for Care, 2013).

Higher Diploma Professional Practice in Leading and Managing Care Services

▷ **Teaching tips: Using accreditation in your HEI**

Academic accreditation is formal recognition of learning achievements gained outside the HEI's main academic programme and is normally delivered by a partner or organisation outside the HEI who retain content and intellectual property of the accredited programme. Accreditation processes are designed to incorporate the HEI's quality processes by ensuring consistency with the institution's level descriptors, teaching, learning and assessment standards. Academic accreditation differs from accreditation by a professional body in that it reflects HE-level credit for a learning activity, whereas professional accreditation involves meeting standards of a specific profession or sector. Academic accreditation offers the potential for higher-level learning occurring outside the HEI to be brought into an HE award by using credit accumulation and transfer (CATS). Having an institutional flexible framework will help you to be responsive to external accreditation requests.

The activity below will help you to analyse your institution's readiness to develop an academic framework.

ACTIVITY

Discuss these questions with key colleagues.

▶ Does your institution have a process by which organisational learning can be accredited, for example, a formal accreditation process and practice?

▶ What is the current provision for recognising prior learning from individuals, for example, processes for inclusion in programmes, teaching and assessor skills, design of programmes to enable claims?

▶ What modules and/or programmes would need to be created and what are already available to be adapted to the needs of work-based learners? How might current modules be adapted to work-based learners' needs and employer requirements?

▶ How might your institution's regulations, procedures and policies respond to a flexible framework? What are the 'given' assumptions within the institution with regard to programme design and construction, and how adaptable could these be?

▶ Who might need to be consulted and involved in developing the appropriate infrastructure to support work-based learners? Particularly consider administrative and registry staff who have to interpret policies, processes and regulations to encompass HEI standard procedures.

▶ **Learning, teaching and assessment in a WBL framework**

These topics are discussed in detail in Chapter 2, but it is worth signposting here that the aims of a WBL programme should align with authentic learning and assessment opportunities within the workplace. For example, creative thought and planning to maximise higher-level learning opportunities through usual work activities combined with assessment activities that reflect realistic work will promote deep learning. Discussions with your learners about their work environment will highlight creative problem-solving opportunities and develop skills of critical analysis. Collaboration with employers and workplace mentors when identifying real learning opportunities can lead to productive partnerships between employers and the HEI, offering professional development opportunities for you and your work-based learners alike. Delivery mechanisms that are flexible in time and location, including distance and blended modes of programme delivery, will maximise your students' learning and responsive tutor and peer support.

SUMMARY

▶ Key approaches to supporting learning, such as reflection on practice, research skills and critical engagement with professional networks, are transdisciplinary in nature, and because of this such work-based frameworks are extremely flexible and useable.

▶ Negotiation is built into the construction stages of WBL programmes, including using the existing HEI mechanisms to recognise higher-level learning.

▶ There is a need for clarity and coherence in relation to the national academic infrastructure within which HE is understood, practised and approved.

▶ A common understanding of academic credit is a powerful building block.

▶ The need for a clear curriculum philosophy has been outlined, including traditional subject disciplines within HEI faculties, but mostly the real-world contexts for learning that most people encounter, namely work.

▶ References

Bravenboer, D. W. (2011) Maximising employer-responsive progression through organisational development, in Tallantyre, F. and Kettle, J. (Eds), *Learning from Experience in Employer Engagement*, pp. 34–44. York: Higher Education Academy.

Bravenboer, D. W. and Workman, B. (2015) Developing a transdisciplinary work-based learning curriculum: A model for recognising learning from work, in Keppell, M., Reushle, S. and Antonio, A. (Eds), *Open Learning and Formal Credentialing in Higher Education: Curriculum Models and Institutional Policies*. Hershey, PA: IGI Global.

Brown, J. S. and Duguid, P. (2001) Knowledge organization: A social-practice perspective. *Organization Science*. 12 (2), pp. 198–213.

Kolb, D. A. (1984) *Experiential Learning: Experience as the Source of Learning and Development*. London: Prentice Hall.

McGregor, S. L. T. and Volckmann, R. (2011) *Transdisciplinarity in Higher Education, Part 7: Conclusion*. Available at http://integralleadershipreview.com/2630-transdisciplinarity-in-higher-education-part-7/ accessed 18 August 2014.

Office of Qualifications and Examination Regulation (2013) *Comparing qualification levels*. Available at http://ofqual.gov.uk/help-and-advice/comparing-qualifications/ accessed 18 August 2014.

Quality Assurance Agency (2011) *UK Quality Code for Higher Education* (incorporates the QAA (2008) *The Framework for Higher Education Qualifications in England, Wales* and Scotland and the Framework for Qualifications of Higher Education Institutions in Scotland (FQHEIS), published by QAA in 2001). Available at http://www.qaa.ac.uk/ Publications/InformationandGuidance/Documents/Quality-code-Chapter-A1.pdf accessed 19 May 2014.

Quality Assurance Agency (2014) *The UK Quality Code for Higher Education.* Available at http://www.qaa.ac.uk/assuring-standards-and-quality/the-quality-code/ subject-benchmark-statements, accessed 18 August 2014.

SEEC (2010) *Credit Level Descriptors.* Available at http://www.seec.org.uk/, accessed 18 August 2014.

Sheehan, J. (1986) Curriculum models: Product versus process. *Journal of Advanced Nursing.* 11, pp. 671–678.

Skills for Care (2013) *New Routes into University for People Working in Adult Social Care,* Leeds: Skills for Care. Available at http://www.skilssforcare.org.uk/Document-library/Qualifications-and-Apprenticeships/Apprenticeships/New-routes-into-univer sity-e-version.pdf.

Uzzi, B. and Dunlap, S. (2005) How to build your network. *Harvard Business Review.* Available at http://hbr.org/2005/12/how-to-build-your-network/ar/1, accessed 8 August 2014.

Wenger, E. (2006) *Communities of Practice: A Brief Introduction.* Available at http:// www.noetikos.org/sitebuildercontent/sitebuilderfiles/copandsituatedlearning. pdf, accessed 8 August 2014.

Willis, K. (2008) Frameworks for work-based learning, in HEA (2008) *Work-based Learning: Workforce Development: Connections, Frameworks and Processes,* pp. 31–41. York: HEA.

Workman, B. (2009) The core components: Teaching, learning and assessing, in Costley, C., Garnett, J. and Workman, B. (Eds), *Work-based Learning: Journeys to the Core of Higher Education,* pp. 189–203. London: Middlesex University Press.

Workman, B. and Garnett, J. (2009) The development and implementation of work-based learning at Middlesex University, in Costley, C., Garnett, J. and Workman, B. (Eds), *Work-based Learning: Journeys to the Core of Higher Education,* pp. 1–15. London: Middlesex University Press.

Workman, B. and White, T. (2015) Build your degree, in Helyer, R. (Ed.), *The Work-based Learning Student Handbook.* 2nd Edn, London: Palgrave.

Wilson, T. (2012) *A Review of Business–University Collaboration.* London: BIS.

▶ **Recommended further reading**

Durrant, A., Rhodes, G. and Young, D. (2009) *Getting Started with University-level Work-based Learning.* London: Middlesex University Press.

Gordon, N. (2014) *Flexible Pedagogies: Technology-enhanced Learning.* HEA. Available at http://www.heacademy.ac.uk/resources/detail/flexible-learning/flexiblepeda gogies/tech_enhanced_learning/main_report HEA York, accessed 30 June 2015.

Graham, S., Helyer, R. and Workman, B. (2008) Accreditation of in-company training provision: An overview of models and issues, in Higher Education Academy (Ed.),

Frameworks for Work-based Learning: Workforce Development: Connections, Frameworks and Processes, pp. 43–55. York, UK: HEA.

Kettle, J. (2013) *Flexible Pedagogies: Employer Engagement and Work-based Learning.* HEA. Available at http://www.heacademy.ac.uk/resources/details/flexible-learning/flexiblepedagogies/employerengagement/report, accessed 30 June 2015.

Quality Assurance Agency (2012) *UK Quality Code for Higher Education: Part C Information about Higher Education Provision.* Available at http://www.qaa.ac.uk/AssuringStandardsAndQuality/quality-code/Pages/Quality-Code-Part-C.aspx), accessed 30 June 2015.

Raelin, J. A. (2008) *Work-based Learning: Bridging Knowledge and Action in the Workplace.* New and Revised Edn, San Francisco: Jossey-Bass.

Skinner, H., Blackey, H. and Green, P. J. (2011) Accrediting informal learning: Drivers challenges and HE responses. *Higher Education, Skills and Work-based Learning.* 1 (1), pp. 52–62.

4 Negotiation and work-based learning

Mike Laycock and Mary Karpel

IN THIS CHAPTER YOU WILL:

▶ Find out what institutional conditions are favourable to the introduction of negotiated work-based learning
▶ See which pedagogical theories underpin negotiated work-based learning
▶ Examine what can be negotiated in a work-based learning project or programme
▶ Consider the practicalities involved in ensuring that negotiated work-based learning can be formalised, documented and approved through learning agreements
▶ Investigate the ways in which the process of negotiation can be experienced by learners and tutors
▶ Look at the potential future of negotiated work-based learning and, particularly, if it could be framed in a new Professional Bachelors (BProf) award

▶ The process of negotiation

Work-based learning (WBL), as an umbrella term, encompasses a wide range of learning environments, each with its own relationship to the formal taught curriculum. When faced with the requirement of facilitating learning that directly results from experiences within the workplace itself, rather than from other forms of teaching, the situation becomes unmediated and the learner becomes central to learning choices. However, these choices need to be closely informed by the demands of higher education (HE) and, where relevant, aligned to the organisational strategies of the workplace. To ensure that the needs of those involved (learners, employers, higher education institutions (HEIs)) are addressed, whilst at the same time establishing a clear learning agenda for the learner, the process of negotiation in WBL takes centre stage.

Brennan and Little (1996) argue that negotiation characterises and distinguishes WBL from other forms of learning:

> the aspect that distinguishes work-based learning from other processes of learning is the part that negotiation between individual, employer and higher education institution plays: negotiation between these three stakeholders in identifying achievable learning outcomes which are meaningful and challenging to the individual, are relevant to the employer and have academic credibility; establishing, through negotiation, appropriate methods of, and criteria for, assessment acceptable to all parties; establishing and maintaining, through negotiation, a supportive learning environment (based primarily in the workplace) (p. 5).

Providing a model of learning, where the learner has a leading role in negotiating the content, level and scope of their intended programme with the academic institution and the employer, challenges the traditional academic, intellectual assumptions of HE, and, as Ramsey et al. (2010) note, 'the process of negotiating work-based learning is crucially important both to the learning journey of the learner and also to the quality control systems of the accrediting university' (p. 46).

▶ What are the institutional conditions for authentic and effective negotiation?

The nature and degree of institutional support for WBL is, in our view, dependent on the presence of six conditions that will either help or hinder the process of negotiated work-based learning. These are:

1. Pedagogic understanding – It is axiomatic that there is a need for institutional understanding of, and support for, the pedagogical underpinning for negotiated WBL. Without support for the theoretical implications of, for example, constructivist and social constructivist approaches to learning, WBL may always be regarded with professional suspicion.

   We argue here that the term 'work-based learning' is reserved for active, purposeful and reflective learning that is derived from the major site of learning – the workplace. It is characterised by a student- or learner-centred pedagogy that is focused on the application and development of learning in the workplace, is built around problems or challenges associated with the learner's current and/or potential work requirements and takes into consideration the capabilities that the learner brings to her or his work practice.

2. Curricula flexibility – It is further important that significant aspects of the curriculum are open and amenable to the process of negotiation. Thus the number and size of work-based projects available to the learner will determine the degree of possibility for negotiation.

3. Relational democracy – It is essential, although there will be variations in the degree of control over the process the three parties will have, that participants clearly demonstrate a respect and concern for the position of the others in the process, and that the relation between them is, so far as is possible, democratic.

   Chapter B5 of the *UK Quality Code for Higher Education* (Quality Assurance Agency, 2012a) is of relevance here. It sets out the expectations of the QAA in 'Student Engagement' and clearly states the relational obligations in 'partnership'. The terms 'partner' and 'partnership' are used in a broad sense to indicate joint working between students and staff. In this context, partnership working is based on the values of openness, trust and honesty, agreed shared goals and values, and regular communication between the partners.

4. Dialogic opportunities – Opportunities for dialogue and discussion must be present in any negotiated learning process. Ramsey et al. (2010) discuss, for example, the need for continuing dialogue in their discussion of ways of approaching the negotiation of the size and credit value of work-based projects:

   Just as dialogue is important in arriving at the initial definition of the size of a work-based project, so continual communication is vital to the ongoing management of that work-based project (p. 56).

5. Boundary clarity – Inevitably, the concept of negotiation in learning also implies aspects of the process that are non-negotiable. These non-negotiable boundaries require clarity. In the main, they will emanate from the institution and, for example, from (in the UK) the Quality Assurance Agency's quality code. As an example, institutions may have created a module with specific non-negotiable learning outcomes but left scope within that module for learners to negotiate, in addition, their own learning outcomes in conjunction with employers.

6. Procedural frameworks and documentation – All WBL programmes have their specific procedures and processes governing the overall structure of the programme. Specific to negotiation are the requisite

tools for planning, monitoring and assessing WBL projects, not the least of which is the ubiquitous negotiated learning contract or agreement.

Of all these conditions, an understanding of the key elements of pedagogical theory is essential to the successful comprehension of negotiated WBL.

▶ New pedagogies for learning

Boud and Solomon (2001) argued that 'though many variants and hybrids of WBL exist, the more "radical" versions "depart substantially from the disciplinary framework of university study and develop new pedagogies for learning"' (p. 4).

Pedagogies for learning include:

▶ Constructivism and social constructivism – Constructivism posits that by reflecting on our experiences, we construct our own understanding of the world we live in. Each of us generates our own mental models which we use to make sense of our experiences. Learning, therefore, is an active process of making meaning from experience by adjusting our mental models to accommodate new experiences. Work-based learning is a modern example of a constructivist approach to learning where *'socially situated individuals relate the familiar contexts of their work environments to the requirements of an academic award'*. (Bosley and Young, 2006, p. 357).

▶ Social constructivism – Social constructivism claims that learning involves participation in a 'community of practice', where people 'learn from observing other people' (Merriam and Caffarella, 1991, p. 134). The workplace is an obvious 'social setting' (also see Smith and Smith, 2015).

▶ Andragogy – Andragogy is the *'art and science of helping adults to learn'* (Knowles, 1984). Knowles introduced the notion of a 'learning contract' or 'contracted learning' as a methodological manifestation of this notion and a means of empowering the learner.

▶ Heutagogy – Heutagogy places emphasis on self-directed and double-loop learning and draws together ideas around learning to learn, situated learning, action learning, experiential learning and reflection in WBL (Kenyon and Hase, 2001).

▶ Situated learning – Rather than viewing learning as the acquisition of certain forms of knowledge, situated learning places it in social relationships – situations of co-participation as might occur in the workplace (Lave and Wenger, 1991).

▶ Action learning – Action learning, like WBL, is predicated around the need for negotiation, through questioning and reflection (Lewin, 1946; Carr and Kemmis, 1986) and as participative inquiry (Reason and Rowan, 1981). The practices of action learning draw heavily on models of experiential learning developed by Kolb (1984) and Boud et al. (1985) and, of course, on principles of reflective practice espoused by Schön (1983).

▶ Experiential learning – Experiential learning theories are based on the idea that understanding is not fixed but is formed and re-formed through experience in a continuous and cyclical process (Kolb, 1984), with participants bringing their own ideas and beliefs to learning situations. The importance of negotiating ways forward through this cycle of learning is prioritised in experiential learning.

▶ Theories of reflection – Reflection is critical to WBL. As Nixon et al. (2006) have noted, *'Students are encouraged to critically reflect on their experiences as a means by which to recognise knowledge creation and development in the workplace'* (p. 9). Schön brought reflection into the centre of an understanding of what professionals do. His notions of reflection-in-action (1983) and reflection-on-action (1987) have been crucial to development in this area. Schön argues that we can link the process of 'thinking on our feet' with reflection-on-action (after an 'encounter' when, for example, work-based learners write up recordings, complete Personal Development Plans and talk things through with their mentors). Reflection-on-action enables work-based learners to explore why they acted as they did and subsequent consequences. In so doing they develop questions and ideas about activities and practice and begin to negotiate, or re-negotiate, subsequent courses of action.

A successful understanding of WBL is one that goes beyond the where and how of the 'delivery' of WBL and, instead, focuses on learning processes. These processes, in turn, need to be supported and underpinned by learning theory and the actuality of learner autonomy in the workplace. All of which emphasise the crucial role of negotiation in any WBL programme.

▶ What can be negotiated?

In the majority of WBL programmes in the UK, the term 'negotiation' includes negotiating the balance and inclusion of 'taught' modules with experiential projects derived from the workplace, as the following Case study 4.1 illustrates:

Case study 4.1 Accreditation of WBL: Work-based and Integrative Studies at the University of Chester*

The University of Chester's Work-based and Integrative Studies (WBIS) programme is a flexible mechanism for the accreditation of WBL, in which learners are expected to use their workplaces as sites for experiential learning. This is a programme where learners can negotiate their programme award titles within certain parameters, so long as these relate to the field of professional practice concerned. Students can also negotiate the modules and credit that make up this programme – these too need to be consistent with both the award title and the area of practice.

The programme is 'work-based', meaning that experiential learning at work can be accredited but it also offers the opportunity for 'integrative studies' – which means that relevant modules from elsewhere (including the wider university 'bank' of modules) can be integrated into a student's negotiated learning pathway where appropriate. These, for instance, may be modules taught face to face or supported online and at distance (current popular examples include Negotiation Skills, and Emotional Intelligence in the Workplace).

A typical negotiated programme will begin with a *Self-review and Negotiation of Learning* module. This enables participants to undertake a self-audit and complete a claim for prior learning, if appropriate. Crucially, *Self-review and Negotiation of Learning* also provides the opportunity for needs analysis and action planning, leading to the negotiation of the wider programme of study. This is captured in an Approved Studies Learning Agreement for each level of study and is agreed by the university. Participants then follow this individually tailored study programme.

Of relevance and significance in the Chester model is the way experiential learning is then captured. This is typically through '*Negotiated Experiential Learning*' modules (or NELMs) of which there are two broad types. The first is '*where academic reward for experiential learning is undertaken in relation to a specific subject matter*' (for example, team leadership/designing websites), and the second, where experiential learning '*arises from planning and completing a specific work-based learning project of some sort*'.

Before starting a NELM, it is important for learners to discuss their ideas with their university tutor and mentor/line manager '*to ensure that the project is feasible, manageable, of value to the organisation and will allow you to demonstrate learning at the appropriate academic level*'. Learners then formalise their proposal in a NELA – a Negotiated Experiential Learning Agreement – which must be signed by '*your University Tutor, mentor/line manager and yourself*'.

Learning within the NELM is always driven by hands-on experience in the workplace; the learning outcomes are negotiable, reflecting the individual nature of the learning involved, and the assessment is also negotiable and flexible – and for the same reasons.

Most learners on negotiated routes at Chester negotiate learning pathways that comprise a combination of recognition of prior learning, relevant taught modules and NELMs.

***Extracts from WBIS Module Handbooks, University of Chester**

Despite the fact that negotiated WBL presents a challenge to the academic assumptions of HE, it is, of course, subject to, and governed by, the same qualification framework as more traditional discipline/subject-centred delivery. But to suggest that there are equally valid sites of knowledge production and co-production is to challenge an identity and value system that has been rooted, until relatively recently, in the 'cultural capital' from which HE has derived its legitimacy (Symes, 2001), and attention to national and institutional quality control frameworks in the design and delivery of negotiated WBL is vital. For UK HEIs, therefore, the *UK Quality Code for Higher Education* is the major reference point. Other examples include the Australian TEQSA's (Tertiary Education Quality and Standards Agency) *Higher Education Standards Framework (Threshold Standards) 2011* or the AUCC (Association of Universities and Colleges of Canada) principles in Canada. Membership of the AUCC requires institutions to meet quality criteria and adhere to set principles of institutional quality assurance that are reaffirmed every five years.

▶ Negotiable elements of a WBL project

The following elements are often negotiable within individually negotiated WBL projects, but much will depend on individual institutional approaches:

Teaching tips	
Content	Dialogue may be required between tutor and student to establish the academic level of the proposed content and may refer to the Qualification Descriptors of the FHEQ (Quality Assurance Agency, 2012b). If the work is at FHEQ Level 6, for example, does the proposed content permit the demonstration of the appropriate descriptors such as the following: ▶ *Apply the methods and techniques that they have learnt to review, consolidate, extend and apply their knowledge and understanding and to initiate and carry out projects* ▶ *Critically evaluate arguments, assumptions, abstract concepts and data (that may be incomplete) to make judgements and to frame appropriate questions to achieve a solution – or identify a range of solutions – to a problem* ▶ *Communicate information, ideas, problems and solutions to both specialist and non-specialist audiences* (Quality Assurance Agency, 2012b, p. 11) *continued overleaf*

Teaching tips *continued*	
Size and scope	Negotiation will clarify an appropriate size for a project in terms of its credit value, and much will depend on the hours that potentially will be devoted to the project, whether the learner has articulated these appropriately and whether all the learning outcomes can be demonstrated given the size and scope of the project and the time available for its completion. Has the student over- or under-estimated what is possible?
Learning outcomes	Shell modules may have their own non-negotiable learning outcomes. However, the learner may be able to add their own in relation to the content and size of the project. Care should be taken to explain how learning outcomes are constructed and written with regard to level and assessment implications.
Resources	Relevant and appropriate HEI resources will normally be available. However, some specialised equipment or information may be required in the work environment. Access to this may require negotiation with the employer.
Assessment materials	The HEI may offer flexibility with regard to materials submitted for WBL assessment, but there may also be non-negotiable materials (written reports, theses, portfolios and so on). Negotiation of assessment materials will take into account learning outcomes, level and content.
Assessment criteria	Some assessment criteria may be non-negotiable. However, scope may exist to negotiate the learner's own criteria. Discussions are thus needed around learning outcomes, level and scope and the importance of the submission of assessment products that are responsive to the application of these criteria.

▶ The practice of negotiation through learning agreements

Although there are many potentially negotiable aspects of a WBL pro-gramme, they may typically involve students in negotiating their aims and learning outcomes, the methods by which those aims and learning out-comes will be met and the means by which those aims and learning out-comes can be assessed in the form of a negotiated learning agreement. The terms 'learning contract' and 'learning agreement' are often used inter-changeably. Laycock and Stephenson (1994) argue that the term 'learn-ing contract' has sometimes been misinterpreted. A learning contract is *generated by the learner* and not meant to imply a legalistic or bureaucratic approach to learning; a 'negotiated learning plan' might better express both the process and the methods involved (p. 17).

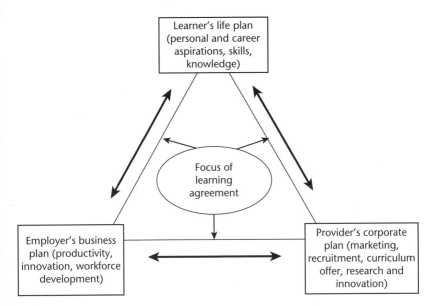

Figure 4.1 Workplace learning interrelationships

Source: Nixon et al. (2006) p.35

To better understand the creation of a learning agreement it is essential to examine the motivations of each party, the consequences of the negotiation, the extent to which all are fully involved and the ways in which learning agreements/contracts can formalise, document and provide appropriate means of approving the outcome of the negotiation.

Penn et al. (2005) suggest that the focus of the learning agreement will depend on the relative predominance of the needs and interests of the different stakeholders. They suggest that the student is influenced by their *life plan*, the learning provider by their *corporate plan* and the employer (or sector) by their *business plan.* In other words negotiation has to be placed in the context of the motivations and needs of the relevant stakeholders (see Figure 4.1)

▶ **The extent of employer engagement in tripartite negotiation**

Some have argued that the degree of employer engagement in the negotiation process is not as strong as the other partners, though their inclusion is essential. Crossan et al. (2010) acknowledge that:

> in order for WBL to be effective, there needs to be open three-way communication between learners, academic institutions and employers in order to increase the likelihood that all parties have a positive learning experience or outcome (p. 33).

But they also note the critics of this accepted wisdom:

> Gleeson and Keep (2004) question the required level of employer engagement. Both Hanney (2005) and Hillier (2006) separately argue that in reality there is less employer involvement in the tripartite relationship (p. 33).

Lester and Costley (2010) examine the ways in which HEIs continue to engage with the tensions that exist between the demands and opportunities provided by the workplace and the need to develop practice, support personal development and maintain academic validity, and are developing more sophisticated approaches than those suggested by the notions of employer engagement and skills development.

Bolden and Petrov (2008) have also suggested that the critical role HEIs play in engaging with businesses needs to be evaluated and improved. They contend that the employer's perspective is:

> more responsive to markets than policy and they may not see the need to invest the necessary time and resources (and that) employers may not necessarily value 'academic' education, showing a preference for on-the-job and work-based learning leading to professional and industry qualifications (pp. 4–5).

Negotiated learning agreements provide a means of facilitating deep learning (Marton et. al., 1984; Hooker and Helyer, 2015) and a high level of student motivation and effective involvement (Boud et al., 1985). Anderson et al. (1996) have noted that they also promote inclusivity. Though we have argued that, in reality, employer engagement in the process may not be as robust as that of the learner and the HEI, the learning agreement is the most obvious way in which employers can demonstrate their engagement. It also needs to be remembered, however, that sometimes a WBL student is attending an HEI in order to change jobs and may not have told their employer. If this is the case the agreements around negotiating award content are simply between the student and the institution.

The process by which tripartite learning agreements can be agreed and their outcomes assessed would involve the preparation and negotiation of a work-based project or projects, approval by the HEI, the implementation of the learning agreement and assessment, mapped against the outcomes of the agreed project and the benchmarked standards of degrees (see Figure 4.2). The mapping process can, of course, also involve whole awards, not just projects (Case study 4.2).

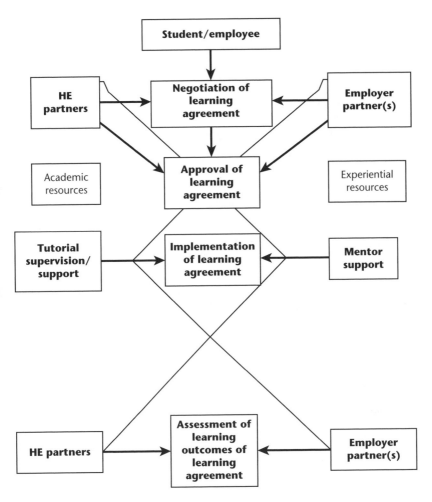

Figure 4.2   Using learning agreements for WBL programmes

Source: Laycock (2011)

Case study 4.2 How learning agreements work in real life: One student's learning agreement for an undergraduate WBL module

Title of study

'An evaluation of the extent to which emotion-gender differences can account for the differential usage of counselling self-referral services in a primary school.'

continued overleaf

Case study 4.2 How learning agreements work in real life: One student's learning agreement for an undergraduate WBL module *continued*

Aims of study

▶ To critically examine how counselling self-referral services are promoted in a primary school
▶ To critically investigate whether counselling self-referral services are perceived differently by boys and girls in the school
▶ To critically review the literature with regard to theories explaining possible gender differences in emotion sharing

How are those aims going to be fulfilled?

▶ Statistics of attendance by gender will be critically evaluated with regard to self-referral to the counselling service.
▶ School staff will be questioned with regard to the promotion of self-referral counselling services.
▶ Primary school children will be interviewed about their familiarity with counselling self-referral services in their school, possible experience of using the services and whether they feel that it is sufficiently promoted; children will also be questioned about possible improvements to the service.

Learning outcomes

By the end of this module I will have:

▶ Critically reviewed current research, that is, books, journals and online resources, which propose gender differences with regard to sharing and expression of emotions
▶ Analysed how theories of 'emotion-gender differences' may account for differential usage of the counselling self-referral service between males and females at a primary school
▶ Analysed how the counselling self-referral service is promoted by primary school staff and how it is perceived by children attending the school
▶ Critically reflected upon my work as a volunteer counsellor
▶ Managed my time effectively throughout the course of the project

Professional skills intended to be developed/enhanced

▶ Self-awareness skills
▶ Time management skills
▶ Learning reflection skills
▶ Critical/analytical skills

How are learning outcomes to be demonstrated and evaluated?

▶ Current research on emotion-gender differences relevant to this study will be referenced and discussed in the report.

continued overleaf

> **Case study 4.2 How learning agreements work in real life: One student's learning agreement for an undergraduate WBL module** *continued*
>
> ▷ Psychological theories of emotion-gender differences, which may explain the differential usage of counselling self-referral services in a primary school, will serve as evidence to support the discussion in the report.
> ▷ Data obtained from interviewing school staff and children on the promotion and perception of counselling self-referral services will build the basis for the discussion in the report and will be attached as appendices.
> ▷ Learning logs will illustrate the processes involved in conducting the study, any difficulties encountered and possible amendments made throughout the course of the project.
> ▷ Learning logs will reflect upon effective time management throughout the course of the project.

▷ What might a learning agreement involve?

A negotiated learning agreement for a module might involve the learner specifying the following:

- ▷ The title of the study/project
- ▷ The general aims of the module and how they will be fulfilled
- ▷ The intended learning outcomes of the module
- ▷ The professional skills the learner intends to develop/enhance and/or the details of a particular work-based project the learner will conduct
- ▷ A timetable for the study
- ▷ A research methodology for undertaking a particular project
- ▷ An indication of the learning resources that will be utilised
- ▷ How the learning outcomes will be demonstrated and assessed
- ▷ Signatures of all parties to the agreement

As can be seen from the above, there are many benefits to developing a learning agreement.

▷ Benefits of learning agreements

Learning agreements require learners to:

- ▷ Be explicit about their learning intentions and set clear and achievable aims (learning outcomes)
- ▷ Justify their plans in terms of their own personal, professional and vocational development

▶ Address key issues such as the level of performance required to demonstrate the learning outcomes at the appropriate programme level (see Chapter 4 regarding level descriptors)

Learning agreements enable universities to:

▶ Focus support and resources on an individual learner's needs, harnessing the resources of all parties and noting the resource gaps (Minton, 2007)
▶ Be explicit about their own assumptions, about what they are prepared to negotiate and the criteria they will use for approving agreements
▶ Provide the context for intellectual rigour and continuing personal support within which students/employees can prepare their plans, review their progress and complete their programmes

Learning agreements can enable employers to:

▶ Participate in the development, approval and assessment of an employee's/student's plans
▶ Plan more effective work placements
▶ Reassure employees/students on the relevance of their programmes

There may also be other benefits that you or your institution would prioritise.

▶ Practitioner experiences of the process of negotiation: Sharing the learning journey, not just the map

Earlier we introduced some of the theoretical frameworks that inform the practice of negotiated learning. However, in the world of professional practice there is a varied topography requiring navigation that contrasts a high ground of research-based theory and technique, which provides solutions to clearly articulated problems, with a swampy lowland of situations which are messy and confusing and incapable of technical solution (Schön, 1987). The reflections here are from the latter and are based upon experiences from teaching on 'shell' WBL modules from within and across different institutions.

Negotiated WBL is driven by context and requires a totally different approach to learning and teaching than that demanded by much traditional subject discipline learning. Nowhere is this more apparent in the process than at the very beginning when the negotiation is taking place. Without successful negotiation there can be no clear articulation of the intentions of the learning for all stakeholders. However, in practice, the skills required to effectively create a blueprint for the learning are highly complex and present interesting challenges to both student and tutor.

▶ Learner challenges

For the majority of students, most learning has emphasised content over process, and this is at odds with the demands of flexibility and creativity required for negotiated learning. In addition to this the tutor role has changed to one of a facilitator who supports the *process* rather than delivering pre-defined content. Many are challenged by this less structured learning environment and may take a while to get used to the differences between attending lectures each week and preparing essays, and self-directed study. Having a choice in what to study might well score high on student-centredness, but it is also so much at odds with their experience of other learning that it is, without doubt, the biggest challenge that many students face. Identifying a learning opportunity and deciding upon a topic of inquiry, which are at the core of negotiated learning, are complex requirements which need to be recognised. The problems and issues faced at work are ill defined, ambiguous and open ended. This has to be contrasted with the more usual experience of clearly prescribed curriculum outcomes and rewards for 'correct' answers.

▶ Tutor challenges

The challenge as a tutor is to recognise the different demands being placed upon students and to support and guide them in the *process* of learning at work. This requires an approach more like a manager of the learning experience rather than an information provider. It means relinquishing the 'sage on the stage' role and actively cultivating and enjoying uncertainty. The tutor's role might best be described as one of 'facilitating the messiness' (Reid, 2010). As each student's ability, circumstances and context of learning will be different, there needs to be a balance between being 'hands off' in order to encourage independence and more directive during times of difficulty such as balancing work requirements with academic activity, understanding ethics and when things go wrong, such as a change of job. Tutors become co-creators of learning, and this requires a negotiation of the role within the student experience. The biggest challenge is helping the learner identify and decide upon a suitable and appropriate topic of inquiry. It is not unusual to be met with blank faces and shrugging shoulders. Often, students are at a complete loss as to how they might direct their own learning. When they seek direction it has to be avoided by the tutor at all costs at this stage. To 'facilitate the messiness' there needs to be a clear strategy to negotiate a learning plan and to foster self-direction.

▶ Strategy for supporting the negotiation process

As a tutor, in many ways the teaching and learning skills that are developed to support the student are mirrored in the learner's skill development because of the 'real life' context of activities. They might best be described as 'wicked' competencies, skills which cannot be precisely defined, take on different shapes in different contexts and keep on developing. They are difficult to teach but can be developed experientially (Knight, 2007). Whilst the student learns the skills of self-directed study in a real-life context, the tutor learns the skills of controlling the process of learning so that at the end of the module, the student meets the required outcomes. In practice, this process is centred upon the creation of the learning agreement. This agreement is the outcome of the negotiation of learning and provides both the *what* and the *how* of the learning that will take place. Interestingly, the 'how' they are going to learn presents little difficulty compared to the task of deciding what to learn. Students, in the formal educational setting, are used to being told what to learn. However, for context-driven learning, the learning needs to be negotiated between the module's learning outcomes, the workplace context, the student's interests and, where appropriate and/or relevant, the employer.

Inexperienced learners and tutors can easily make the mistake of expecting 'perfect' learning agreements, but as the learning evolves there needs to be flexibility to address the ensuing messiness of real-life circumstance, and some HEIs re-visit learning agreements every year, semester or term. Facilitating the process of moving from vague idea to submission of an agreement proposal is best achieved by group dialogue and discussion led by the tutor in a workshop environment. The template (see p. 85, 'What might a learning agreement involve?') for the learning agreement can provide a framework for the questions the tutor needs to ask in order to foster critical engagement with the learner's workplace. Even students who have a clear idea of what they would like to examine have to negotiate to ensure that the scope and level of learning is appropriate. Students should be invited to suggest any ideas for learning they may have. Sometimes the most bizarre ideas can turn into important learning opportunities, so a safe learning environment where students can feel free to 'play' with ideas creatively is necessary. Not all students' ideas can be addressed in a workshop, but the observation and participation in the process of a few examples provide enough direction for all students to then negotiate their own. Listening to how an ill-defined idea can be turned into a project proposal or learning agreement is a fundamental part of the learning experience.

Negotiation of learning, in practice, requires creativity and initiative by both student and tutor. Only once the student has taken the initiative to pursue a learning experience, and accepted responsibility for their own learning, are they able to follow it through to its conclusion. The negotiated learning agreement is paramount in the process. Once created, agreements should be assessed promptly for both summative and formative feedback and be constantly used as a reference point for all further learning on the module or programme.

▶ The future of negotiated learning in HE

Negotiated WBL involves the transfer of authority over the way knowledge is organised into academic curricula away from the HEI and towards the learner. In so doing it is more than a simple economic exchange or mere training in skills. As Costley and Armsby (2008) note:

> Many work-based learners enter programmes of study to develop them-selves in new ways of thinking. They are already experts within their own fields and know how to access familiar, paradigmatic professional and subject based knowledge (p. 12).

Negotiated learning should be designed to be emancipatory and trans-formational whilst also being formally recognised by a particular award that clearly signifies its educational orientation. Laycock (2008, 2010) has argued that an appropriate award that reflects and recognises the growth, status and orientation of negotiated WBL is now needed and proposed a BProf or Professional Bachelor's award. The BProf would be reserved for pro-grammes where participants had developed high-level occupational skills such as:

▶ project and programme management skills,
▶ teamwork skills and, where appropriate, leadership skills,
▶ oral and written communication skills and
▶ organisational skills

and, in addition, had made a significant contribution to the enhancement of an occupational area informed by the application, development and test-ing of theoretical and conceptual frameworks, and had demonstrated an ability to exercise moral and ethical judgements (see Appendix for more information on ethics).

Importantly, the BProf would signify that the programme had com-prised a negotiated WBL project or projects formulated by the learners themselves according to their own and the organisation's long-term goals. The respective interests of the three parties would be protected by the use of three-way negotiated learning agreements. The learner would negotiate the purpose, direction and content of the learning, the HEI providing specialist supervision and access to accreditation, and the employer providing opportunities to learn through work with access to resources and help.

SUMMARY

▶ As negotiated WBL becomes more systematically embraced it presents more challenges to traditional orthodoxies where legitimacy in terms of control over objectives, content, timing, pace, location and forms of assessment is weakened.

▶ The principal challenge is to make the 'architecture of higher education' (Boud and Solomon, 2001) work for WBL.

▶ There are important theoretical foundations which support the understanding of the principles of negotiation.

▶ There are established approaches in assuring the quality of learner-directed learning and the place of negotiation within that learning.

▶ The process of negotiation presents tutors with challenges but also exciting opportunities.

▶ References

Anderson, G., Boud, D. and Sampson, J. (1996) *Learning Contracts: A Practical Guide*. London: Kogan Page.

Association of Universities and Colleges of Canada. *Principles of Institutional Quality Assurance in Canadian Higher Education* Available at http://www.aucc.ca/wp-content/uploads/2011/03/Principles_of_institutional.pdf accessed 16 May 2015.

Bolden, R. and Petrov, G. (2008) *Workforce Development: Employer Engagement with Higher Education*. London: CIHE. Available at http://business-school.exeter.ac.uk/research/areas/topics/leadership/outputs/publication/?id=399 accessed 15 May 2015.

Bosley, S. and Young, D. (2006) Online learning dialogues in learning through work. *The Journal of Work and Learning*. 18 (6), pp. 355–366.

Boud, D., Keogh, R. and Walker, D. (1985) *Reflection: Turning Experience into Learning* London: Kogan Page.

Boud, D. and Solomon, N. (Eds) (2001) *Work-based Learning: A New Higher Education?* Buckingham: SRHE and OU Press.

Brennan, J. and Little, B. (1996) *A Review of Work-based Learning in Higher Education*. London: Department for Education and Skills.

Carr, W. and Kemmis, S. (1986) *Becoming Critical. Education, Knowledge and Action Research*. Lewes: Falmer Press.

Costley. C. and Armsby, P. (2008) Critiquing work-based learning in higher education – a review, in Garnett, J. and Young, D. (Eds), *Work-based Learning Futures II* Proceedings from the Work-based Learning Futures II Conference, pp. 7–21. Middlesex, May 2008. Available at www.uvac.ac.uk/wp-content/uploads/2013/09/WBLFII-FINAL. pdf accessed 15 May 2015.

Crossan, M., McTavish, A. and Bayley, V. (2010) The reality of employer engagement in work-based learning. *Assessment, Teaching and Learning Journal* (Leeds Met). 10 (Winter), pp. 33–36.

Gleeson, D. and Keep, E. (2004) Voice without accountability: The changing relationship between employers, the state and education in England. *Oxford Review of Education*. 30 (1), pp. 37–63.

Hanney, R. (2005) Competence or capability: Work-based learning and problem-based learning. *Journal of Media Practice*. 6 (2).

Hillier, Y. (2006) *Education, Education, Education or Employers, Education and Equity: Managing Employer and Employee Expectations of Foundation Degrees*. Paper for Higher Education Close-up Conference, University of Lancaster, 24–26 July 2006.

Hooker, E. and Helyer, R. (2015) Planning and negotiating learning, in Helyer, R. (Ed.), *The Work-based Learning Student Handbook*, 2nd Edn, pp. 120–141. London: Palgrave.

Kenyon, C. and Hase, S. (2001) *Moving from Andragogy to Heutagogy in Vocational Education. In Research to Reality: Putting VET Research to Work*. (ERIC Document Reproduction Service No. ED456279). Melbourne: Melbourne Institute of Technology, December. Available at http://www.lindenwood.edu/education/andragogy/andragogy/2011/Kenyon_2001.pdf accessed 15 May 2015.

Knight, P. (2007) *Fostering and Assessing Wicked Competencies*. Paper: The Open University's Centres for Excellence in Teaching and Learning. Available at http://www.open.ac.uk/opencetl/resources/pbpl-resources/knight-2007-fostering-and-assessing-wicked-competencies accessed 15 May 2015.

Knowles, M. S. (1984) *Andragogy in Action. Applying Modern Principles of Adult Education*. San Francisco: Jossey-Bass.

Kolb, D. (1984) *Experiential Learning*. Englewood Cliffs, NJ: Prentice Hall.

Lave, J. and Wenger, E. (1991) *Situated Learning. Legitimate Peripheral Participation*. Cambridge: University of Cambridge Press.

Laycock, M. (2008) Why we need a BProf: The case for a new UK award. *Educational Developments*. 9 (3), pp. 1–6.

Laycock, M. (2010) A 'BProf' for negotiated work-based learning: The case for a new, 'signature' award. *Learning and Teaching in Higher Education*. 4 (2), pp. 114–132.

Laycock, M. (2011) *Learner engagement: A guide to negotiated work-based learning* SEDA Paper 29 Staff and Educational Development Association, Birmingham.

Laycock, M. and Stephenson, J. (Eds) (1994) *Using Learning Contracts in Higher Education*. London: Kogan Page.

Lester, Sand Costley, C. (2010) Work-based learning at higher education level: Value, practice and critique. *Studies in Higher Education*. 3 (5), pp. 561–565.

Lewin, K. (1946) Action research and minority problems. *Journal of Social Issues.* 2 (4), pp. 34–46.

Marton, F., Hounsell, D. and Entwistle, N. (Eds) (1984) *The Experience of Learning.* Edinburgh: Scottish Academic Press.

Merriam, S. and Caffarella, R. (1991) *Learning in Adulthood. A Comprehensive Guide.* San Francisco: Jossey-Bass.

Minton, A. (2007) Negotiation of learning contracts and assessment in work-based learning, in Middlesex University, *UALL Work-based Learning: A Multidimensional Approach to Knowledge.* (unpublished).

Nixon, I., Smith, K., Stafford, R. and Camm, S. (The KSA Partnership) (2006) *Work-based Learning: Illuminating the Higher Education Landscape.* York, UK: Higher Education Academy. Available at https://www.heacademy.ac.uk/node/4817 accessed 15 May 2015.

Penn, D., Nixon, I. and Shewell, J. (2005) *Workplace Learning in the North East.* Report to HEFCE by The KSA Partnership.

Quality Assurance Agency (2012a) *The UK Quality Code for Higher Education. B5 'Student Engagement'.* Gloucester. Available at http://www.qaa.ac.uk/en/Publications/Pages/Quality-Code-Chapter-B5.aspx#.VVXYNZZwbIU accessed 15 May 2015

Quality Assurance Agency (2012b) *The UK Quality Code for Higher Education. Part A: Setting and Maintaining Threshold Academic Standards. Chapter A1: The National Level.* Gloucester. Available at http://www.qaa.ac.uk/en/Publications/Pages/Quality-Code-Part-A.aspx accessed 15 May 2015.

Ramsey, R., Harvey, M., Partridge, S. and Workman, B. (2010) *Negotiating the Size and Credit Value of Work-based Learning Projects,* Higher Education Academy. Available at http://www-new1.heacademy.ac.uk/assets/documents/employability/employerengagement/EEL_chapter3.pdf, York accessed 15 May 2015.

Reason, P. and Rowan, J. (Eds) (1981) *Human Inquiry: A Sourcebook of New Paradigm Research.* Chichester: Wiley.

Reid, K. (2010). *Co-creating Learning: Tutor Perspectives of Work-based Learning.* Final Report Practice-Based Professional Learning Centre, The Open University. Available at http://www.open.ac.uk/opencetl/resources/pbpl-resources/reid-k-2009-co-creating-learning-tutor-reflections-practice-based-pedagogy-and-assessment-final-report accessed 15 May 2015.

Smith, S. and Smith, L. (2015) Social learning: Supporting yourself and your peers, in Helyer, R. (Ed.), *The Work-based Learning Student Handbook,* 2nd Edn, pp. 184–204. London: Palgrave.

Schön, D. A. (1983) *The Reflective Practitioner.* New York: Basic Books.

Schön, D. A. (1987) *Educating the Reflective Practitioner: Toward a New Design for Teaching and Learning in the Professions.* San Francisco: Jossey-Bass.

Symes, C. (2001) Capital Degrees: Another episode in the history of work-based learning, in Boud, D. and Solomon, N. (Eds), *Work-based Learning: A New Higher Education?* Buckingham: SRHE and OU Press.

Tertiary Education Quality and Standards Agency (2011), *Higher Education Standards Framework (Threshold Standards) 2011* Available at http://www.comlaw.gov.au/Details/F2013C00169 accessed 15 May 2015.

▶ Recommended further reading

Chisholm, C. U., Blair, M. S. G., Northwood, D. O. and Johrendt, J. L. (2009) Characterisation of work-based learning by consideration of the theories of experiential learning. *European Journal of Education.* 44(3), pp. 319–337.

Nixon, I. (2008) *Work-based Learning: Impact Study.* York , UK: HEA. Available at https://www.heacademy.ac.uk/sites/…/impact_work_based_learning.pdf accessed 15 May 2015.

White, T. (2012) Employer responsive provision: Workforce development through work-based learning. *Higher Education, Skills and Work-based Learning.* 2 (1),pp. 6–21.

5 Recognising and accrediting prior experiential learning

Pauline Armsby and Ruth Helyer

IN THIS CHAPTER YOU WILL:

▶ Clarify the importance of RPL/APL in WBL programmes through an overview of current pedagogic practices and theories of learning
▶ Be offered illustrations of ways that credit can be used in WBL programmes
▶ See the role of the tutor in supporting and assessing these accreditation processes
▶ Be given an example of how technology has been utilised to manage these processes
▶ Be introduced to the place of accredited company training activity in WBL programmes
▶ Explore some common issues for tutors working in this area and some approaches for dealing with them

▶ Learning from experiencing work and life

This chapter focuses on recognising and, if appropriate, accrediting prior learning which students have already undertaken before they embark upon a formalised programme of study with a university or other higher education institution (HEI). Often work-based learners will have amassed considerable learning from their experiences of work and life; if they can adequately evidence this learning and if it has some relevance to their current learning pathway, there are established processes in place within education to award credit for this learning. These processes are commonly referred to as the recognition of prior learning (RPL) and the accreditation of prior learning (APL). Recognition of existing learning as a foundation to further work-based study is important, but using RPL and APL can be extremely beneficial for work-based learners as it can reduce the time they need to spend on campus and also reduce the fees they might have to pay, due to undertaking less modules overall. The majority of the chapter will examine RPL and APL within work-based learning (WBL) programmes for individual students, but one of the final sections explores the accreditation and use of in-company programmes. Case studies are offered throughout to provide practical examples and real-life context to the ideas being discussed. Student performance is rigorously judged against academic standards; RPL effectively links assessment from learning elsewhere with assessment from programme learning and the key features of sound practice still apply. We hope that the chapter will convince you of the importance of RPL/APL in WBL programmes and provide you with some guidance on how to incorporate and manage RPL/APL processes.

▶ The RPL/APL process and why it is important in WBL

Many WBL programmes begin with some kind of recognition and accreditation of prior experiential learning. There is a range of reasons for this, including its alignment with the lifelong learning agenda (OECD, 1996), acknowledgement that learning arises from contexts and practices (Lave and Wenger, 1991) and an ontological turn in HE that foregrounds who the student becomes (Dall'Alba and Barnacle, 2007). Perhaps most important is the philosophy of WBL that puts the learner and his or her learning requirements central to the programme. These learning requirements may be guided by organisational priorities, but it is the learner, as a productive worker, who must take the work-based developments forward and is therefore seen as the central agent of action. The RPL process offers the opportunity to accredit the learner's relevant learning from prior experience and can act as a kind of training needs analysis (TNA) of areas that may still need development in order to complete the WBL programme. In addition, the process of making the claim requires the ability to reflect on experiences to define what has been learnt and is often facilitated in HE via a self-audit module. RPL offers the following:

▶ The opportunity to accumulate and recognise a foundation of relevant credit towards the WBL programme
▶ A mechanism for auditing and evaluating current knowledge, skills and abilities required to complete the programme
▶ A learning process to develop reflective practice skills that will be invaluable in supporting learning through the rest of the programme

Experiential learning has a long philosophical history, but in more recent times its importance in HE has been asserted (Kolb, 1984) and connected with reflection as a process to develop practitioners (Schön, 1987). These ideas have, in turn, been built on constructivist theory which argues that individuals develop knowledge through building meaning from their experiences. These conceptual frameworks underpin WBL pedagogies, and modern teaching and learning principles such as student-centred learning have also evolved from these approaches. It helps to clarify the difference between:

▶ Specific credit – credit achieved through meeting explicit learning outcomes, for example, on a named module, and
▶ General credit – credit achieved through showing alignment to broad, universal-level outcomes.

Learning from experience is not a causal relationship because learning does not automatically emerge; rather experience provides a context in which learning may happen. The recognition of prior learning (RPL) helps students to claim for this experiential learning, if it meets certain specified levels, and is always aligned to the discernible learning, never merely the experience.

Furthermore, RPL claims do not attempt to capture all learning but rather that which is relevant to current learning plans. Good RPL facilitation seeks to capture key insights that give a flavour of deeper learning and which in turn help to suggest at what level the learning can be claimed. The focus here is on facilitation. This is a pedagogic activity; there are several pedagogic metaphors (Wall, 2013) which might help to think about this (Table 5.1):

Table 5.1 Pedagogic metaphors

Meticulous accountant	This is the most common pedagogy in the UK and US and involves learners accounting for their knowledge against known and specified outcomes from an existing academic framework. It may involve minor re-organisation of what is already known, but its facilitation focuses on ensuring that the learner is able to express their learning in terms of academic standards. Handled badly this can feel like an administrative process, but done well it enables less confident learners to structure and organise their learning. Similarly, it can be very useful for learners who understand the framework being used and are capable of making an independent and self-directed claim or for those who wish to explicitly make a claim against the learning outcomes of an existing module. This is called 'specific credit'.
Creative sculptor	To help the learner become more aware of their learning, or more specifically, their tacit knowledge, more open-ended, exploratory facilitation is used. This helps learners to take responsibility for the structure of their learning and is valued by those who want to reflect more deeply or make sense of what they know in a more formal or academic sense. This is less common in traditional HE but can be the mainstream practice on negotiated WBL programmes in HE. The credit gained from this practice is usually 'generic credit', as the learner has identified his or her own learning in relation to generic-level outcomes. *continued overleaf*

Table 5.1   Pedagogic metaphors *continued*

Creative accountant	This metaphor includes both of the above sets of practices. Here, the first facilitation task is focused on enabling the learner to explore and select existing knowledge frameworks or standards they want to use to help them account for their learning. The second task is then to systematically account for the learning, much like the meticulous accountant metaphor. This is particularly useful for those who want to account for their learning against formal, recognised standards or bodies of knowledge.
	To use RPL to its full potential it must be viewed as a pedagogic task: it can enable individuals to become aware of their existing learning whilst also producing opportunities to re-organise that learning in generative ways, creating new linkages and dynamic connections.

Source: Based on Wall (2013)

▶ Accumulation of credit and recognition of learning

In relation to HE's 'recognition' of learning, Butterworth (1992) asserted that the accreditation of prior experiential learning should be seen as more than just an opportunity for credit accumulation. As Trowler (1996) commented, the 'developmental' model which focuses on extending the learners understanding of their experiences is more appropriate for the context of HE. This is particularly pertinent for negotiated WBL that situates the learner as central to the agreed learning programme.

By utilising an HE accreditation process, learners' existing knowledge, skills and abilities are recognised and legitimated (Armsby et al., 2006). This has served to improve access to HE for those from non-traditional backgrounds. In addition, recent research has pointed to the importance of this for the development of self-realisation (Sandberg and Kubiak, 2013), and self-understanding can provide a solid basis for planning a successful WBL programme in which the learners' abilities are central. The importance of the candidate, tutor and assessor in the recognition process is clear (Hamer, 2012), but Sandberg and Kubiak (2013) assert that a range of other actors, for example, co-students, colleagues, managers, family and friends, have an important influence. The claimant's experiences, together with others' past and current perceptions of it, provide an opportunity for the learner to explore the social context of their learning, much as Lave and Wenger (1991) describe in their seminal work on situated learning. Understanding others' views of one's learning is important in WBL studies because the learner must influence and impact on their work-based context.

▶ Evaluating knowledge claims

Theories of knowledge creation, such as Gibbons et al.'s (1994) 'modes of knowledge', have prompted debate about what is being taught and assessed in WBL studies (Costley and Armsby, 2007). It is argued that work-based knowledge and practice are transdisciplinary in nature (Costley, 2015), but as Trowler (1996) noted, most academics are sceptical about accrediting knowledge gained from experience, preferring the propositional knowledge of their disciplines. More recent research suggests that this may be changing, at least in some subject areas (de Graaff, 2014), although the prevalence of RPL/APL in HE generally remains low. We will return to this issue later in the common misconceptions section. Negotiated WBL programmes set out to recognise the kinds of knowledge that arise from work practices; other uses of APL, for example, to provide accreditation for an existing subject-based module, may not.

De Graaff concludes that 'RPL is a bridge between the workplace and the academy' (2014, p. 13). Given what has been described as a 'practice turn in contemporary theory' (Schatzki et al., 2001) it seems appropriate that HE has ways of recognising and accrediting knowledge arising from practices of the professional groups they seek to educate. Debates about the place of different types of knowledge, theory and practice are not new to HE, and the use of APEL in WBL is central to these. The ontological turn, mentioned on p. 95 (Dall'Alba and Barnacle, 2007), which foregrounds education for personal and professional development, is also important in relation to WBL APL claims as it offers the opportunity to explore the learning that arises from being a professional. Both 'turns' fit comfortably with APEL in WBL and illustrate its cutting-edge position in contemporary HE as well as some of the reasons for its controversy.

The APEL process gives students the opportunity to self-assess their learning and negotiate how this learning will be gauged by HE. This innovative practice, where students gain knowledge and understanding of the HE credit system, level descriptors and learning aims and outcomes, means that students' assessment literacy is developed, along with enhanced professional judgement around how standards are derived – including regulations, policies and processes (QAA, 2014, p. 15).

To uphold the recognised standards your institution will have its own regulations around RPL and APL processes. Try undertaking the following activity to familiarise yourself with these:

ACTIVITY

HEIs differ and you need to find out within your own HEI:
▶ Whether prior learning is graded?
▶ Are fees charged for either the process and/or the ensuing credits? And if so, what are these?
▶ What are time limitations around claims (for example, does the claim have to be before the programme commences)?
▶ The timeframe within which previous learning must have occurred (for example, within five years)?
▶ The limits around amount and level of credit claimed?
▶ Who are the key contacts who will facilitate the process?
▶ How feedback on RPL will be provided? If successful do students still get feedback? (If rejected they must be provided with full reasons and details of re-study, re-submission and appeals.)
▶ How any credit achieved will be represented on the eventual transcript?

▶ Assessment and evidence

Assessing specific credit claims is straightforward. Evidence should prove that the student has met the learning outcomes for the specific module or programme at the appropriate level. Deciding on the level of general credit to be awarded is also usually straightforward; universities use their own already established level descriptors, which outline the features of each level of study. APL tutors need to use to assess if the evidence provided will prove that the learning has taken place. Assessment criteria are usually based on the generic level descriptors (also see Chapter 3).

Determining the *volume* of credit to be claimed is more difficult (Workman, 2008; Pokorny, 2012). Within UK HE, one credit represents ten hours of learning, although precise measurements of this are not possible, and this rule differs around the world. Some HEIs give word count advice for experiential learning claims, using more standard modules for comparison. This does bring some precision but may place too much emphasis on outputs rather than prior achievements (Prince, 2004). For example, if credit claims are to be around 'areas of learning', these areas might be compared to the size of a written assessment for a module, for example, carrying 20 credits. This kind of comparison is only an approximation and should not be used to slavishly require the student to produce the same amount of words. With APL claims, quality always comes before quantity; that is, a piece of high-quality evidence can say a lot more about a student's prior learning than, sometimes, many thousands of words. Structured CVs can often be used to help define 'areas of learning'; some ways to evidence these areas of learning are suggested below:

Teaching tips: Providing evidence

▶ Student's own professional writing such as reports, evaluations, handbooks, budgets, briefing papers and so on
▶ Workplace performance appraisals and testimonials
▶ Correspondence proving involvement
▶ Products and artefacts
▶ Minutes/actions from meetings
▶ Project outlines
▶ Procedures developed
▶ Initiatives created

Further suggested assessment tools can be found in QAA publications (QAA, 2014).

This kind of evidence is required for experiential learning claims, but some claims rely entirely on prior certificated learning, which involves comparing the learning outcomes of the completed award (ranging from a single module to a full qualification) with those of the proposed course of new study, against which credit is being claimed. Sometimes, if the tutor involved feels there is not an adequate match they may require a 'mixed' portfolio that includes certificated and experiential evidence.

Evidence needs to clearly demonstrate:

▶ Relevance (significance, match to, and implications for, contents of programme)
▶ Sufficiency (amount and strength of evidence, balance of quality and quantity)
▶ Authenticity (valid and clearly their own)
▶ Currency (current, intrinsic value, equivalence)

The following Case study 5.1 outlines a situation in which experiential learning was claimed and illustrates the role of the tutor in facilitating this learning:

Case study 5.1 Assessing prior learning: Developing a portfolio of evidence

As part of her BA in work-based studies (innovative leadership), Lucy, an executive officer, was asked to compile a portfolio of evidence to support her APL claim. She approached the task positively and confidently as she was accustomed to writing many complicated, formal reports within her job role; however, she was surprised when she received a lot of constructive criticism of her first draft.

continued overleaf

Case study 5.1 Assessing prior learning: Developing a portfolio of evidence *continued*

Lucy's initial portfolio used formal language and factual information (which she assumed the university would require), listing her formal duties at work and so on. Unfortunately the portfolio was so precise and objective that the passion and intensity she had demonstrated at her admission interview had been omitted, along with content that would demonstrate her learning of new skills and knowledge and the application of this to the workplace. Furthermore, examples of accolades such as 'Employee of the Year', which potentially could result in a significant amount of credit being awarded, were only briefly mentioned.

When pressed on the 'Employee of the Year' accolade Lucy was initially very shy but eventually through discussion with her tutors, she was able to provide more detailed evidence of why she had received the award (for example, starting a voluntary group within her organisation to help disadvantaged people within her community). This more detailed evidence enabled her to demonstrate her learning in several areas, including:

- ▶ Leadership
- ▶ Strategic planning
- ▶ Time management
- ▶ Problem solving
- ▶ Analytical reflection
- ▶ Financial management
- ▶ Effective communications
- ▶ Working with others
- ▶ Coordinating skills
- ▶ Writing skills

In addition there was also ample evidence of Lucy's ability to empathise, encourage and care for others.

Lucy's tutors suggested that she discussed her voluntary work with a trusted friend or colleague and recorded the conversation to capture connections the activity had with her skills, how she came to have these skills initially and how it was further enhancing and developing her skills and knowledge.

After taking on board the comments made by her tutors Lucy managed to successfully claim 200 credits for her prior learning by structuring 'areas of learning' around what she had learnt in creating and developing the voluntary group.

Madeline Fisher, Cranfield University

The above Case study 5.1 demonstrates that writing a claim for credit for previous learning is not a one-stage writing exercise. To get the most from the task it is important that your students allow plenty of time for compilation of the claim and receiving your feedback on their drafts, along with time for them to re-draft the submission before the final assessment hand in date.

Within HE, RPL focuses on recognising, 'learning at the equivalent level (to HE learning) achieved outside the defined programme of study' (QAA, 2014, p. 3). Tutors need to offer feed forward in order to focus on prior and current, but also further, learning. These students have not had the benefit of feedback during the learning process, which more traditional students enjoy, but they do need feedback now. In giving this feedback you must evaluate and develop your own practice, drawing on scholarship, research and professional activity. Furthermore, you must build reflection into your own practice (as your RPL candidates are expected to reflect effectively and will rely on you to help them).

▶ Reflective practice

The ability to reflect on practice has long been seen as essential to develop practitioners, and Schön's work (1987) consolidated understanding of the importance of analytical reflection for educating modern-day professionals. The content of the narratives that typically accompany evidence of practitioners' experiential learning, often presented in an 'RPL portfolio', will vary but will require the claimant to have reflected on the meaning, extent and importance of their practices. It is the RPL tutors' responsibility to clarify what should be included in a claim and, importantly, to help the candidate develop this capability. A developed ability to reflect *on* practice is important as it enables the learners to learn more effectively from their past experiences and prepares them to reflect *in* practice and for *future* practice (Schön, 1983 and also Chapter 11). Reflective practice is therefore a cornerstone of WBL and is required throughout the WBL studies curriculum, for example, in:

▶ Considering the perspective of all the key stakeholders in the candidate's learning agreement (Chapter 4)
▶ Selecting an appropriate methodological approach for a work-based project
▶ Analysing the implications and possibilities arising from a work-based project

Reflective practice begins with the individual but the individuals' reflections relate to the social context and endeavours of their everyday work, and it is also exemplified in WBL programmes of study. The social element of reflection is important in facilitating productive work (Boud et al., 2006). The following case study illustrates some of the issues involved for a student and a tutor facilitating reflection on practice (Case study 5.2).

Case study 5.2 Preferred learning styles: How they affect articulation of prior knowledge

Meta-cognition is at the heart of RPL: the tutor acts as facilitator enabling the learner to recognise and articulate their prior experiential learning. Questionnaires can help the learner to recognise their preferred learning styles as they prioritise self-awareness and encourage reflective practice.

Although work-based learners eventually become *knowing subjects* who can identify how they learn best, initially RPL claims, requiring articulation of prior learning, then measured against rigid learning outcomes, can still prove too difficult for them. To resolve this and inform pedagogical practice, I hypothesised that learning typologies may affect the ability to present prior experiential learning in an academic written form (often the reflective portfolio).

I tested this with a comprehensive questionnaire considering learning types and linking the skills of meta-competence, reflective practice and articulation of tacit knowledge.

The use of learning typologies is not universally praised (Coffield et. al., 2004); however, patterns did emerge from the research to support the hypothesis. There was clear evidence that strong activists and weak reflectors (Honey and Mumford, 2006) found the greatest difficulty in articulating prior learning experiences. Activists (who enjoy the immediacy of new learning experiences) found reflecting on 'old' learning, especially that which is tacit, challenging to the point of demotivation:

> *My learning style was primarily activist with pragmatist close behind ... I found the (RPL) process did not sit well with me as I tend to want to move on rather than look back.*

The majority of activists found critically examining former situated learning within the workplace was easier and cited practical demonstration as beneficial in providing evidence of learning. This would make the learning from the RPL process self-directed from an andragogical perspective and more liable to improve and develop professional practice.

Weak reflectors found the greatest difficulty with articulation of tacit knowledge, where the situatedness of the learning gained through experience in specific contexts is known but cannot be easily communicated through a written text:

> *I found it difficult to articulate what I learnt as I had learnt it over time honing my skills ... learning within the structure of academic theories is difficult.*

Written portfolios inhibit claims for some, leaving them unable to maximise prior learning. A choice of assessment mode, negotiated between student and tutor, should be considered.

Ideally the RPL process should be delayed until the essential skills of reflection, meta-competence and understanding of complex theory are established.

Norma Sutcliffe, Teesside University

▶ UK and international terminology and practice

Trowler (1996) traces the origins of APEL back to the USA where there has been an established practice of awarding credit to assessed learning. He suggests that the UK's post-1992 universities with their focus on modularisation, accreditation of WBL and 'credit frameworks' have led in its implementation. A survey of HE credit practice in the UK appears to support this (Atlay et al., 2012). However, the practice of APEL is still not widespread in the UK and is minimal in Europe. Whilst there are some positive frameworks in Europe for enabling APEL such as the V*alidation des Acquis de l'Experience* in France, and there has been some sharing of practices in Europe, Schmit and Gibbs (2009) conclude that APEL and WBL are only very slowly advancing in Europe.

International terminology and practice varies, but UNESCO's (2012) published *Guidelines for the Recognition, Validation and Accreditation of the Outcomes of Non-formal and Informal Learning* illustrate a widespread drive to use RPL to deliver on the access and lifelong learning agenda and give 'value to the hidden and unrecognised competences that individuals have obtained through various means and in different phases of their lives (p. 3). The Bologna Process and European Higher Education Area (http://ec.europa.eu/education/policy/higher-education/bologna-process_en.htm) address the issue of different national frameworks, which obviously influence the opportunity for APEL. Taken together, these initiatives suggest that APEL may continue to advance. The following Case study 5.3 illustrates how one APEL development in Lithuania progressed following initial consultations with APEL experts in one French and two UK modern universities. This network of HEIs was chosen due to their experience in assessing adults' learning in diverse environments outside of academia. As a result of the development, individuals, with evidence of prior learning, can now be enrolled to the Lithuanian University and be awarded credit towards a professional programme (Republic of Lithuania, 2009).

Case study 5.3 Assessment and recognition of non-formal learning: Experience in HE in Lithuania

Assessment and recognition of non-formal and informal learning (ARNIL) in Lithuania has been on the policy agenda since 1998; however, legal acts regulating the process in HE were adopted only in 2009/10. Some HEIs have gained experience in this field during the last decade resulting in the introduction

continued overleaf

Case study 5.3 Assessment and recognition of non-formal learning: Experience in HE in Lithuania *continued*

of assessment procedures for ARNIL. Recently, a network of HEIs has been established to assess and recognise non-formal and informal learning.

This study analysed ARNIL in HEIs to examine learners' perception of their participating in the procedure of assessment of their prior learning with a particular focus on their experience of portfolio development.

Prior learning of 27 learners, in four Lithuanian colleges, was assessed. The HEIs and learners were novices, in that they did not have any previous experience of assessing this type of learning or preparing for this type of assessment.

Analysis of responses to 'What was the biggest challenge in the process of portfolio development?' revealed three categories of challenge:

▶ Analysing and documenting learning
▶ Understanding the procedure of assessment/portfolio development
▶ Managing own time

The respondents perceived analysing and documenting their learning as the major challenge. They did not have any previous experience of doing this; the challenge was caused by lack of ability to distinguish between experience and learning. Evans (1992) suggests that the most demanding intellectual task for learners is the shift from describing experience to identifying learning. It also reinforces Pokorny's (2013) recommendation that during the process of preparing claims for assessment of prior learning, emphasis should be shifted from artefacts and products of practice presented in portfolios to the creation of mutual understanding between assessors and learners, which could open better opportunities for disclosing learning.

These findings lead to the assumption that a strong institutional emphasis on the complexity of ARNIL in general and on the process of portfolio development in particular is required. This strengthens Burkšaitienė and Šliogerienė's (2010) findings that institutional support–provided in the format of portfolio development courses and long-term consultations– leads to students' success.

The study concluded that ARNIL can be supported by raising awareness of how learning is understood and interpreted in HE and by increasing institutional responsiveness to the difficulties that learners face in preparing for assessment.

Nijolė Burkšaitienė, Mykolo Romerio University

▶ Using technology to facilitate claims

RPL is often cited in academia as time consuming and resource heavy. This is based upon the notion of academic staff dealing with each individual's claim. In response to this several HEIs have developed online tools to facilitate electronic claims. Technology can enable economies of scale to be made in the RPL/APL process. The massification of HE has required academics to find efficient, cost-effective ways to work with learners. Case study 5.4 from the University of Derby showcases an innovative online tool for facilitating initial APEL claims:

Case study 5.4 e-APEL: Negotiated learning at the University of Derby

In the early 2000s the University of Derby experienced a rapid growth in demand for higher-level negotiated WBL from employed learners; almost 90 per cent of these individuals wanted to achieve recognition for existing levels of knowledge and expertise.

The Negotiated Work-based Learning Scheme used the accreditation of prior learning (APL); learners avoid repetition of learning by submitting claims for academic credit. Staff noticed, however, the disproportionate amount of work and effort undertaken by both the students and those guiding them, with cases where it seemed easier for them to undertake modules and requisite assessments. Some students needed considerable support with the APL process, even before they had committed to study, or paid any fees (Minton and Malone, 2010). Post-enrolment these frequent tutorials usually had no revenue attached to them.

Staff with RPL expertise felt that some initial structured support and guidance, encouraging reflection on learning to date and looking at matches for experiential learning with level indicators and learning outcomes, could be achieved electronically using the existing virtual learning environment (VLE). The VLE offered potential for building student confidence, helping with HE terminology and preparing students for in-depth discussions about their WBL. Students identified their own level of competency by matching prior learning to the university's levels (in the electronic tool) and explaining how they were meeting the criteria, along with citing sources of evidence to support their claim.

The tool was designed to be accessible with a logical flow; however, students can go back to add additional information when they become more immersed in the reflective process. Registered students can log in and out, building up their proposal in their own timeframe. A workflow structure guides the student through the process; this clearly illustrates progression as sections are completed, with those left to complete highlighted.

The system includes an Advisor tool, which facilitates reviews, comments and focused, specific guidance on how to develop the claim as well as advice about the required supporting evidence. Pre-set evaluation criteria ensure consistent feedback across the tutor team.

The e-APEL tool has:

▶ Helped APL students successfully make their claims
▶ Enhanced awareness of APL to other learners and staff across the whole university
▶ Promoted APL to new students
▶ Served as a useful marketing device
▶ Attracted non-traditional and part-time students to study

Ann Minton, University of Derby

▶ Accreditation

Within APL claims candidates are encouraged to claim credit for any relevant past training that they may have undertaken in the workplace, which can be proved to be at HE level (although it did not carry credit at the time). This accreditation of workplace training is popular. However, the philosophy of RPL has also encouraged many HEIs to look creatively at how they can acknowledge training and development that is happening in the workplace at HE level *prior* to any students presenting it as a retrospective claim. Often in-house training can be mapped across an HEI's own level descriptors and awarded credit; this means that employees undertake the in-house course knowing that they will gain HE credits for it. This activity also facilitates relationship building between the HEI and the organisation. The following Case study 5.5 exemplifies this activity.

Case study 5.5 HE accreditation: Partnership development between work-based learners, employers and HEIs

HE has a large role to play in workforce development (Lester and Costley, 2010; Hordern, 2014). The Department for Business, Innovation and Skills (2010) support this need as part of their response to the changing demands of both learners and employers.

In 2007 I initiated a partnership with the Defence College of Policing and Guarding (DCPG) at MOD Southwick Park, Portsmouth, several hundred miles from the university. It is a combined military police school being the training facility for the Royal Navy Police, the Royal Military Police and the Royal Air Force Police. The university link was initiated by an article I had written, promoting programmes which military personal could study. A relationship based on trust developed between both partner organisations and the discussions evolved into the eventual accreditation of a number of courses taught at DCPG. This was facilitated by aligning the established course learning outcomes with the Framework for Higher Education Qualifications in the UK (FHEQ) learning outcomes and jointly evolving appropriate academic and work-based assessments.

Through the partnership, military police personnel completed a number of short specialist courses accredited by the university as 30 and 60 credits at FHEQ Levels 4 and 5. The courses varied in level and content and allowed their study to be formally acknowledged, useful for their continuing military career but also giving them recognised qualifications for when they leave the services. Over several years more than 1,200 learners completed university-accredited courses.

I engaged with the partners in their own workplace, geographically distant, rather than requiring them to travel to the campus, and offered flexible timescales – for example, fast academic approval of the accreditation process and year-round delivery. Gaining access to, and developing the trust of, both the decision- makers and the practitioners within police organisations can be challenging, an aspect

continued overleaf

Case study 5.5 HE accreditation: Partnership development between work-based learners, employers and HEIs *continued*

that Westmarland (2011) identified when attempting to conduct research within the police service.

I have found it to be imperative that the context, needs and subject-specific language of the discipline is understood, and the expertise of the learners valued, in order that their trust be developed over a period of time.

Ian Pepper, Teesside University

In conclusion, the following box revisits some of the most common misconceptions about RPL/APL, together with some further detail to explain the reality of each situation (Table 5.2).

Table 5.2   Some misconceptions about RPL/APL

It gives credits away and makes getting a degree too easy; it's dumbing down.	Using RPL is a different, but not easier, way of gaining HE qualifications. The processes designed to facilitate it are rigorously quality assured and in line with all other HE regulations and standards.
It makes getting a degree too cheap.	It is true that some HEIs do not charge for credits gained through RPL – but most do, although this will be at a reduced rate when compared to the equivalent module. However, RPL candidates have not attended the module/s, with all of the attached resources and costs.
The process is very labour intensive.	Because each student is treated as an individual case there is a perception that endless hours of staff time will be involved. However, as with all things, the more often something happens, the better we become at dealing with it, and those institutions who regularly award large amounts of credit via RPL have developed efficient systems to make it cost-effective, whilst still giving the candidates the personalised service they deserve (see the case studies in this chapter).
The process is very complicated and convoluted; it is always easier to do a module.	The ethos of RPL is simple; it is aiming to avoid forcing students to re-learn anything that they have learnt already – with this in mind the system is simplified because all we are trying to achieve is proving the candidate's learning – in a way that meaningfully demonstrates its level and relevance. Usually those who state that the process is complicated have never actually attempted to understand the process or have some deep-seated lack of information about the credit system itself. The criticism 'it is easier to do the module' is usually a giveaway that the student is being asked to do far too much to prove their previous learning. It is true, once the students are expected to write a long narrative they almost may as well be writing the essay or report a similar module might require (see elsewhere in chapter for more details on how to evidence a claim).

continued overleaf

Table 5.2   Some misconceptions about RPL/APL *continued*

By giving people an alternative you are losing students or taking them away from other courses.	Almost without exception the kind of student who benefits significantly from RPL would not have come to the HEI without a work-based-studies-style route. They are probably working full time and these kinds of programmes tend to have an 'out of hours' offering. They are often mature learners whose sector has become a graduate profession since they joined (although there are many, many other reasons) but their age and stage of their career makes them 'in a hurry' as well as very experienced, so what they have learnt from this experience is the ideal tool to give them some advanced standing, which also helps them to – in their eyes – catch up a bit more quickly. This is the route they want; they are not somehow 'stolen' from a more traditional one.
It messes up awards – in terms of class of degree and so on.	It is true – RPL credits do not carry a mark or class – this would be very difficult to do – although probably not impossible; for this reason HEIs define what they MUST do in terms of taught modules which consequently limits how many credits a student may bring in. This is clearly written in individual institution's quality regulations and is not the 'black art' that some colleagues think.
It isn't academic or scholarly; for example, it doesn't include theory.	The learning that RPL candidates' evidence is marked against the institutions' level descriptions and learning outcomes – so it will be as academic as these are.
It didn't happen in my day; I didn't study like this.	It is called innovation! Our students are subject to a rapidly changing world and work environment; nothing stays the same and we all have to learn to cope with changes. There are now many ways to study and many conflicting theories about how knowledge is created. RPL is a different, but equally good, way to gain HE recognition. It is about individual appropriateness.
It is impossible to prove.	This simply is not true. See elsewhere in this chapter for ideas around evidence. All RPL claims have to be proved and backed up by evidence; it is as easy to map this against descriptors and outcomes as it is an essay, report or presentation. Education needs to be creative, not stagnant.
It fragments my class; I cannot treat everyone exactly the same.	Well, that's a shame! The news is your class are not all the same – even if they want to study the same topic, are roughly the same age or come from the same background; all students are individuals and deserve to be treated as such. It is the only way to ensure they maximise their learning experience.
Students can't learn anything if they are not in the classroom with me.	Unfortunately for our egos this has been proved to clearly not be the case. Work-based students frequently embark upon projects where they are found to be far more expert in the topic than any of the HEI staff, because they have been working in that area, in a real-life scenario for a number of years, solving problems, analysing performance and innovating.
You just have to prove you have a job, or work experience, and you get a degree.	This is one of the widest-held falsehoods. RPL credits are awarded for LEARNING from experience; nothing is awarded for merely having an experience. Once academics realise and accept this they are much more interested in the potential of the process.

continued overleaf

Table 5.2   Some misconceptions about RPL/APL *continued*

Students are wasting time, looking backwards when they should be learning here and now.	Psychologically, as stated above, these students do tend to want to quickly get on, perceiving themselves to be behind already. However, once they have been shown the process of proving their learning is at HE level, they feel empowered that they have already been operating at this level and are therefore NOT behind. They learn about, and feel the power of, reflective practice and become reflective practitioners – capable of looking back, but also capable of reflecting on the present and reflecting forward to future activity. Some enlightened institutions allow work-based learners to keep making RPL claims throughout their programme of study.
Nowhere accepts or acknowledges it.	The Bologna process means that HE credits are part of a recognised global currency – CATS. http://ec.europa.eu/education/policy/higher-education/bologna-process_en.htm
There are no experts to help you with this.	Membership bodies such as SEEC and NUCCAT offer expert advice and support around HE credit. http://www.seec.org.uk/ http://www.nuc.ac.uk/ Also, there is a UK Credit Forum that shares information about credit and recently published a review of practice (Atlay et al., 2012).
It is only about low-level learning.	This can't be true: it is used at undergraduate and postgraduate level. In fact, the PhD by published works is a kind of RPL, and professional doctorates and professional doctorates by public works also use it (Armsby, 2012); so it's available right up to Level 8.
The difference between specific and general credit is very confusing.	It's no more confusing than any other terms in learning and teaching. Specific credit is easily understood as connecting with already validated modules or programmes; that is, the credit is specific to them. General credit is not confusing; it's just not well used and hence known about. This is probably because many academics think that they should deliver the particular knowledge they think is important, rather than facilitate the development of students' own existing knowledge.

SUMMARY

▶ Academic credit is awarded for learning, not experience; experience provides the context where learning might occur.
▶ RPL allows WBL students to progress their studies logically by building on existing learning and without repeating learning.
▶ Awarding academic credit for prior learning helps to create truly flexible, often individually negotiated, WBL programmes.
▶ Credit arising from RPL can be used for existing modules or as a foundation for individually negotiated programmes.
▶ RPL tutors are facilitators, helping their students to articulate evidence what they have already learnt.

continued overleaf

SUMMARY *continued*

▶ Assessing the level of RPL claims is supported by the use of level descriptors. Determining the volume of credit can be more difficult.

▶ Reflective analysis is key to the RPL process, and this comes more naturally to some than others.

▶ RPL can be used for workplace training by mapping learning outcomes to HEI level descriptors.

▶ **References**

Armsby, P. (2012) Accreditation of experiential learning at doctoral level. *Journal of Workplace Learning*. 24 (2), pp. 133–150.

Armsby, P., Costley, C. and Garnett, J. (2006) The legitimisation of knowledge: A work-based learning perspective of APEL. *International Journal of Lifelong Education*. 25 (4), pp. 369–383.

Atlay, M., Bridges, P. and Flinn, M. (2012) *A Survey of Higher Education Credit Practice in the United Kingdom 2012*. UK Credit Forum Report No 1. Derby: University of Derby.

Boud, D., Cressey, P. and Docherty, P. (2006) *Productive Reflection at Work*. Oxford: Routledge.

Burkšaitienė, N. and Šliogerienė, J. (2010) *Assessment and Recognition of Non-formal and Informal Learning Outcomes at the University*. Vilnius: MRU.

Butterworth, C. (1992) More than one bite at the APEL. *Journal of Further and Higher Education*. 16 (3), pp. 39–51.

Coffield, F., Moseley, D., Hall, E. and Ecclestone, K. (2004*) Learning Styles and Pedagogy in Post-16 Learning*. London: Learning and Skills Research Centre.

Costley, C. (2015) Educational knowledge in professional practice: A transdisciplinary approach, in Gibbs Paul, (Ed.), *Transdisciplinary Professional Learning and Practice*, pp. 121–133. Switzerland: Springer International Publishing.

Costley, C. and Armsby, P. (2007) Work-based learning assessed as a field or a mode of study. *Assessment and Evaluation in Higher Education*. 32 (1), pp. 21–33.

Dall'Alba, G. and Barnacle, R. (2007) An ontological turn for higher education. *Studies in Higher Education*. 32 (6) pp. 679–691.

de Graaff, F. (2014) The interpretation of a knowledge claim in the Recognition of Prior Learning (RPL) and the import of this on RPL practice. *Studies in Continuing Education*. 36 (1), pp. 1–14.

Department for Business, Innovation and Skills (2010) *Higher Education Funding for 2011–2012 and Beyond*. London: Department for Business, Innovation and Skills.

Evans, N. (1992) *Experiential Learning: Its Assessment and Accreditation*. London and New York: Routledge.

Gibbons, M., Limoges, C., Nowotny, H., Schwartzman, S., Scott, P. and Trow, M. (1994) *The New Production of Knowledge*. London: Sage Publications.

Hamer, J. (2012) An ontology of RPL: Improving non-traditional learners' access to the recognition of prior learning through a philosophy of recognition. *Studies in Continuing Education.* 43 (2), pp. 113–127.

Honey, P. and Mumford, A. (2006) *The Learning Styles Questionnaire 80 Item Version,* Revised Edn, Maidenhead: Peter Honey Publications.

Hordern, J. (2014) Workforce development, higher education and productive systems. *Journal of Education and Work.* 27 (4), pp. 409–431.

Kolb, D. (1984) *Experiential Learning: Experience as the Source of Learning and Development.* New Jersey: Prentice Hall.

Lave, J. and Wenger, E. (1991) *Situated Learning: Legitimate Peripheral Participation.* Cambridge: Cambridge University Press.

Lester, S. and Costley, C. (2010) Work-based learning at higher education level: Value, practice and critique. *Studies in Higher Education.* 35 (5), pp. 561–575.

Minton, A. and Malone, S. (2010) *The e-APEL Tool: Developing Informed Conversations About Prior Learning.* York: HEA Exchange Group Publication.

Ministry of Education and Science of the Republic of Lithuania (2010) (Order No V2319). *On Recommendations on the Assessment and Recognition of Competences Acquired through the System of Adults' Non-formal Education [interactive].* Available at http://www3.lrs.lt/pls/inter3/dokpaieska.showdoc_l?p_id=389755&p_query=Neformaliojo%20suaugusi%F8j%F8%20%F0vietimo%20sistemoje%20%E1gyt%F8%20kompetencij%F8&p_tr2=2 accessed 18 April 2014.

Organisation of Economic and Cultural Development (1996) *Lifelong Learning for All.* Paris: OECD.

Pokorny, H. (2012) Assessing prior experiential learning: Issues of authority, authorship and identity *Journal of Workplace Learning.* 24 (2), pp. 119–132.

Prince, C. (2004) University accreditation and the corporate learning agenda. *Journal of Management Development.* 23 (3), pp. 256–269.

Quality Assurance Agency (2014) *UK Quality Code for Higher Education, Part B, Chapter B6.* Available at http://www.qaa.ac.uk/assuring-standards-and-quality/the-quality-code/quality-code-part-b accessed 24 November 2014.

Republic of Lithuania (2009) *Law on Higher Education and Research (No. XI-242).* Available at http://www3.lrs.lt/pls/inter3/dokpaieska.showdoc_l?p_id=366717 accessed 18 April 2014.

Sandberg, F. and Kubiak, C. (2013) Recognition of prior learning, self realization and identity within Axel Honneth's theory of recognition. *Studies in Continuing Education.* 35 (3), pp. 351–365.

Schatzki, T., Knorr, C., Von Savigny, K. and Von Savigny, E. (Eds) (2001) *The Practice Turn in Contemporary Theory.* London and New York: Routledge.

Schmit, R. and Gibbs, P. (2009) The challenge of work-based learning in the changing context of the European higher education area. *European Journal of Education.* 44 (3), pp. 399–410.

Schön, D. (1983) *The Reflective Practitioner.* New York: Basic Books.

Schön, D. (1987) *Educating the Reflective Practitioner.* San Francisco: Jossey-Bass.

Trowler, P. (1996) Angels in marble? Accrediting prior learning in higher education. *Studies in Higher Education.* 21 (1), pp. 17–35.

UNESCO (2012) *United Nations Education, Scientific and Cultural Organisation Guidelines for the Recognition, Validation and Accreditation of the Outcomes of Non-formal and Informal Learning.* UNESCO Institute for Lifelong Learning.

Wall, T. (2013) *Leading Transformation in Prior Learning Policy and Practice*, 2nd Edn, Charleston, SC: CreateSpace.

Westmarland, L. (2011) *Researching Crime and Justice: Tales from the Field.* London: Routledge.

Workman, B. (2008) Beyond boundaries: Value and assessing experiential learning outside module templates, in Garnett, J. and Young, D. (Eds), *Work-based Learning Futures 2* (pp. 72–83). Bolton: UVAC.

▶ Recommended further reading

Garnett, J., Portwood, D. and Costley, C. (2004) *Bridging Rhetoric and Reality: Accreditation of Prior Experiential Learning (APEL) in the UK.* Bolton: UVAC

Higher Education Academy (2012) *A Marked Improvement: Transforming Assessment in Higher Education.* Available at https://www.heacademy.ac.uk/node/3950 accessed 13 May 2015.

Higher Education Academy (2013) *Review of Credit Accumulation and Transfer Policy and Practice in UK higher education.* Available at https://www.heacademy.ac.uk/node/7613 accessed 13 May 2015.

Lester, S. (2007) Professional practice projects: APEL or development. *Journal of Workplace Learning.* 19 (3), pp. 188–202.

Perrin, D. and Helyer, R. (2015) Make your learning count: Recognition of Prior Learning (RPL) in Helyer, R. (Ed.), *The Work-based Learning Student Handbook*, 2nd Edn, pp. 96–119. London: Palgrave.

Pokorny, H. (2011) APEL research in English higher education, in Harris, J., Breier, M. and Wihak, C. (Eds), *Researching the Recognition of Prior Learning*, pp. 106–127. Leicester: PLIRC/NIACE.

Pokorny, H. (2013) Portfolios and meaning-making in the assessment of prior learning. *International Journal of Lifelong Education.* 32 (4), pp. 518–534.

Quality Assurance Agency (2012) *UK Quality Code for Higher Education, Chapter B3: Learning and Teaching.* Available at http://www.qaa.ac.uk/en/Publications/Documents/quality-code-B3.pdf accessed 13 May 2015.

Skinner, H., Blackey, H. and Green, P. J. (2011), Accrediting informal learning: Drivers challenges and HE responses. *Higher Education, Skills and Work-based Learning.* 1 (1), pp. 52–62.

6 Turning practitioners into practitioner-researchers

Tony Wall

IN THIS CHAPTER YOU WILL:

▶ Find that undertaking practitioner research can be viewed as developing an additional identity for work-based learners, whereby they learn further ways of thinking, feeling and acting
▶ Be offered a multipurpose pedagogical scaffold for adult work-based learners, which provides initial boundaries but also acts as a springboard to key concepts and new ideas
▶ Be given a way of conceptualising practitioner research that foregrounds and values practical change and practical outcomes within the work-based learner's own context
▶ Be introduced to a way of thinking about 'reality' that encourages change and action
▶ Gain an understanding of pedagogical tools for facilitating practitioner-research learning with work-based learners

▶ Becoming a 'practitioner-researcher'

Learners on work-based learning (WBL) courses will usually start their research experience with notions more or less formed about what it means to be a researcher. They will have ideas about typical daily tasks, patterns of thinking, down to what a researcher should wear, perhaps sitting in a sterile laboratory, wearing a protective white coat and glasses, examining statistical data. Bourdieu (and later Lave and Wenger, 1991; Holland et al., 1998; Wenger-Trayner and Wenger-Trayner, 2014) argue that such internalised notions are formed over time, perhaps from previous educational, work and social experiences, particular to the social spheres frequented by the learner. At the same time as developing these understandings, affective responses and fears of being unable to take on such a self-identity can emerge; learners can have a deep-seated anxiety towards their ability, or even right, to present themselves as researchers. They are, more often than not, much more confident in their identity as a practitioner (or professional). However, Baxter (2012) alerts us to just how important it is, to student learning and academic success, for learners to take on particular self-concepts, because the identity drives patterns of thinking, feeling and acting.

What does it mean to think, feel and act as a practitioner-researcher? This is a difficult question because there is no one clearly defined field or community of practice; teachers of research methods are acutely aware of the different research worlds that exist, with diverse, potentially oppositional ways of thinking, acting and feeling in practice. Although work-based learning might be conceptualised as a discipline (Costley and Gibbs, 2006), this is not a widespread or typical model, and there can be strong disciplinary influences brought to bear on work-based learning practitioners from more established disciplines. For example, some courses favour reflective methods used in education, whilst others use more statistical methods typical of business research. Yet this complexity is not just an issue for work-based learning courses (Cameron and Molina-Azorin, 2014). Hammersley (2012) points out the challenges in teaching social research methods:

> The problem of the sheer amount and difficulty of the material that could be covered, and the question of what should be taught to whom and when … the deep methodological divisions now to be found among social researchers, not just quantitative versus qualitative but also within each of those camps. These sometimes extend beyond differences in view about how to pursue research to disagreement about its goal and value…

Importantly, he concludes:

> It is not just that it is now very difficult to teach social research methods well, but that there is actually little agreement about what this would mean – even as regards what is to be taught.

Where does this leave the teacher of practitioner research? Wenger-Trayner and Wenger-Trayner (2014) offer some possible navigation through the complexity. They argue that rather than learning one set of practices from a singular field, humans identify with some aspects of a landscape of practice more than others. This is comparable to Lévi-Strauss's (1966) concept of the 'bricoleur': someone who combines potentially disparate ideas or methods according to the purpose of a given situation. Thinking that helps make sense of this includes 'parsimony' or Occam's razor (Sorensen, 2014), 'accommodation' (Checkland and Poulter, 2006) and 'satisficing' (Simon, 1997). The idea crossing these notions is to not necessarily attempt to actively deal with the full complexity of a situation; indeed, this is often impossible, but instead, try to develop a 'working model' which is claimed to not necessarily represent a social reality or 'best approach' but is sufficient to move out of the potential analytical paralysis of complexity towards a genuine opportunity to 'learn through doing'. In other words, it provides an initial 'rule of thumb' or heuristic which enables us to start our action somewhere, to actually do something, and learn more about what happens when using that working model in our own landscape of practice.

▶ Pedagogical scaffolds: Educational's and pits' or 'skeletons'

So the pedagogical question is not, which research community of practice or genre do we want our work-based learners to subscribe to and learn to be part of? But instead how can we construct a pedagogical space in which work-based learners can engage and learn key concepts from a broader landscape of communities. This space is a working model, or pedagogical scaffold, which enables the learning of key ideas and practices as springboards to further learning, which offer practical pedagogic approaches to facilitating serious play (Vygotsky, 1979). This pedagogical approach emphasises the need for the teacher of practitioner research to be flexible and open to a patchwork approach like the bricoleur. Within Wall's (2014) adoption of this approach, the pedagogical scaffold has a number of aspects:

▶ **Perspectives**: It is useful to be clear and explicit about what particular views of practitioner research you are looking to promote, but which also then direct other pedagogical structures in addition to what your teaching team is specifically looking for in assessment. That might include valuing practical change and outcomes (a pragmatic axiology), thinking about reality in a way that facilitates change (a pragmatic ontology) and thinking about how we can learn about that reality in pragmatic ways (a pragmatic epistemology). These ideas are discussed below.
▶ **Processes**: It is also useful to be explicit with your learners about how these perspectives might translate into a thinking or 'research proposal' writing process, which will partly determine the selection of terms, concepts and the particular interpretation of those. An example practitioner-research proposal is outlined later in this chapter.
▶ **Flexibility and boundary-crossing as 'learning assets'**: Although we may establish boundaries about the type of thinking, acting and feeling you are wanting to promote with your learners, it is important to recognise these boundaries as scaffolds to allow your learners to springboard into other areas (such as discipline-specific ideas or resources).

This may cause confusion and frustration at points, but such moments can act as 'learning assets' (Wenger-Trayner and Wenger-Trayner, 2014) which prompt additional discussion and insights for learners, perhaps to clarify a particular stance.

▶ A pragmatic axiology: Valuing change and practical outcomes

In many forms of academic research, learners are expected to find a gap in a literature with a view to generating new data or theory to fill that gap. The academic literature therefore legitimately has a central role within the initial stages of scoping out the research with a high value placed on theory generation. When what is valued by the researcher, their axiological stance, shifts from theory generation to making a change, or creating practical outcomes, in a real-world setting, then the dynamic changes. Rather than starting within a literature, the starting point can shift towards the practitioner-researcher, situated in a real context, with a history and expected trajectory; they are an insider researcher rather than an independent researcher 'looking in' to an organisation. What the practitioner (researcher) then experiences as problems to solve, and/or opportunities to seize, become the centre of attention and the purpose of practitioner research. The role of literature then becomes a way to learn alternative ways of thinking about the problem or opportunity in order to move forward in some way through the vehicle of the research. This describes the difference between Mode 1 knowledge production (as defined by academe, through its literature) and Mode 2 knowledge production (as defined by practitioners, through solving problems and seizing opportunities) (Nowotny et al., 2003).

Axiology is about what is valued in research. Within practitioner research, change and practical outcome are valued, and shape its purpose, for example, reducing absenteeism at work, deciding how to expand into a new market and so on.

There are a number of heuristics (shortcuts to exemplify or prompt the type of thinking required at a particular point) that can enable learners to focus attention on their own context. One of the most powerful is identifying 'killer statistics' within the learner's local context. The idea is that a statistic has a major communicative utility across specialist silos (Wenger-Trayner and Wenger-Trayner, 2014) and can demonstrate the strategic need for a particular research focus, even to a non-specialist audience. For example, a 50 per cent decrease in an organisation's sales over the last year makes it

Teaching tips: Introducing practitioner research

Link to the familiar – explain practitioner research to your learners in terms of everyday activities, for example, purchasing a high-value item such as a holiday or a car:

▶ Focus on:
   • Who needs to be convinced by the research?
   • Who needs to be involved in the research?
   • The implications or consequences of only using one source of data?

▶ Steer away from common starting points such as:
   • a literature base, without any grounding in their practical setting
   • a method, without a grounding in its wider practical purpose
   • a personal interest, without consideration of broader perspectives
   • a particular 'answer' or 'finding' in mind, which provides their investigation with the frame of 'proving' rather than 'discovering'

▶ Acknowledge the starting point with the learner and bring them back to the specific change or practical outcome needed within their context

logical to investigate further. The killer statistic is also a heuristic to check whether a research approach is needed at all or whether relatively quick and simple action (without research) could be taken. For example, if a hospital ward needs to inform its patients of a new procedure for booking appointments, a 12-month research approach to design a poster is probably not the most efficient and effective approach. The task is to guide your learners towards a strategic issue that would benefit from a research approach.

Teaching tips: Helping learners find a focus

In helping learners find their focus it is important to:

▶ Draw boundaries and explain that the purpose of practitioner research is to change practice and/or create practical outcomes
▶ Compare practitioner research with other axiological bases such as theory generation to drive discussion around boundaries and overlaps
▶ Use focused questions such as:
   • What needs to change in your workplace?
   • What problem needs to be solved?
   • What opportunity needs to be seized?

▶ Establish the principle of 'Before-During-After' foci in conducting research and what form this might take
▶ Introduce the concept of killer statistics – the key data that quickly communicates the significance of a workplace problem or opportunity

continued overleaf

Teaching tips: Helping learners find a focus *continued*

▶ Establish the power of setting the scene; for example, your learners role-play a research fund pitch.

Activity

▶ Draft some questions that will help your work-based learners establish some focus
▶ Examine what 'Before-During-After' foci might look like, for example, a research project which:
  • Identifies the costs and benefits of various options before a decision is made
  • Develops/enhances a new workplace system
  • Evaluates the outcomes of a training programme
▶ Consider using role-playing to help set the scene for your work-based learners

---

▶ Ontologies and epistemologies: Routes to alternative practices

If axiology is about the 'why' of research, ontology and epistemology are the 'what' and 'how' of research. Ontology concerns the assumptions made about (or way of thinking about) what 'reality' is, or perhaps where it is, and therefore shapes how we might find out about that reality or do research at work. Epistemology concerns the assumptions made about *how* we learn about that 'reality', which in turn shapes what methods practitioner-researchers use. It is intimately linked to ontology (what/where reality is).

Many learners start higher education (HE) assuming there is a singular, objective reality; discussing this provides a route into different ways of thinking about the practical problems and opportunities work-based learners want to investigate through their research. Ontology and epistemology can be viewed as two different sets of assumptions that the practitioner might have when designing and conducting their research: realist and relativist (Stokes and Wall, 2014).

As a 'realist', the practitioner-researcher might adopt assumptions which are typical in natural sciences, technology, engineering and mathematics disciplines. Here, they would assume that the world they work in is an objective world that exists outside and independent from their perception (ontology). A practitioner-researcher tackling an absenteeism problem might, for example, be aspiring to find out the objective truth ('what's really happening?') about what is causing the absenteeism. In order to learn about it, they might measure numerical levels of absenteeism across their organisation and try to find any links with other objectively measured factors they predict might have an impact, such as workload levels, management style inventories, branch postcodes and so on (epistemology). The practitioner-researcher might even aspire to measure the relative and precise impact of each of these factors on absenteeism.

As a 'relativist', the practitioner-researcher might adopt a set of assumptions which are typical in action research and qualitative and participatory research. Here, the practitioner-researcher assumes reality exists subjectively within each and every person and is therefore a social construct, which is generated through interaction. If so, a practitioner-researcher seeking to tackle absenteeism might be aspiring to access the multiple and varied social constructs that employees within their organisation use when talking about the causes of absenteeism (ontology). The researcher might have an open mind to discover what the employees think is 'really happening' (from their particular angle) and be very aware that just simply asking questions is shaping the responses they get from employees. They would learn about what is happening by generating discussion, capturing multiple perspectives and then potentially reaching a social consensus about the causes of absenteeism within their place of work (epistemology).

In practice, the learner might adopt either or both (as will be shown next) and will tend to reflect their own personal assumptions. However, as a teacher of practitioner research, it is important to recognise that classifying research assumptions into two camps, such as realist and relativist, is a simplification to emphasise difference and aid communication. There are fuller classifications; Guba and Lincoln (2005, pp. 191–216), for example, propose five camps of research assumptions. Importantly, both two- and five-camp classifications are not being used to state an objective fact about what really happens in practice (a realist ambition); they are being used as heuristics to approximate the complexity of assumptions used in research practice (a relativist, social construction). Practically, as heuristics are simplified versions of a presumed reality, they give your learners a quick and convenient route to talking and learning about the complexity existing in practice. To use heuristics to facilitate learning in this way rests on the tutor's own accommodation of it as a strategy; it is not that we accept it as 'what really happens in practice' but rather that we can accept it is a useful device for learning about assumptions in research. This is a subtle difference, but an important one to facilitate communication and move forward with learning. If we agree to use this heuristic, there are three ways your learners can utilise these assumptions to shape their research towards change and/or practical outcomes.

Taking a relativist stance to explore minds and build consensus for action

When the practitioner-researcher needs to create some sort of change with others, or to create practical outcomes which require the input or agreement of others, a relativist approach can be useful. This is because the relativist approach seeks to reveal or generate the multiple, and potentially oppositional, views in the workplace and work towards approximations of those views that people within the workplace can accommodate. For example, a researcher might want to find stakeholders' views about the impact of a training programme to reach a consensus from different perspectives about that impact before more is invested in the programme. Alternatively, it might be reaching a consensus view on how a website should be designed, before it is built. Generating a consensus enables moving forward into action. This is the stance taken in much action research and participatory research (Checkland and Poulter, 2006; McNiff, 2013). An example of a relativist approach is provided below in Case study 6.1:

Case study 6.1 A relativist approach to research: An eDelphi study of leadership needs

Suada is the HR director for a company operating across Europe and Asia. She was tasked with re-developing their leadership development provision; the Board was unhappy with the current outsourced training.

Taking a realist stance, she might have used 360 degree questionnaires which involved each leader's managers, peers and clients objectively rating them on a numerical scale. She may also have supplemented that with her own observation of each leader. Triangulating the numerical scores in this way is driven by an aspiration to get to an objective measure (truth) of the leaders' behaviours.

For her results to be valid, she would need to ensure that she had a representative sample of leaders and their managers, peers and clients. She would also need to make sure her observations were representative of the leaders' daily work so would have to spend at least a week with each leader.

However, to work towards this realist aspiration was unrealistic in terms of access to participants (they were spread across Europe and Asia and some would not have enough time to be involved) and in terms of timescales and budget to fund such extensive work.

Instead, she decided to adopt an eDelphi approach, which asked the top leaders to anonymously prioritise their own collective leadership needs on a secure online space.

Within the eDelphi process, she collated the statements made by the top leaders, found themes within the statements and wrote new statements which attempted to capture all of the statements made by the leaders.

She circulated the new statements and asked the leaders to comment on and tweak them again. This cyclical process of writing and developing different/broader

continued overleaf

Case study 6.1 A relativist approach to research: An eDelphi study of leadership needs *continued*

statements of leadership needs was continued until all leaders reached a consensus of what their needs were.

In this way, the relativist stance freed up Suada to attempt to make objective claims about the leadership needs, which would have been unrealistic given her resources, and allowed her to get a consensus which enabled buy-in and commitment to subsequent action.

The outcome was a list of leadership needs which each of the leaders had agreed represented their collective leadership needs, and therefore had buy-in to invest in particular leadership development training.

Taking a realist stance to find an evidence base

There are situations where a realist stance needs to be adopted within the workplace, so that research findings move forward to action. Medical or clinical settings are classic examples, where decisions are often made with scientific evidence from clinical trials of new drugs or new procedures. Another example is when a work-based research project does not require agreement or accommodation but rather evidence of discrete events. The study might be testing a new information system in a supermarket, with the researcher interested in whether or not a system calculates the correct total. Similarly, if the researcher is finding out ways to increase profitability, by conducting an intricate analysis of accounting information, they might be interested in the expenditure trends across different areas of the business. Neither of these are subjective calculations. The following Case study 6.2 gives an example of a work-based practitioner taking a realist approach to their research project:

Case study 6.2 A realist approach to research: A study into improving digital marketing performance

Mason is a marketing manager for an online education company in the US. The company relies heavily on its digital marketing campaigns and its website to promote its products. Although the company was increasing in profit, its directors have ambitious plans to grow annually.

In order to boost sales, the company invested in different promotional channels including adverts in various web-based magazines and search engine adverts. However, they are expensive, and Mason needs to manage his budgets much more efficiently to maximise sales.

Within this context, Mason was tasked with finding out which of the three channels, if any, should be continued.

Mason initially considered a relativist approach, which examined the opinions of experts in digital marketing, accessing knowledge he would never be able to

continued overleaf

Case study 6.2 A realist approach to research: A study into improving digital market performance *continued*

develop alone. He also considered collecting the opinions of possible customers (market research).

He discounted both options as they both generated data about opinions of what potential customers might do and were therefore not subject to the authentic conditions of potential customers making decisions amongst live competitors.

Mason decided on a realist approach, so he could make claims about how many clicks had been made and the amount of sales income that could be accurately attributed to those sales – according to the promotional channel used.

Mason adopted Google Analytics, which enabled him to track the source of each visit to the company's website, plus whether someone continued to click on the 'purchase' button.

As a result of his approach, he found that one channel (a search engine advert) attracted the most hits but also the least number of purchases. He also found that one particular magazine attracted most purchases.

Overall, the magazine channel of advertising provided the greatest return on investment in terms of sales. As a result of the research, promotional expenditure increased in this magazine, and other channels were discontinued.

Mason's realist approach was appropriate to measure and track discrete events such as a potential or actual customer clicking on a button, which was relevant to his research.

Had he been interested in how easy the process was, or why the customer selected his product rather than a competitor's, then a relativist approach would have given him different information.

Taking a mixed stance to answer diverse research questions

The practitioner might also use a mixed stance to encompass the different aspects or stages of a research project. For example, one stage of their research might be finding out which team member has sold which line of products to which postcodes (a realist question), but another stage might be related to generating a consensus as to how to improve sales processes (a relativist question). This is why it is particularly important to get the research questions of a study as clear and well formed as possible; they act as guides to when you might consider taking a mixed stance. The following Case study 6.3 illustrates this:

Case study 6.3 Using a mixed stance in research: Exploratory study of what a new product might look like

Olayinka was based in the UK but was setting up an educational business in Accra, Ghana. Before he invested heavily in marketing and staff he wanted to find out which programmes would be most likely to generate an operating surplus.

continued overleaf

Case study 6.3 Using a mixed stance in research: Exploratory study of what a new product might look like *continued*

His research was interested in two aspects: the design features that customers would like for an educational product and how much profit that design might create.

Stage 1: Exploring design features (relativist)

In the first part of his study, Olayinka undertook market research through focus groups with his target customers and asked them questions to elicit the design features they would like and how much they might pay for such features.

This was based on a relativist approach, as he was interested in eliciting customer opinion and reaction to potential design features. Here, the aim was to explore (and approximate) the views of the participants, rather than capture views which he would then claim to be representative of the entire target market.

This representative approach, a realist ambition, would have required hundreds of participants (to then be able to say that the data was probabilistically representative). Olayinka did not have the resources to organise and conduct so many focus groups distributed across Ghana.

Instead, he employed three focus groups within Accra (with a specific target market), which was a more practical way to get enough data for him to test his ideas and then take action, that is, to be able to get a unique product to the market relatively quickly and efficiently.

Stage 2: Calculating potential profits (realist)

The next stage was about calculating how much profit would be made, given the prices customers said they might pay, what other competitors were charging and the costs of delivering the product.

Olayinka used a realist approach here, as the data he was dealing with were not subject to opinion, but rather, the result of a clearly defined calculation: total predicted revenue minus total predicted costs.

Here, he used opinion data (relativist) alongside discrete cost/price data (realist) to help him make a decision. The outcome was that he did not continue with the venture; it was unlikely to create a worthwhile level of profit given the high expectations of quality but low pricing within the market he had identified.

▶ Explorations (vs representations)

As a teacher of practitioner research, it is important to recognise that these alternative assumptions shape what counts as legitimate in terms of sampling and sample size and to guide the learner appropriately. From a realist stance, the aspiration is to capture and represent an objective reality, and there are various sampling practices which provide legitimate ways to do this with varying degrees of accuracy (or specific levels of confidence). Typically these are probabilistic and raise the question: how probable will it be that the research findings represent a wider population? Within an axiological stance, geared towards change and practical outcome, and the important role of accommodating approximations in relativism, this can legitimate exploration rather than representation. This type of thinking has featured in many forms of practitioner research such as 'straw polls' or 'quick and dirty' forms of market and marketing research. It is important to recognise this difference and not to impose the requirements of representation when the learner is practically aiming for exploration to aid action.

Teaching tips: Teaching key concepts

▶ Keep an easy-to-access glossary (see Addendum for some research terms) to manage misconceptions or comprehension difficulties – generate understanding of terms through open discussion at various points in teaching.
▶ Explain similar concepts to illustrate there is no singular reality within research, for example:
  • *Parsimony* or *Occam's razor* – the simplest explanation usually gives the most accurate one (Sorensen, 2014)
  • *Accommodation* – considering a current situation which allows different perceptions to be encompassed enables action (Checkland and Poulter, 2006)
  • *Satisficing* – dealing with the information you have, accepting it's not a full picture of reality (Simon, 1997)
  • *Action learning and action research* – broad range of methodologies including, activity, collaboration, problem solving, aiming to change practice for the better

▶ Give practical examples of how *approximation* is used on a day-to-day basis:
  • A member of staff trusts what one of their colleagues tells them about a dispute at work (an *approximation*), and adjusts how they interact with colleagues as a result
  • A company forms an opinion about their brand or product packaging based on a small number of influential industry leaders

▶ Give *oppositional* examples of research using topical or relevant issues (that may be sector specific).
  • Encourage the learners to compare two research pieces that present *oppositional* findings, for example, 'coffee is good for you, coffee is bad for you. Discuss'.

▶ A process for practitioner research

As Hammersley (2012) points out, learners can struggle to make sense of the multitude of terms and concepts which do not have shared meanings. These can include 'methods', 'methodologies', 'design', 'philosophy', 'aims', 'objectives', 'purpose', 'approaches' and 'strategies'. Within a single text, each term might be very well defined and linked together, as is the case within Saunders, Lewis and Thornhill (2012, p. 103), who use the idea of the research 'onion' to layer and connect different ideas. However, complexity is exacerbated when learners read multiple texts by different authors who do not adopt a practitioner-research stance (Wall, 2013). Although insider research is a powerful tool capable of causing major personal and professional impact, the complexity it causes can frustrate and negatively affect the student experience of very busy professionals who are undertaking a work-based learning course in addition to working full time.

In order to navigate this challenge, it is useful to introduce a clear and logical process which acts as an initial pedagogic scaffold of key concepts and ideas, which is specifically designed for practitioner research (Wall, 2014). This becomes a kind of 'working model' which can act as a springboard from which the learner can lead other ideas and concepts – the pedagogic boundaries of their own 'sand pit' or 'skeleton' mentioned at the start of this chapter. To this end, the practitioner-research process outlined below is presented as a 'working model'; it is acknowledged that different work-based learning courses or institutions may require different processes or documents, particularly in relation to ethical approval (see Chapter 4 and Appendix). Despite the different higher education institutions' (HEIs') ethical processes, there will be some commonalities such as:

▶ Has your learner written permission to use that data for their research purposes?
▶ What are the consequences of their research for their colleagues and respondents?
▶ How will the change or practical outcomes they create through their research affect others in their workplace/sector?
▶ What will they do to manage any of the risks from the above?

▶ Facilitating the research process

Heuristics (prompts) and coaching questions (open ended) guide the learners' thoughts and facilitate the research process. The following stages (Table 6.1) will be helpful in this process:

Table 6.1   Facilitating the research process

Stage	Questions*
Review of professional context An analysis of the practitioner-researcher's current (and/or future) situation which outlines a strategic problem or opportunity. As an introduction it draws on a 'killer statistic' to quickly communicate the importance of a particular problem or opportunity.	What needs to change? How do you know? Who needs to be convinced of what?
Research focus A statement about the broad focus of the practitioner-researcher's work, in terms of what they want to 'find out'. It is expressed as '*The focus of my project is to find out...*'	What do you need to find out?
Review of literature An analysis of what published sources report about the practitioner-researcher's focus. It should help them to be very specific about what they want to focus on and what they want to find out. It is 'thematic' rather than 'descriptive' in that it reports key 'themes' or 'insights'. Each theme reports the similarities or differences from different authors.	Who has said what about your focus? What are the key insights in the literature? What are the key themes in the literature?
Research purpose A specific statement about the actionable outcome of the practitioner-researcher's research. It sets boundaries and can be expressed as '*The purpose of this research is to identify recommendations...*'	What will the practical outcome be from your research? What will you deliver to who?
Research questions Precisely what the practitioner-researcher needs to ask in order to fulfil their research purpose. The answers should cover all aspects of the research purpose.	What specifically do you need to find out to fulfil your purpose? What else? What do you need to ask to fulfil your purpose? What else?
Research approach A statement of the stages of the research, plus a justification of whether each stage will be qualitative, quantitative or mixed.	What type or broad approach do you need to take?
Methods for data collection The tools and techniques the practitioner-researcher will use to gather or generate data to answer their research questions.	How will you answer your research questions? What methods will you use to collect the data you need to answer your research questions?
Methods for data analysis The tools and techniques the practitioner-researcher will use to identify the patterns or themes in the data they gather or generate. Data analysis is about turning raw data into something meaningful that can be acted upon.	How will you turn your raw data into something meaningful to help make decisions? What methods will you use to do this?

continued overleaf

Table 6.1 Facilitating the research process *continued*

Stage	Questions*
Ethicality check A cross reference to principles of ethics (such as autonomy, beneficence and justice) to ensure it has approval and that it can be trusted. (see also Appendix)	Might anyone possibly be emotionally or physically harmed by this research? What could happen that might create such harm?
Schedule A list of practical tasks that the practitioner-researcher will need to plan and complete. (for example, a Gantt chart – see Case study 6.4)	Specifically, who will do what, and when?

Source: Wall (2013; 2014); Stokes and Wall (2014)

The following Case study 6.4 exemplifies the use of the above stages:

Case study 6.4 Applying practitioner research: Enhancing coaching product outcomes

Review of professional context

I am the owner of a small coaching firm. Business has become difficult because of increasing competition and intensifying rivalry.

Sales of my coaching product have decreased by over 50 per cent over the last 12 months, and potential clients say I need strong evidence of how my product makes a difference to them.

Research focus

The focus of my research is to find out the impact of my coaching product.

Review of literature

There are many frameworks for assessing the impact of coaching (Passmore and Velez, 2012) including the Kirkpatrick four-level model (Kirkpatrick and Kirkpatrick, 2006). This has been criticised by various authors (Impact and Evaluation Group, 2012; Phillips et al., 2012) who have expanded the original framework (Berg and Karlsen, 2012):

▶ Inputs – people, funding, policy/strategy (Impact and Evaluation Group, 2012)
▶ Level 0 – *foundations*: investment in the infrastructure to deliver the experience (IEG, 2012)
▶ Level 1 – *reaction*: a subjective assessment of the learner's satisfaction of the learning experience
▶ Level 2 – *learning*: the extent to which the learner believes they have learnt something
▶ Level 3 – *behaviour*: the extent to which the learner's behaviour has changed as a result of the learning experience
▶ Level 4 – *result*: the extent to which the experience has influenced the achievement of organisational goals, such as sales and profits

continued overleaf

Case study 6.4: Applying practitioner reseach: Enhancing coaching product outcomes *continued*

▶ Level 5 – *return on investment*: calculating the value of a particular intervention, including (but not limited to) economic value (Phillips et al., 2012; Sweet, 2013)

Given feedback from potential clients, I will focus on Level 4.

Research purpose

The purpose of my research is to identify recommendations to enhance the outcomes of my coaching.

Research questions (RQs)

RQ1 What are the perceived outcomes of my current coaching product?
RQ2 What areas might be developed to change these outcomes?
RQ3 What design options might be developed to enhance outcomes?
RQ4 Which design is most feasible within my current resource base?

Research approach

Stage 1: Assessment of Coaching Impact: this will be qualitative to collate the perceptions of the participants (my coachees) (RQ1, RQ2).

Stage 2: Coaching Product Refinement: this will also be qualitative, but predominantly action based (RQ3, RQ4).

Methods for data collection and analysis

Stage 1 data will be collected through ten in-depth, semi-structured interviews with previous clients who have experienced my coaching product – four coaching sessions over three months. This sample is 33 per cent of my current client base (population). The structure for the interview will be based on theory by Kirkpatrick and Phillips above. Because of the close, personal relationship I have built with participants, an independent qualified coach has agreed to conduct the interviews. Data will be analysed using thematic analysis and will be verified with participants. Stage 2 is an action stage which refines my coaching.

Ethicality check

This research adheres to the following principles (Sales and Folkman, 2000):

▶ Autonomy – participants can 'say no' to participation or withdraw at any point. Participant identity and data will be kept confidential at all stages.
▶ Beneficence – participants will not be put in the way of any additional emotional or physical harm during the research. Coaching skills will manage any unintended emotionally disturbing experiences during the interview.
▶ Justice – one group is not expected to bear the costs or benefits disproportionately.
▶ Intellectual property rights – I have a written agreement from the HEI that I will own the intellectual property rights of the new product I develop as a result of my studies.

continued overleaf

Case study 6.4 Applying practitioner research: Enhancing coaching product outcomes *continued*

Schedule

Activity	Month number									
	1	2	3	4	5	6	7	8	9	10
STAGE 1 Assessment of Coaching Impact										
Design interview framework	▓									
Design participant information sheets	▓									
Agree access	▓	▓								
Hold interviews			▓	▓						
Analyse data			▓							
Verify data with participants					▓					
Amend analysis					▓					
STAGE 2 Coaching Product Refinement										
Develop options							▓			
Analyse resources for implications							▓			
Agree final design							▓			
Write up final reports						▓	▓			

As the above case study suggests, teaching practitioner research is a complex matter, not least because it transcends disciplinary boundaries to facilitate the learning of business professionals who are in full-time work. Using the planning stages suggested above in Table 6.1 will help you to facilitate and support practitioner research.

SUMMARY

▶ It is useful to develop and use relatively simple scaffolds and heuristic devices as springboards to further learning.
▶ Use everyday examples to demystify the research process for your work-based learners.

continued overleaf

SUMMARY *continued*

▶ Involve work-based learners in compiling a glossary of frequently used terms so that they become familiar with them.

▶ There are multiple practices which you can use, adapt and blend in your own teaching of practitioner research.

▶ Develop 'sand pits' or 'skeletons' and enable your learners to build their own sandcastles or decide how their skeleton should be fleshed out.

▶ Addendum: Some research terms

Approximation – is about purposively utilising simplified working models of a situation or of something in order to help the practical act of representing or communicating the complexity of that situation or something, typically to progress action.

Axiology – this concerns our assumptions about what is important to us, or in other words, what we value. Within practitioner research, the outcome of practical outcomes and change are typically valued over the creation of theory for no other gain (though theory generation might contribute in some way to helping people create change). Axiology might be considered to be assumptions about the broad 'why' of research.

Epistemology – our assumptions about how we can legitimately learn about 'reality', for example, by measuring it through instruments (realist) or by creating opportunities to co-create it in conversations (relativist). Epistemology is intimately connected with the idea of ontology; ontology sums up what humans take for reality. It might be considered to be assumptions about the broad 'how' of research.

Exploratory sampling – a strategy of selecting participants which is based on capturing approximations of a wider population in order to facilitate pragmatic action. Generally aligned to a relativist stance and as opposed to representative sampling.

Ontology – our assumptions about what 'reality' is or, perhaps more specifically, where it is: for example, is it 'outside' of and independent of the observer (realist), or is it created in the minds of those investigating (relativist)? Ontology is intimately connected with the idea of epistemology, which is about how to learn about reality. It might be considered as the assumptions about the broad 'what' of research.

Realist – assumes that the world exists outside and independent from perception and can be accurately measured using clearly defined instruments.

Relativist – assumes that reality is a social construct and that it is not just accessed through, but also generated through, interaction.

Representative sampling – a strategy of selecting participants in a way so that the participants and therefore findings are said to be probabilistically representative of the wider population. Generally aligned to a realist stance and as opposed to exploratory sampling.

▶ **References**

Baxter, J. (2012) Who am I and what keeps me going? Profiling the distance learning student in higher education. *The International Review of Research in Open and Distance Learning.* 13 (4), pp. 107–129.

Berg, M. E. and Karlsen, J. T. (2012) An evaluation of management training and coaching. *Journal of Workplace Learning.* 24 (3), pp. 177–199.

Cameron, R. and Molina-Azorin, J. F. (2014) The acceptance of mixed methods in business and management. *International Journal of Organizational Analysis.* 22 (1), pp. 14–29.

Checkland, P. and Poulter, J. D. (2006) *Learning for Action: A Short Definitive Account of Soft Systems Methodology, and Its Use for Practitioners, Teachers and Students.* Chichester: John Wiley & Sons.

Costley, C. and Gibbs, P. (2006) Work-based learning: Discipline, field or discursive space or what? *Research in Post-Compulsory Education.* 11 (3), pp. 341–350.

Guba, E. G. and Lincoln, Y. S. (2005) Paradigmatic controversies, contradictions and emerging confluences, in Denzin, N. and Lincoln, Y. S. (Eds), *The Sage Handbook of Qualitative Research*, 3rd Edn, (pp. 1–42). Thousand Oaks, CA: Sage Publication.

Hammersley, M. (2012) *Is it possible to teach research methods well today?*, paper presented at the Higher Education Academy Social Sciences Summit, June 2012. Available at http://blogs.heacademy.ac.uk/social-sciences/2012/09/10/teaching-research-methods/ accessed 20 June 2014.

Holland, D., Lachiocotte, W., Skinner, D. and Cain, C. (1998) *Identity and Agency in Cultural Worlds.* Cambridge, MA: Harvard University Press.

Impact and Evaluation Group (2012) *The Impact Framework 2012: Revisiting the Rugby Team Impact Framework.* Cambridge: Vitae.

Kirkpatrick, D. L. and Kirkpatrick, J. D. (2006) *Evaluating Training Programmes*, 3rd Edn, Berrett-Koehler Publishers, San Francisco.

Lave, J. and Wenger, E. (1991) *Situated Learning: Legitimate Peripheral Participation.* Cambridge: Cambridge University Press.

Lévi-Strauss, C. (1966) *The Savage Mind*, 2nd Edn, Chicago: University of Chicago Press.

McNiff, J. (2013) *Action Research: Principles and Practice*, 3rd Edn, London: Routledge.

Nowotny, H., Scott, P. and Gibbons, M. (2003) Introduction: 'Mode 2' revisited: The new production of knowledge. *Minerva.* 41 (3), pp. 179–194.

Passmore, J. and Velez, M. (2012) SOAP-M: A training evaluation model for HR. *Industrial and Commercial Training.* 44 (6), pp. 315–325.

Phillips, P. P., Phillips, J. J. and Edwards, L. A. (2012) *Measuring the Success of Coaching: A Step by Step Guide for Measuring ROI.* Alexandria, VA: Association for Training and Development.

Sales, B. D. and Folkman, S. (Eds) (2000) *Ethics in Research with Human Participants.* Washington, DC: American Psychological Association.

Saunders, M. N. K., Lewis, P. and Thornhill, A. (2012) *Research Methods for Business Students*, 6th Edn, London: Financial Times Prentice Hall.

Simon, H. A. (1997) *Administrative Behavior: A Study of Decision-making Processes in Administrative Organizations*, 4th Edn, New York: The Free Press.

Sorensen, R. (2014) Parsimony for empty space. *Australasian Journal of Philosophy.* 92 (2), pp. 215–230.

Stokes, P. and Wall, T. (2014) *Business Briefings – Research Methods.* Basingstoke: Palgrave-Macmillan.

Sweet, P. E. (2013) Improving results through measuring 'return on investment', in Wall, T. and Knights, J. (Eds), *Leadership Assessment for Talent Development* (pp. 219–238). London: Kogan Page.

Vygotsky, L. S. (1979) *Mind in Society: The Development of Higher Psychological Processes.* Cambridge, MA: Harvard University Press.

Wall, T. (2013) Transcending the relevance gap: The accelerated practitioner research approach. *The Macrotheme Review: A Multidisciplinary Journal of Global Macro Trends.* 2 (1), pp. 298–301.

Wall, T. (2014) Transforming the research-learning performance of professional lifelong learners. *Procedia – Social and Behavioral Sciences.* 116, pp. 189–193.

Wenger-Trayner, E. and Wenger-Trayner, B. (2014) Learning in a landscape of practice, in Wenger-Trayner, E., Fenton-O'Creevy, M., Hutchinson, S., Kubiak, C. and Wenger-Trayner, B. (Eds), *Learning in Landscapes of Practice: Boundaries, Identity, and Knowledgeability in Practice-Based Learning*, pp. 13–30. London: Routledge.

▶ Recommended further reading

Bell, J. and Waters, S. (2014) *Doing Your Research Project: A Guide for First-time Researchers*, 6th Edn, Maidenhead: Open University Press.

Cameron, S. and Price, D. (2009) *Business Research Methods: A Practical Approach.* London: Chartered Institute of Personnel and Development.

Cathcart, T. and Klein, D. (2007) *Plato and a Platypus Walk into a Bar: Understanding Philosophy Through Jokes.* New York: Abrams Image.

Costley, C., Elliott, G. C. and Gibbs, P. (2010) *Doing Work-based Research: Approaches to Enquiry for Insider-Researchers.* London: Sage Publication.

Dawson, C. (2009) *Introduction to Research Methods: A Practical Guide for Anyone Undertaking a Research Project*, 4th Edn, Oxford: How To Books.

Denscombe, M. (2009) *Ground Rules for Social Research: Guidelines for Good Practice*, 2nd Edn, Maidenhead: Open University Press.

Denscombe, M. (2014) *The Good Research Guide: For Small-scale Social Research Projects*, 5th Edn, Maidenhead: Open University Press.

Gaarder, J. (2012) *Sophie's World: A Novel About the History of Philosophy*, Special Edn, London: Phoenix (Orion).

Kara, H. (2012) *Research and Evaluation for Busy Practitioners: A Time-saving Guide.* Bristol: The Policy Press.

Walsh, A. (2011) Beyond a naturally occurring ethnography: The work-based researcher. *Higher Education, Skills and Work-based Learning.* 1 (1), pp. 38–51.

7 Supporting work-based learners

Ann Minton and Anita Walsh

IN THIS CHAPTER YOU WILL:

▶ Examine student support specifically related to the pedagogical differences in WBL

▶ Learn to offer support that maintains a student-centred and student-led approach

▶ Find tips for empowering learners to take charge of their learning to maximise the benefit for them and potentially their organisation

▶ Think about working with employers to put in place support mechanisms within the organisation as well as the HEI

▶ Acknowledge the role of the tutor (you) as a resource

▶ Learn about structures, signposts and mechanisms which can be used to maintain momentum in your pedagogic relationship with work-based learners

---

▶ Differences and challenges of being a work-based learner

All students need support; however, the support required by work-based learners will differ from campus-based learners and possibly vary individually. Existing approaches to learning and teaching have to be adapted or developed to support students who are learning in the workplace. There are some specific considerations that differ between each group; for example, individual learners undertaking self-initiated study will expect support from the higher education institution (HEI), whilst those undertaking a programme designed to meet their organisation's needs will probably expect their employer to be actively involved in support mechanisms in order to ensure a successful outcome for all parties. The work-based learning (WBL) tutor needs to be able to work with learners across these differing contexts.

Different students have varying opportunities to learn from their work in different ways; the common element underlying these differences is experiential learning. For example:

▷ A classic WBL student as described in this book will be an employed student integrating their workplace experiential learning into their HE course (either individually or as part of a company cohort).

▷ However, you may already be accustomed to full-time students who benefit from experiential learning in the workplace via internships, placements or part-time jobs (more on this in Chapters 10 and 11).

In both cases it is the workplace that is providing a lens through which the students can focus their learning, and the underlying pedagogical principles are the same. Therefore, with either category of these students you will find, when supporting them, that they need help with:

▷ identifying the learning that they have gained from their experience
▷ developing skills of analysis and evaluation, rather than basic description of activities
▷ challenging their own assumptions

▷ How can tutors support work-based learners?

The WBL curriculum is student centred and student led and provides a strong contrast to the more established discipline-led and university-centric model. It is designed to respond to the students' and/or their organisation's needs and to offer support mechanisms to help students to identify and articulate these needs. This emphasis on the students' own construction of meaning echoes the constructivist approach; it is not what you as the teacher teaches, but 'what the learner has to do to create knowledge [that] is the important thing' (Biggs, 2003). You should encourage work-based learners to take an active role in their own learning and development, rather than the more usual passive learner role, where the teacher will, 'take full responsibility for decisions about what is to be learned, how it is to be learned, when it is to be learned and if it has been learned' (Laycock, 1993, p. 24). Facilitating learning, rather than teaching is key. As Boud and Symes point out, 'Work-based learning puts an important new focus on learning as distinct from teaching: it is called work-based learning *not* teaching' (Boud and Symes, 2000). Most learning and teaching interventions are based upon pedagogic models developed in the context of compulsory education and therefore originally designed for children. Knowles argues that, rather than thinking in terms of pedagogy, higher education (HE) tutors, like yourself, should think in terms of andragogy, which he defines as 'the art and science of helping adults learn' (cited in Jarvis, 2004), and this seems particularly relevant for work-based learners.

Learners more familiar with conventional models of education may have developed a tendency to rely on the tutor's expertise, and this new and growing expectation for them to take responsibility for their own learning and development will present a challenging transition. In traditional learning the main question from a student to you might be, 'What do I need to know?' This question cannot be easily answered in WBL scenarios; what work-based learners need to know develops as they progress through their course. Work-based learners, therefore, are required to act with autonomy from the beginning of their HE course of learning. This has implications for the way that you structure the learning experience, the amount of access to you your students will need and the clarity of information needed about activities to be undertaken. You should consciously make links between new learning and familiar work contexts; this will facilitate making sense of the relationships between different types of learning and further develop the lines of inquiry and techniques which will enable your work-based students to work independently successfully.

▶ Developing autonomy

The development of individual autonomy is integral to HE graduates, furthermore, individuality and self-direction flow from the formative social nature of work (Beckett and Hager, 2002). WBL is an active, experiential model of learning, in which theoretical knowledge is used to interrogate workplace practice (Wenger, 1998). Acknowledging the importance of experience as a basis for learning emphasises the need to harness metacognitive skills and reflective practice, as part of achieving effective learning (Dewey (1997); Kolb (1984); Schön (1983)). The term 'reflection' can mean reflection 'outwards' (thoughtful and critical evaluation of disciplinary material) and reflection 'inwards' (on the professional assumptions and attitudes which inform workplace practice). Reflection often requires 'an external sounding board (ideally with the objectivity and authority of a facilitator or supervisor role) and it is necessary to both manage defensiveness and determine optimal learning from challenging experience' (Lizzio and Wilson, 2007). With your WBL students you often become this 'sounding board'. See the teaching tips below for some ideas about supporting these students further:

Teaching tips

In order to support your learners you need to understand:

▶ How the boundaries of the academic disciplines relate to their work context (the concept of 'transdisciplinarity'; see also Chapter 1)
▶ What language and terminology your students regularly use and build this into your programme documentation alongside the academic phrases
▶ How you can make your students aware of the informal experiential learning that takes place in the workplace

---

ACTIVITY

Taking the above into consideration, think about how you will:

▶ Enable your learners to articulate what disciplines they need to consider when undertaking their programme
▶ Encourage your students to begin to understand academic terminology for themselves
▶ Help them to evidence and articulate this learning so that it is recognisable as HE practice, thereby building their confidence

---

As a tutor of work-based learners you need to be able to help your students to articulate their own learning needs within the context of their role and career aspirations. At the same time that this is happening they will be familiarising themselves with the academic conventions of writing and referencing. As well as support from you they will also rely heavily on the information made available to them. This can be done in a number of ways including:

▶ Using induction programmes to make clear links between working and learning, highlight support available, clarify expectations and explain availability of HEI systems. For many learners this will be their first experience of HE. It is important that these links are made to help:
  • build confidence
  • explain the expectations of academic writing
  • clarify submission dates
  • enforce the formality of the assessment process
  • set clear expectations around your role as the tutor and equally their role as student
  • give the student a clear and logical structure to utilise
▶ Using clearly structured handbooks and assessment guidance so that students easily find the information that they require and in learner-friendly language.

If your programme has been developed in conjunction with an employer, then using the organisation's terminology and format for reports should be considered. Information should be quickly available without having to follow a series of links or find other documents. Work-based learners are often experience rich and time poor, so finding information easily is vital to keep them engaged. Make sure that your handbooks include a series of student-generated frequently asked questions, and consider using these questions as the structure for your handbook – with the assessment hand-in dates always on the front page.

▶ Using learning agreements to capture the planned structure of an individual WBL programme. Case study 7.1, below, offers an example of this; in addition, there is much more information in Chapter 4:

Case study 7.1 Planning learning activity: Developing learning agreements

All students following individual programmes in Work-based Professional Studies within the Institute for Work-based Learning at Middlesex University are required to complete a Programme Agreement, which spells out their planned learning activity and the precise amounts (and levels) of academic credit required for the award they are aiming for.

This can be a daunting and complex process for students and careful encouragement is needed. Support and explanations are required from the tutor, as the student gradually becomes both architect and builder of their programme of learning, embedding the concept of autonomy and independent learning.

Students are encouraged to consider the opportunities that exist for them within their workplace to drive their learning forwards. This process is supported by the tutor learning about the organisation, together with the student's role; part of this is scoping out opportunities for the student to undertake work-based research projects or maximise work-based projects they have to do anyway.

Tutors need to be knowledgeable about the university requirements and adept in advising students on programme structure. They do not necessarily have to be subject experts within their students' fields; indeed this is often not possible with widely diverse mixed cohorts of work-based learners.

Advice on programme design is provided by WBL tutors beginning with the admission and induction of work-based learners, through to the submission of their Programme Agreement.

Keith Buckland, Middlesex University

▶ Specific WBL modules integrated into an academic programme.

It is important for you to explain to your students why there are different requirements for WBL modules (especially as they may be simultaneously undertaking conventional modules). Students from a range of disciplines are often present in WBL classes, where they will draw on theory from different academic contexts. This can be accommodated by using 'empty box' modules, which let you utilise generic outcomes, usually focusing on capabilities and leaving the content to be determined by your students' workplace activities (see Chapter 3).

Case study 7.2, below, illustrates the use of specific WBL modules:

Case study 7.2 Support for learners: Support through structured modules

Within negotiated WBL programmes it is important that students are given the opportunity to critically examine their past, interrogate their present situation and then make plans for the future with effective tutor support. The University of Chester uses two specially devised modules to support negotiated WBL students at the early stages of their programme:

▶ 'Self-Review and Negotiation of Learning'
▶ 'Skills and Approaches for Work-based Learning'

The modules enable students to undertake an in-depth personal review and audit, which in turn identifies their personal and professional development opportunities and the associated skills and knowledge required to support this (see Case study 4.1 in Chapter 4). They also provide an 'intellectual toolkit' to develop the key skills of reflection, project planning, teamwork, referencing and academic writing. This is crucial, as many students will be unfamiliar with learning (and learning opportunities) outside of the formal classroom environment.

Tutors support these processes by entering into a structured dialogue designed to empower students to recognise their experiential learning and the value of the workplace as a site of learning, whilst enabling them to articulate this in a way that is recognisable as academic work.

The modules are designed so that the students start with the familiar – their role and their experience – and then go on to relate this to the unfamiliar context of academia. This develops their confidence in being able to recognise learning opportunities and encourages them to be proactive in seeking help from their tutor. The tutorial relationship established via these modules fosters facilitation and guidance on thinking, rather than simply delivering knowledge didactically.

Students attend an initial self-review tutorial, to establish the tutorial relationship, with subsequent tutorials being organised according to student needs. This process of (usually) one-to-one contact supports the process of personal review, with the tutor facilitating reflection on development and learning so far, to clarify and add depth to the review process. Tools such as the Myers-Briggs Type Indicator (MBTI), learning styles theory and Belbin's team roles are typically used and students are encouraged to relate these to the way they think and work.

For their first assignment, students are asked to configure a learning-focused CV and an annotated job description for their current role, where they can identify the skills and knowledge needed to carry out their work and reflect on how they practically keep these up to date. The 'Self Review' module ultimately leads to the negotiation of a coherent learning pathway and award title based on the development needs identified and the likely future direction of the work role (as discussed in Chapter 4). The 'Skills and Approaches for WBL' module provides them with the intellectual toolkit that can support the rest of their study as a work-based learner and reflective practitioner.

David Perrin, University of Chester

▶ Students who are experts

It is also important to acknowledge that your WBL students will very often be experts in their jobs, working at advanced levels within the workplace. Jarvis (2004) points out that, in the context of practice, professionals use theory pragmatically, and when working as a tutor with work-based learners, you need to be able to adopt a pragmatic approach to your use of theory and recognise that work-based learners submit work that is theoretically informed, not theoretically driven. Your academic role is the design and structuring of the learning process and to include demonstration of metacognitive processes which ensure that, in the absence of disciplinary coverage, an appropriate learning experience is achieved.

One good way to address this is to get your students to think about professional 'stories' that can be used to illustrate the way their learning links to their work, providing a catalyst to share thoughts and ideas and build credibility and confidence in each other as you get to know each other more. Naish and Minton (2015) suggest that 'storytelling within a professional context is a powerful tool'; it can bring a rather dry theoretical concept to life and provide a framework to help your students to identify for themselves ideas arising from their practice, which, with further encouragement, can be linked to the literature. Figure 7.1 depicts the ways in which storytelling can be structured to facilitate learning and encourage the integration of theory and wider reading into learning.

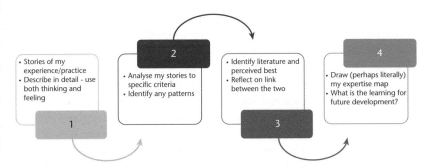

Figure 7.1   Using stories to build rapport and link theory to practice

Source: Hadfield (2014)

Supporting assessment

Your work-based learners will need your support as they tackle HE-level assessments for the first time. As Boud and Symes (2000) point out, 'Work-based learners typically want to be assessed in ways and on matters that are related to their work needs and interests', rather than tested on the detail of an academic discipline. As a tutor of work-based learners you need to move away 'from seeing [yourself] as a person who inducts students into a disciplinary culture to one in which [you] accept a role as learning consultants, actively engaged in mediating work, context and academic expectation' (Boud and Tennant, 2006). Undertaking such a role effectively requires a learner-centred response to experience-based learning from you, whilst at the same time you address academic standards and the knowledge needs of the workplace. This requires you to develop:

▷ skill in learning consultancy
▷ understanding of relationships between work and context
▷ appreciation of transdisciplinarity
▷ ability to foster inquiry
▷ knowledge of reflexivity and review

(Based on Boud and Tennant, 2006)

In Jenny Moon's work (2002) on learning outcomes and assessment criteria she notes the importance of seeking a balance to ensure that the quality, and innovation in student learning is not stifled by assessment criteria that are too precisely written. It is important that your criteria make it clear what is expected for your students to pass the module, and in the case of WBL they also ensure that there is a balance between underpinning theory and application in practice. Above all it is essential that your criteria are written in student-friendly language, avoiding academic jargon, whilst still retaining HE-level standards and benchmarks.

Work-based learning students also need clear guidance around the demonstration of an appropriately professional stance in assessment; this is key as it can be difficult to separate personal and professional aspects of work activities. You might address this by providing examples of personal and professional judgements. Reflective commentaries are often part of WBL assessments, where it might seem natural for your students to adopt a personal, conversational tone; normally in HE this would be deemed too informal, but in these circumstances it may well be appropriate. Showing your WBL students past examples of WBL assessment can help them to build their confidence. One very positive point to take into account when assessing work-based learners is that the content for their assessments develops as they progress through the programme with you, as they continue to work and learn in the workplace. This means that they are in a strong position to produce exciting, innovative and relevant work.

Teaching tips: Support methods for assessment

▶ Remember to match the assessment method with what you are assessing.
▶ When designing an assessment method consider what activities your students are engaged in at work. Can these be used to evidence the application of their learning in practice?
▶ When setting deadlines try to avoid busy work periods when your students will face additional pressure.
▶ It is important to alleviate pressures that are faced by WBL students, wherever possible.

ACTIVITY

Using profiles of your work-based learners consider how they can demonstrate their theoretical basis for the assignment, for example, reflective diary, annotated bibliography, guide for readers and critical review.

▶ Other support mechanisms

Workplace support

If your WBL students are undertaking individual programmes of study then their employer may take a fairly passive role; for example, they might facilitate their employee's learning by allowing appropriate access to organisational resources, and so on, but would not otherwise be involved in the learning experience. Indeed in some cases where WBL students are undertaking higher-level study to facilitate their career progression, and perhaps a move of employment, their employer can be unaware that their employee is even undertaking a course of study. Obviously in these cases it is not feasible to ask the employer to provide support.

However, it seems logical that an employer who has instigated a programme of learning will want to be involved and they can often be fundamental in ensuring learner success on some WBL programmes. It is intrinsic to well-designed, employer-instigated programmes that the workplace should be the focus of the learning and that real-work activity is used for assessment purposes (Boud and Solomon, 2003, p. 48). As a WBL tutor you need to accept that the primary purpose of the workplace is not education and to establish a worker/learner distinction. Try to capitalise on the learning aspects of the workplace experience without intruding unnecessarily onto your student's role as *worker*.

So that you can develop successful employer support mechanisms, consider what employers can usefully provide; for example:

▶ Access to the company intranet to post important messages about your course and provide a 'hot link' to the HEI's course resources and library
▶ Coordination of communication
▶ IT support and help with computer skills
▶ Opportunities for real-work assessment
▶ Line manager support
▶ Mentoring
▶ Setting up 'buddy' groups

Using real work, rather than additional tasks, for HE assessment, obviously saves some time and effort; however, balancing study with work and home remains a key challenge for work-based learners (Edwards and Minton, 2009, p. 104). Having support in the workplace, from someone who understands both the context and culture of that workplace and also the requirements for the HEI, is an invaluable resource for both work-based learners and tutors. In many cases this may be your learner's line manager; however, in some cases they may not be the right person as they may inadvertently provide blocks to the learning process. Before the programme is implemented, you should work with a range of people within the workplace to identify any tensions and help to put in place a range of focused support for learners, in addition to the usual student support package. Often work-based learners have little experience of HE and may initially be reluctant to contact a university tutor, feeling that they should be able to resolve issues for themselves, as they do at work. It is therefore important for you to emphasise the collaborative nature of HE and to explain that effective self-managed learning includes knowing when to ask for advice or guidance. The following Case study 7.3 exemplifies utilising line managers as a resource in supporting work-based learners and shows that this develops both the students and the line managers themselves:

Case study 7.3 Support for learners: Engaging with line managers

A large manufacturing company collaborated with the University of Derby to create a Management Development Programme for its team leaders on the production line. To demonstrate the application of their learning in practice, these work-based students put together a portfolio of evidence which included details of leading their team in a work-based project which addressed a problem that had arisen within their job role.

Although many of the students were highly experienced within the company, several had not undertaken any education since compulsory schooling and were daunted at the prospect of attempting a university qualification. The line managers, prospective students and company's training and development department were consulted as part of the programme development to ensure that the programme met the business need and the university's quality assurance requirements.

Support materials were developed for the learners and the line managers to help them to understand the aims of the programme and the assessment process. Separate induction sessions were held for line managers explaining:

- how they could support their employees to utilise opportunities occurring within the workplace
- how to compile evidence in a portfolio
- how to identify an appropriate project
- other sources of support such as access to basic computer skills tutorials, preparation for presentation skills, mentoring programmes, university tutors and their role

The consultation/discussion at the outset of the programme meant that the line managers:

- understood the programme requirements
- viewed the programme as a way to enhance the performance of the production line, rather than something that would take time away from the work
- understood the range of support available for students and how students could access it

At the end of the programme, every student completed the assessment. The line managers reported that:

- where there had been challenges with regard to workload, they had worked with the tutor and the learners to identify ways in which this could be addressed. This included refocusing the project, using university systems for extensions and intercalation
- the learners had applied their learning in practice
- the work-based projects undertaken had visible impacts on performance in their area, by direct efficiency savings and also by the increased confidence of the learners in dealing with the team
- they had improved their confidence in delegating to the learners, and for some this had extended their confidence in supporting other line reports to solve problems, even those not on the programme

▶ Mentors

Your work-based learners might appreciate a mentor to guide them through their programme and provide support and advice when needed. For traditional students this may be a fellow student or friend; however, for work-based learners it is more likely to be a fellow colleague (usually not their line manager). A mentor can act as a 'sounding board' for the learner who tests out their ideas in the context of their business, as well as suggesting enhancements or signposting key people within their organisation who may help and support them as a learner. It is important, however, that the mentoring relationship is explained clearly to both mentors and mentees, with stated roles and responsibilities for each party, and a support mechanism in place for the mentors (Clutterbuck, 2004, p. 57). The following Case study 7.4 discusses the use of workplace mentors for HE learning:

Case study 7.4 Support in the workplace: Using workplace mentors

At the University of Derby, specific training is provided for mentors, and this can be a credit-bearing mentoring qualification if the individual chooses. The training covers the concepts and principles of mentoring, including how people learn, and useful tools and techniques to support learners in the workplace.

A local authority developed a programme for its managers to help them to understand how to manage a mobile workforce. Recognising that many people within the organisation had little experience of HE and there would be some resistance from a workforce who were facing challenging times, with staff cuts, redundancies and increasing workloads, the council and the university agreed that empathetic support from within the organisation was required.

A group of managers, who had previously undertaken an HE WBL management development programme, were trained as mentors to support the students. Their training programme was specifically designed to focus on different models of mentoring and the practical application of mentoring to support learning in the workplace, rather than traditional forms of mentoring, which focus on the whole job role.

The students had a number of questions about applying the learning in the context of their own organisation and specialism. As role models for the impact of HE WBL, the mentors encouraged engagement with the programme and articulated the benefits to the students themselves. They were able to signpost and facilitate access to key information within the organisation, highlight topics where students could support each other, share resources and 'troubleshoot' some key IT issues.

▶ Buddy systems

Buddy systems are another good and useful way of supporting your individual learners by using previous learners or those at higher stages to support each other. Buddy systems can be used within cohorts to encourage peer support and mutual learning, maintaining motivation and helping to overcome the challenges faced. In the context of an organisation, buddies can be selected from those who have done the course previously, and therefore understand the process from the learner's perspective. They can provide helpful hints and tips about seeking advice within an organisation as well as useful resources, such as journal articles and reading materials. Case study 7.5 (below) exemplifies using a buddy system to good effect:

Case study 7.5 Support from peers: Using social media for buddy groups

A retail organisation developed an online learning programme with a university to develop business awareness for supervisors aspiring to become store managers.

The geographical distribution and size of the cohort led to learners feeling isolated.

The tutors decided to put in place a series of buddy groups so that the students could contact each other by phone, email or a closed Twitter account to share thoughts and ideas. The tutor initially promoted discussions and answered questions on the Twitter account, and the learners became accustomed to using the system and gained confidence in asking question of the group.

Whilst the tutor remained active in the group, he was gradually required to contribute less and less as the learners began to support each other and answer each other's questions and signpost advice that was available.

Using buddy groups in this way can develop a community of practice (Wenger, 1998), where students:

▶ Develop meaning – *learning as experience* – explain how their experience has contributed to the learning of themselves and others
▶ Undertake practice – *learning as doing* – apply their learning and share ideas about resources and perspectives of the application of their learning
▶ Develop a community – *learning as belonging* – identify areas for development in pursuit of furthering professional competence both individually and collectively
▶ Develop their professional identity – *learning as becoming* – students talk about the way in which their learning has had an impact on them personally and professionally

The students found that these communities of practice did not stop at the end of the programme; instead, the mutual understanding developed went on to continue to provide a supportive network outside the formal learning context.

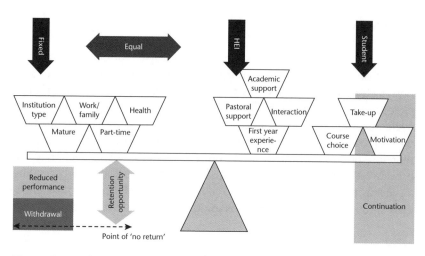

Figure 7.2   Edward's retention scales for part-time distance learners

Source: University Vocational Awards Council, 2009

▶ Maintaining momentum

One of the biggest challenges for your WBL students will be keeping up the momentum when they are 'set loose' on their independent journey. This is when the challenges of time management and keeping focus are at their height. There can be many conflicting calls on your students' time and there are some simple, but effective measures (such as scheduling tutorials, providing interim formative feedback at specific points or using 'patchwork text' assessment methodology (Winter, 2010)) that you can take to facilitate engagement, keeping a watching eye, rather than a straightjacket, to allow your learners to develop their own learning and drive it, whilst you keep them focused.

Edwards and Minton (2009) discuss key factors that affect momentum and engagement for part-time learners, presenting it as a balance beam upon which 'weights' – factors affecting momentum – are placed. This recognises that some fixed structures, such as work, family life, health and institutional requirements, can be 'counter balanced' by interventions such as academic and pastoral support, to increase your students' motivation (Figure 7.2).

The following Case study 7.6 offers some ideas for maintaining momentum, especially if your WBL students are learning at a distance:

Case study 7.6 Maintaining momentum: Utilising key milestones in online learning

A 60-credit programme at Level 4 was developed for a fashion organisation. As the learners were geographically spread, after the initial face-to-face induction event, the programme was wholly supported online with tutorial support from individual tutors.

The programme lasted for six months and had a number of discrete units to complete. Assessment activity was embedded throughout the programme, built into a portfolio of evidence and summarised through a final reflective essay.

The students were 'fired up' and enthusiastic after the induction event and managed to work through the first few units. As the programme progressed a number of the learners fell behind but did not get in touch with their tutors. Often, when a tutor did manage to contact them, they cited pressure of work, feeling somewhat 'lost'. Some noted that the final submission date felt such a long way off they did not feel that the work was pressing, whilst they had other workplace deadlines which *did* feel pressing.

The programme team reviewed their support strategy and put in place a series of target milestones for the various units to be completed; this involved the learners receiving formative feedback. Monthly Skype calls were scheduled in with every learner to check on progress, offer support and provide feedback.

The learners soon realised that an incremental approach to the work was required and that leaving everything to the last week before assessment was not helpful to their learning process. A small number of students highlighted specific issues that had prevented them from engaging with their work (change of work role, increase in duties, ill health and so on), and the tutorial team were able to use the various support mechanisms within the university to support these learners, including extensions to deadlines for extenuating circumstances.

These interim measures helped the learners to deal with assessment activities in achievable units and facilitated and aided their planning skills. In the context of Edwards and Minton's 2009 article the programme enabled the students to space out the 'weights' of assessment across the 'bar', rather than end-loading it.

Young and Stephenson (2007) reviewed the online exchanges between work-based learners and their tutors and identified the following themes:

▶ Learner control – planning, self-monitoring and requests for help
▶ Opportunities at work and how they can be integrated into the course
▶ Making decisions and seeking reassurance that they are 'on the right track'
▶ HE culture and terminology
▶ Clarification of understanding

They note that effective tutoring requires:

1. Knowledge of credit systems and academic regulations
2. Confidence to support generic skills, for example, academic writing, referencing, research, personal development planning
3. Willingness to work outside subject comfort zones
4. Capacity to help learners maintain momentum

They go on to note that the tone of discourse is critical, balancing friendliness and a degree of informality with clarity and precision when providing guidance. As with any tutorial discussion, the guidance should facilitate, rather than direct, allowing the student to choose their own direction, with you as tutor providing support by identifying the academic parameters within which the learning is taking place.

SUMMARY

▶ WBL students are doing the same thing as other students – developing graduate skills through HE; the inclusion of experiential WBL can deliver an enriched curriculum for all students (see Pearce, 2011; Walsh, 2011a; Walsh, 2011b).

▶ Integration of experiential WBL in context into HE can provide transformational learning to those who may not otherwise be able to access HE.

▶ In order for such learning to be fully utilised, in a context where unfamiliar pedagogies and assessment practices are used, it is important that you do not assume that you already know what is needed (based on the delivery of conventional courses).

▶ The 'traditional' HE model which concentrates on teaching 'content' is tutor-centred and often inappropriate in a workplace context.

▶ You need to take a learner-centred approach, recognising the pedagogic importance of putting in place structures to support your student's journey whilst acting as a 'critical friend'.

▶ References

Beckett, D. and Hager, P. (2002) *Life, Work and Learning: Practice in Post Modernity.* Abingdon, Oxon: Routledge.

Biggs, J. (2003) *Teaching for Quality Learning at University*, 2nd Edn, Maidenhead: Society for Research into Higher Education (SRHE) and Open University Press.

Boud, D. and Solomon, N. (2003) *Work-based Learning: A New Higher Education?* Maidenhead: Society for Research into Higher Education (SRHE) and Open University Press.

Boud, D. and Symes, C. (2000) Learning for Real: Work-based education in universities, in Symes, C. and McIntyre, J. (Eds), *Working Knowledge: The New Vocationalism and Higher Education,* pp. 14–29. Buckingham: SRHE and Open University Press.

Boud, D. and Tennant, C. (2006) Putting doctoral education to work: Challenges to academic practice. *Higher Education Research and Development.* 25 (3), pp. 293–306.

Clutterbuck, D. (2004) *Everyone Needs a Mentor,* 4th Edn, London: Chartered Institute of Personnel and Development.

Dewey, J. (1997) *Experience and Education.* New York: Touchstone Books (originally published 1938).

Edwards, S. and Minton, A. (2009) Re-thinking the retention of students in part-time distance learning. in Young, D. and Garnett, J. (Eds), *Work-based Learning Futures III.* Bolton: UVAC.

Hadfield, P. (2014) *Linking Theory to Practice Through the Use of Lived Experience Stories. Resources for Postgraduate Certificate in Professional Practice in Higher Education.* University of Derby (unpublished).

Jarvis, P. (2004) *Adult Education and Lifelong Learning: Theory and Practice,* 3rd Edn, London: Routledge Falmer.

Kolb, D. A. (1984*) Experiential Learning: Experience as the Source of Learning and Development.* London: Prentice Hall.

Laycock, M. (1993) Enterprise in higher education and learner-managed learning: The use of learning contracts, in Graves, N. (Ed.), *Learner Managed Learning: Practice, Theory and Policy Higher Education for Capability,* pp. 24–30. Abingdon, Oxon: Routledge.

Lizzio, A. and Wilson, K. (2007) Developing critical professional judgement: The efficacy of a self-managed reflective process. *Studies in Continuing Education.* 29 (3), pp. 277–293.

Moon, J. (2002) *Linking Levels, Learning Outcomes and Assessment Criteria.* Available at http://www.cemp.ac.uk/people/jennymoon.php accessed 26 September 2014.

Naish, J. and Minton, A. (2015) Support and guidance for work-based learning students, in Helyer, R. (Ed.), *The Work-based Learners Handbook,* 2nd Edn, pp. 84–97. London: Palgrave.

Pearce, D. (2011) *A Critical Review of Contemporary Practice: Experiential and Work-based Learning in the Hospitality, Leisure, Sport and Tourism Subject Area.* York: HEA.

Schön, D. (1983) *The Reflective Practitioner: How Professionals Think in Action.* New York: Basic Books.

Walsh, A. (2011a) *A Critical Review of Experiential Work-based Learning in the Undergraduate Curriculum of the Business, Management, Accountancy and Finance Subject Area.* York: HEA.

Walsh, A. (2011b) *A Critical Review of Experiential Work-based Learning in the Postgraduate Curriculum in the Subject Areas of: Business, Management, Accountancy and Finance, and of Hospitality, Leisure, Sport and Tourism.* York: HEA

Wenger, E. (1998) *Communities of Practice: Learning, Meaning and Identity.* Cambridge: Cambridge University Press.

Winter, R. (2010) Contextualiazing the patchwork text addressing problems of coursework assessment in higher education. *Innovations in Education and Teaching International.* 40 (2), pp. 112–122.

Young, D. and Stephenson, J. (2007) The use of an interactive learning environment to support learning through work, in Young, D. and Garnett, J. (Eds), pp. 84–97. *Work-based Learning Futures.* Bolton: UVAC.

▶ Recommended further reading

Eraut, M. (2004) Informal learning in the workplace. *Studies in Continuing Education.* 26 (2), pp. 247–274.

Ions, K. and Minton, A. (2012) Can work-based learning programmes help companies to become learning organisations? *Higher Education, Skills and Work-based Learning.* 2 (1), pp. 22–32.

Kinsella, E. A. (2007) Embodied reflection and the epistemology of reflective practice. *Journal of Philosophy of Education.* 41 (3), pp. 395–409.

8 Quality enhancement and work-based learning

Helen Corkill and Mark Atlay

IN THIS CHAPTER YOU WILL:

▶ Explore themes of quality enhancement in education, in particular with regard to work-based learning

▶ Be offered some illustrations of this via a series of case studies drawn from the enhancement of work-based learning in a variety of contexts

▶ Be shown key aspects of quality enhancement in action

▶ Explore the contested definition of enhancement in the context of higher education and its relationship to work-based learning

▶ Exploring quality enhancement in a work-based learning context

In Europe the definition of quality enhancement used for the Tuning Project is 'a constant effort to improve quality of programme design, implementation and delivery' (Tuning Project, 2014). This provides a basis for an exploration of enhancement in a work-based learning (WBL) context. Implementing enhancement in any context is problematic but perhaps more so in the case of WBL where the learning experience is made up of a complex interplay between the educational institution, the students and their workplace. Employers are a key stakeholder in WBL delivery and so continuous improvement needs to consider the impact of any changes on the work context, and in some cases changes in the work context may itself drive change. Continuous improvement is thus often more complex to effect in a work-based setting than in more traditional educational settings where tutors have more direct control.

▶ Approaches to quality enhancement

We identify three broad approaches to help frame a consideration of enhancement processes in action:

1. In evolutionary change, enhancement comes about through the continuous development of existing practices. This can lead to minor, but significant, changes in the nature of WBL or how it is delivered and supported. Most higher education (HE) providers will have processes in place to review and enhance provision as part of continuous improvement, and these will apply as much to WBL as to other contexts. Such processes are important, helping to keep the provision fresh and responsive to changing needs.

2. Occasionally there is a need to stand back from existing provision and effect a more radical step change in what is provided. It is with this revolutionary quality enhancement that we are particularly concerned in this chapter because it helps to illustrate some of the key drivers for effective WBL. Unlike traditional, classroom-based approaches to learning, the WBL activities of students can themselves lead to enhancement both of WBL itself and of workplace practice. The learning that comes from a step change in the approach to WBL may be transferable to other settings, but it cannot be assumed that this will be so. Thought needs to be given to generalisation from particular instances, especially given the tripartite nature of WBL and its key stakeholders, student/employee, higher education institution (HEI) and employer/organisation.

3. The third type of enhancement is systemic change illustrated by the UK's Quality Assurance Agency, which defines enhancement as 'taking deliberate steps at provider level to improve the quality of learning opportunities' (Quality Assurance Agency, 2014). This definition would mean actions that enhance the quality of WBL across the whole of a provider's provision, rather than in one particular context and involves changes to institutional policy or procedures.

▶ Principles of effective quality implementation

There are five key principles that lead to the effective implementation of quality enhancement initiatives in WBL contexts (and broadly to any quality enhancement initiative):

1. First, there needs to be clarity about the rationale for change. This may come from intrinsic factors such as a need to improve the student learning experience and to respond to changes in employer requirements,

or extrinsic factors such as a change in government or institutional policy. A lack of clarity about the rationale for change can lead to activities that enhance the learner experience without meeting the core requirements of the drivers for change or can lead to mixed understandings of the enhancement amongst the various stakeholders contributing to a dilution of its effectiveness.

2. Second, consideration needs to be given to possible enhancements to address the reasons for the change and their likely impact on the three key stakeholders: the institution, the employer and the student. We include within institutional and employer considerations implications for tutors, workplace mentors and others who support WBL interactions. The impact is not likely to be equally shared across these, but successful enhancements start by considering the likely impact across all three and engaging stakeholders in discussions from an early stage and ideally before a decision is taken about planned actions.

3. The third factor is a consideration of the resources available and required to implement the change. In a world of unlimited financial and human resources we could deliver high quality and effective work-based learning that met the needs of all stakeholders across a multitude of contexts. In reality resources constrain the 'when' and 'how' of WBL so any enhancement activity should carefully consider the short-, medium- and long-term resource implications.

4. Fourth, there is a need, at the outset, to consider issues of sustainability. How will the enhancement be incorporated into the routine after the initial development and implementation phase? Many enhancement initiatives are developed with pump priming of money or other resources and simply stall once the funding is removed because they are not self-sustaining. In addition, successful change is often driven by the commitment and enthusiasm of key individuals. If they move on then there is a loss of direction and drive to fully embed the change in practice.

5. Finally, consideration needs to be given to the means and mechanism for the evaluation of the change both to see if it has met its original objectives and to identify those other, unforeseen, implications of any change intervention.

Table 8.1 illustrates some of the main differences between the five key principles depending on the type of enhancement activity planned.

Table 8.1 Types and key principles of quality enhancement

Types of enhancement	1. Rationale	2. Envisioning actions and impact	Five key principles		
			3. Resource needs	4. Embedding and sustainability	5. Evaluation
A. Evolutionary change	Driven by internal factors	Imagines a modified practice Impact marginal on some or all stakeholders	Limited	Incremental nature means sustainability not an issue	Through normal monitoring processes
B. Revolutionary change	Often driven by external factors or by a major change in leadership or key staffing	Imagines a different practice Impact major on all stakeholders	Often significant at least in the short term	Maybe an issue if change is related to interests of staff or has major medium- or long-term resource implications	Needs consideration from the outset and may need specific and planned activity
C. Systemic change	Institutionally or externally driven	Imagines a different future across a range of contexts Impact major on some stakeholders or minor across many	Varied but institutional commitment means that resource requirements should be met	Institutional commitment means that it is sustainable	Institutional responsibility

---

Teaching tips: Changes and interventions

▶ Think about outputs before inputs: possible enhancement before change

Activity

Think of a change/intervention you wish to make to your programme. Using the template in Table 8.1 above, consider the type of enhancement and then sketch out the considerations/actions required under each of the five key principles.

The case studies and exercises in this chapter illustrate the application of the above three enhancement types and five key principles in a variety of work-based contexts.

▶ Working at the boundaries

The case studies are drawn from different higher education and workplace contexts: large and small, public and private, student and tutor, UK and USA. They illustrate programmes which occupy very different places on a continuum of WBL, from those with *employee-students* (Quality Assurance Agency, 2004) using their full-time work context as a primary component of their learning to *student-employees* (Association for Sandwich Education and Training, 2014) undertaking extended periods of placement (UK) or cooperative learning (US). In all examples, the main location for the learning is the workplace, and WBL forms a planned and integrated part of the programme of study. Some form of tripartite relationship between the student, the provider and the employer is in place, and the learning 'uses the immediacy of the work context to provide practice and to encourage reflection on real issues leading to meaningful applicable learning' (Ball and Manwaring, 2010, p. 4).

Work-based learners become involved in various cycles of activity generated in or by the workplace: identifying and recommending a solution to a workplace problem, using reflective models to consider new skills and competencies or introducing and evaluating a workplace intervention. The iterative process of introducing a quality enhancement initiative into a work-based programme and then monitoring and evaluating it, mirrors many of the experiences of the work-based learners themselves. In one sense, tutors in turn become *work-based learners* as they introduce changes and review these on a cyclical basis. A quality enhancement process at programme level might be effected through an action research approach (Lawrence and Corkill, 2013) or through the use of a widely used quality improvement model, such as the Deming Cycle (adapted in Case study 8.1).

▶ Case studies

Case study 8.1 Implementing quality management: The Toyota Production System

Enhancement type: A/B

A Year 1 workplace assignment for my FdA Business Management evaluates the quality management system used within Toyota Manufacturing UK (TMUK).

Problems with quality systems were identified in 2009 when there was a recall of Toyota cars. A systematic change was introduced from 2010, driven by new senior management. There was a need to revisit and adhere to original principles so that quality levels could again be assured and customer confidence regained. TMUK, as all Toyota plants, has always operated under a very comprehensive quality management system, the Toyota Production System (TPS), that applies heavy focus on the 'right first time' theory. TMUK employs a detailed standardisation system for *members*[1] to follow. Quality management tools used within Toyota are extensive but based on three main principles:

1. Customer expectation determines quality.
2. High quality is 'built in' at every stage.
3. Quality is continually improved.

Most quality models originate from the same sources as TPS, these being the work of Deming (1986) and Juran (1970). 'We're constantly looking for the next thing without realising that we already had it … the underlying PDCA concept was there to begin with' (Liker, 2004).

Toyota applies a quality cycle originating from Deming (1986), the PDCA Cycle – Plan, Do, Check, Act.

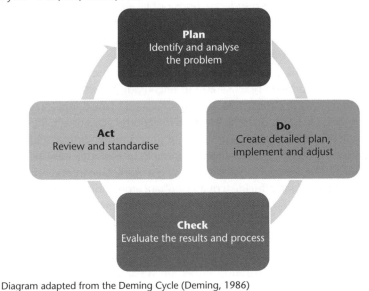

Diagram adapted from the Deming Cycle (Deming, 1986)

---

[1] Toyota employees

continued overleaf

Case study 8.1 Implementing quality management: The Toyota Production System *continued*

TMUK implemented an improvement activity for its suppliers, in which QA (Quality Assurance) personnel supported the supplier. The fundamentals are: go back to basics, understand your concerns and find the root cause of a problem. One could question if TMUK's QA members, for whom quality is their fundamental role, are sufficiently trained to advise on TPS. Whilst TMUK members are experienced, not all are TPS experts, and if the problem is process or logistics based then perhaps they aren't suitably qualified to advise on TPS. However, *members* are empowered through TPS and expected to be responsible for their own processes and not pass on poor quality to the next stage.

Toyota has a very detailed quality system that delivers a high-quality product to customers. However, as shown during the recall of 2009, failure to follow their own philosophy regarding organisational development resulted in quality concerns reaching the final customer. Following the crisis they investigated the root cause and have returned to their original principles.

Key messages

▶ Ensure correct level of training for *members* if they themselves are to train internal and external colleagues in assuring and enhancing quality.

▶ Follow original quality principles and philosophy. Strict adherence to these made Toyota into a hugely successful company, so by following these a high level of quality will be delivered to the customer.

Nick Vale,
FdA Business Management, University of Derby Corporate and Toyota Manufacturing UK

Work-based students may be key players in the introduction of quality enhancement initiatives. They may be instrumental in requiring change (Scott, 1999) but also in becoming partners in that change (Higher Education Academy, 2014). Quality enhancement or improvement measures may be very familiar to work-based learners. *Employee-students* are likely to work in highly regulated professions such as health, education or engineering or may work in businesses where cycles of continuous improvement are embedded into the organisational culture. *Employee-students*, and their employers, may have valuable contributions to make to the enhancement of work-based programmes. One caveat here must remain that for commercially driven organisations, the imperatives concerning the quality enhancement of learning programmes may be different – the value of learning as it impacts on the bottom line is essential (Garnett, 2008).

Case study 8.1 firstly, serves as a workplace example of a Type A quality enhancement model as illustrated in Table 8.1. Secondly, it illustrates how an *employee-student* undertaking a work-based foundation degree has developed a detailed understanding of this enhancement model – in this case embedded within his organisation's complex layers of quality improvement systems. In negotiation with his employer, the student is then enabled to offer recommendations as to how these quality systems could be enhanced in an industry where there is a necessity for tight quality control.

Teaching tips: Introduction, monitoring and evaluation

▶ In relation to any interventions selected it is important to consider how you will introduce, monitor and evaluate them.

ACTIVITY

Thinking back to the intervention you selected earlier:

▶ How are you going to introduce, monitor and evaluate this (for example, action research, a quality cycle like the PDCA cycle in Case study 8.1)?
▶ Identify the training needs required, including for staff and students

---

Case study 8.2 provides an example of Type A enhancement. Tottenham Hotspur Foundation (THF) is a small private provider in London. It offers two foundation degrees delivered within a very distinctive workplace, the White Hart Lane Stadium, home of Tottenham Hotspur Premier League Football Club. Due to the unique setting and wide range of community, business, sporting and educational partners, a wealth of different workplace learning opportunities is on offer to the mostly full-time student body. As a young and aspiring HE provider, with quality driven by its parent organisation, iterative processes of change for quality enhancement are frequent. THF is gradually developing its own distinctive approach to embedding WBL, and students are viewed as key partners in the change process.

As well as being well versed in quality systems (Case study 8.1) and partners in change at programme level (Case study 8.2), work-based learners may also become change agents within the workplace as a direct result of their higher education study. The following two linked studies

Case study 8.2 Students as partners: Sports-based foundation degrees

Enhancement type: A

Context

THF offers two sports-based foundation degrees which have a strong focus on placement and WBL. In 2010, we had a very quick turnaround time from approval to delivery. The vast organisation and management required for effective placement modules was not anticipated initially.

Through using a continuous cycle of student feedback and module enhancement we devised a new and structured student-led process for the organisation of WBL through placements. The innovative scheme includes a Student Placement Committee where students are credited with placement hours for helping to organise supervised placements for peers.

Rationale

Student feedback on the work-based modules was consistent: the organisation of placements was challenging and unclear. There was no systematic process for applying for placement opportunities. The original modules provided little guidance for either students or supervisors. There was no foundation for aiding students' experiences of reflecting and learning. Measures used to determine the quality of the placement experience were 'loose' and 'ad-hoc'.

Envisioning actions and impact

As an HE team we decided to introduce procedures that would enhance the quality of placement experiences for both provider and student. We also wanted to empower students to peer observe and support each other. Measures were introduced based on feedback from students and the module leader, and on the QAA benchmarks for foundation degrees and for hospitality, leisure, sport and tourism. The main themes chosen for enhancement were:

1. Impact on achievement of module learning outcomes
2. Quality of the learning experiences to enhance employability within the sports coaching and development industry

The most innovative part of the scheme was the development of a Student Placement Committee. Students volunteer to be part of the committee, and in return they can log hours for their placement module. The committee now works with many different projects within the foundation.

The module tutor trains the committee on procedures and systems within the foundation and acts as director to it. The tutor sets objectives for the committee and then works with members to create their own objectives and to record completed ones. After week eight the committee is trusted to create its own objectives.

continued overleaf

Case study 8.2 Students as partners: Sports-based foundation degrees *continued*

The committee's first task is to organise placement applications and to nominate students for available places. The committee works together to read applications and match students to appropriate placements. The tutor does not attend committee meetings for fear of influencing outcomes. Afterwards, the tutor deals with conflicts and then confirms placement allocations. The effectiveness of the committee's objective-based decision making and task completion improves with experience, evidenced by committee meeting minutes. Active learning takes place as committee members engage with external agencies, negotiating about timing, location, product or price. The committee has developed new communication procedures to inform peers of events and placement contacts.

Resource needs

Enhanced resources and materials were developed as an iterative process, including an application pack, safety and risk assessment checklists, agreements and mentoring guide. A WBL workbook was created, now being developed as an online tool.

Sustainability

Students successfully achieve 90 placement hours, typically gain a quality learning experience and benefit from thorough testimonials from their supervisors. Students identify key skills development for future careers and gain excellent experience within the sports coaching and development industry. Many students go into employment through their successful placements.

The new scheme is now embedded. The challenge was to create a Student Placement Committee that would support a self-regulation concept and manage good communication channels with peers.

Evaluation

Module feedback in both years one and two has improved significantly. Eighty-four per cent of students believe the modules to have improved career prospects; one hundred per cent of students agreed that changes in the module have been communicated effectively.

Feedback from students and tutors is that the committee system is very effective. The committee received feedback describing placements as 'priceless' and 'invaluable', underlining the importance of active learning and enhancing employability. The experience of being a committee member developed students' people skills, which were invaluable in the organisation of tournaments and communication with local schools. However, the committee needs to grow the size and range of projects in order to test out conceptual skills. Observations suggest the committee is becoming an effective learning mechanism, but there are many aspects yet to be analysed and evaluated.

Key messages

▷ Include students in the planning and implementation phase of any WBL enhancement.

continued overleaf

Case study 8.2 Students as partners: Sports-based foundation degrees *continued*

▶ Encourage students to take ownership over their personal development; they feel more empowered to achieve success.

▶ Conceptualising and question setting at the start of any placement activity is vital to generate an 'active learning' experience.

▶ Permit students to become cognitively engaged throughout the activity; reflection will then have greater clarity.

These key factors help to enhance WBL experiences and separate those that are simply 'satisfactory' and 'good' from those that are 'outstanding'.

John Hyatt and Laura Cornell, THF

Teaching tips: Students as partners in quality

▶ Ensure that student feedback mechanisms are embedded into enhancement.

ACTIVITY

Consider how you will involve students in the introduction, monitoring and evaluation of your enhancement initiative.

(Case study 8.3 and Case study 8.4) illustrate how a significant quality enhancement initiative introduced at the University of Sunderland had a direct impact on students' workplace settings. The university programme is a bespoke, work-based bachelor degree for law enforcement investigators and was developed as a direct response to national policing requirements in the UK. Change was required in the way that investigating police officers are taught, alongside how they analyse, reflect and question.

Case study 8.3 Enhancing reflective practice: The diverse approaches of one work-based BA

Enhancement type: A/B

Context

The work-based BA Applied Investigation programme focuses on developing the reflective and reflexive practices of serving police investigators, encouraging them to think, analyse and question differently.

continued overleaf

Case study 8.3 Enhancing reflective practice: The diverse approaches of one work-based BA *continued*

Rationale

There was observed resistance from police students to the use of reflective practice and critical incident technique, which are both used effectively in other sectors.

A deliberate change in approach was identified by teaching staff, encouraged by the university and agreed by police advisers, including the UK national police lead for investigative interviewing.

Envisioning actions and impact

A facilitated creative storytelling workshop was introduced, using a transformative learning approach. This introduced concepts of reflective and reflexive practice, encouraging students to take alternative perspectives through storytelling and incorporating artistic media (Lawson et al., 2013).

Student response to the workshop was mixed, with some immediate engagement and some hesitance. By the end of the facilitation all students engaged in the process, producing high-quality reflections and artefacts.

Evaluation

This creative intervention has enhanced the quality of this WBL programme and has exceeded all expectations. A multi-methods approach of auto-ethnography and action research was used for evaluation. The quality of assessed work on the programme improved, both in terms of higher grades and progression. Several students achieved first class degrees and, due to demonstrated impact on practice, have progressed directly onto professional doctorate programmes. The intervention has been transferred into workplaces.

One of the police students introduced the approach in a prize-winning innovative project working with school children in the North-East. (Case study 8.4).

Key messages

Professional work-based students often encounter challenges in their studies that take them outside their comfort zones. The facilitated nature of this intervention helped students work through disorientation and insecurities to make transformations in their learning and professional practice.

Ron Lawson, University of Sunderland

Case study 8.4 Enhancing professional practice: New approaches to road safety education

Enhancement type: B/C

I am a roads policing officer and recent graduate of a work-based degree programme specifically designed for law enforcement investigators. Whilst studying on the programme, a new pedagogical approach was introduced,

continued overleaf

Case study 8.4 Enhancing professional practice: New approaches to road safety education *continued*

aimed at widening perspectives, transforming learning and enhancing our professional practice.

Road death remains the biggest killer of young people in the UK. Law enforcement agencies and road safety educators are increasingly challenged to identify innovative ways to encourage safer road use amongst young people. Findings suggest that educational interventions designed without a theoretical learning model may inadvertently increase exposure to risk.

As part of my degree programme, I tackled an assignment around professional identity using digital storytelling. I adapted the technique to successfully implement a new approach to a road safety education programme with young drivers. I facilitated a workplace project which moved away from traditional instrumental teaching of road safety education. Locally, nothing like this type of arts-based learning model had been tried before. Internationally, the nearest approach was the use of theatre-in-education.

Working with six schools across north-east England, the project encouraged students to develop creative artefacts to express alternative narratives of a fatal collision story through the eyes of the characters involved. One school, situated in a challenging city demographic, allowed the participation of a group of students with low educational expectations and a fragile position within mainstream schooling. Using digital storytelling the students created a compelling and sensitive short film, carefully avoiding sensationalising the topic whilst exposing and examining the issue of peer pressure. Both the film and the re-engagement of the pupils exceeded all expectations of the school. The students showcased their artefacts to an audience of parents, teachers, staff from the emergency services and road safety educators.

Following the successful launch of the pilot project, it will continue on a larger scale for a second year. Whilst the students submitted evaluations and testimonials, it is too early to measure the project's impact accurately. A research study investigated one of the short films, examining the social significance of the themes identified and how these were conveyed to the audience.

Pupils from the school won a special award for business and enterprise. I was awarded the High Sheriff Cup at the Northumbria Police Excellence Awards 2014 for introducing an innovative approach in this project.

Key messages

Road death amongst this age group is such a complex and significant issue that it requires an approach that reflects the digital age and utilises imagination and creativity, which allows young people to be producers of their own learning.

Jami Blythe, Northumbria Police and University of Sunderland

Teaching tips: Reflecting on reflection

▶ Higher-level work-based study designed to challenge and change established thinking and practices may impact on a complexity of relationships.

continued overleaf

> **Teaching tips: Reflecting on reflection** *continued*
>
> ▶ These may include relationships with colleagues and line managers as well as perceptions of self.
>
> **Activity**
>
> In relation to your planned enhancement, what consideration needs to be given to the role of reflection and the emotional engagement of the learner?

Case study 8.5 demonstrates a model of enhancement necessitated by external government policy change and internal demand both from students and staff. In this example, the students had come to the end of the third year of their four-year practice-based course in the latter stages of which some significant but additional experiential learning had been identified as being required. The case study clearly demonstrates the five key principles (Table 8.1) within a Type B enhancement model. The outcome has synergies with Case study 8.3.

> **Case study 8.5 Adding a specialist placement: Incorporating learning from real work**
>
> *Enhancement type: B*
>
> **Context**
>
> Education students at the University of Bedfordshire undertake a four-year initial teacher training course. A deliberate change was introduced to the programme. Students were given the opportunity to enhance knowledge and experience of special educational needs and disabilities (SEND) by undertaking an additional four-week placement in a special school. The participating third-year students had all successfully passed mainstream placements and a 15-week module on supporting pupils with SEND.
>
> **Rationale**
>
> The internal and external influences that triggered the enhancement were the following:
>
> ▶ Student evaluations highlighted the need for more practical experience of working with SEND pupils. Staff identified that a SEND placement presented an advantage in terms of employability.
> ▶ Major SEND reforms were underway, a government national priority.
>
> This type of placement had not been a priority before. There was also a lack of staff confidence and competence in this area. The coordinator addressed this through training sessions, coaching staff and being observed/shadowed to ensure a better outcome for student learning and experience.
>
> *continued overleaf*

Case study 8.5 Adding a specialist placement: Incorporating learning from real work *continued*

Envisioning actions and impact

Students had to submit a rationale to be considered for a placement, along with a reference from their tutor. Prior to the placement, students were informed about the nature of pupils' needs in each school, ranging from specific learning difficulties (SpLD) to profound and multiple learning difficulties (PMLD).

Resource

Funding for these placements was secured via the National College for Teaching and Learning (NCTL). Upon completion of the placements, an evaluation was undertaken and written reports submitted to all stakeholders.

Sustainability

The way in which placements are secured has changed. The coordinator and students now work in co-creating the opportunities. Students make initial contact with new schools and refer to the coordinator for guidance and support as required. This is a transformative approach as students now take the placements forward. This has also been a transformative experience for staff who, for the first time, have observed specialist teachers and therapists whilst visiting students. This enables staff to reflect on their learning in order to incorporate this into future teaching. This is organisational learning.

The placements have had immediate and long-term impact. Students all reported that they had grown in confidence with regard to meeting pupils' needs. Some chose to undertake final-year dissertations in SEND; a few secured newly qualified teacher (NQT) posts in special schools. This was previously unheard of. The number of partnerships with special schools has increased and resulted in guest speakers presenting on a range of university units of study.

Key messages

To ensure success:
- ▶ Work with all staff to provide a training programme for students
- ▶ Ensure all students attend a school of interest for a few days before submitting an application for placement. This will help determine whether severe needs are within students' capabilities
- ▶ Pair students in each placement school for support and opportunities to reflect

Lisa Gallimore, Institute of Education, University of London (formerly of the University of Bedfordshire).

Teaching tips: The ripple effect

- ▶ Introducing change into a programme often leads to unexpected or additional changes.

ACTIVITY

Think about the enhancement you wish to make and what further changes might be envisaged as a result.

Case study 8.6 offers a very different perspective on quality enhancement. The Steinbright Career Development Center at Drexel University, Philadelphia, US, runs one of the largest cooperative education (co-op) programmes in the world, involving some 6,000 students and 60 staff (see Chapter 10 for more information on co-op). The university has clear strategic quality enhancement measures (Table 8.1: Type 3), which permeate academic-related areas of the organisation. Cooperative learning is no exception. The drive to improve employability and coherence between university and workplace learning is key, being informed by ongoing student and employer feedback. The mutual benefits, or otherwise, of data generated are monitored closely. Emphasis is placed on evaluation of activity and change within that activity and on exploring different ways to undertake this.

Case study 8.6 University and programme learning assessment: Using cooperative education evaluation data

Enhancement type: C

Context

At the Steinbright Career Development Center, student and employer participants complete evaluations at the conclusion of each six-month work experience. These support the curriculum review and revision process.

Rationale

Prior to the 2009–2010 academic year, student evaluations had not been revised since 2002, and employer evaluations not since 2005. The evaluations were heavily aligned with discipline-specific questions. Changes to institutional student learning assessment priorities and departmental recognition called for improvement. Written communication was also identified as a competency that needed to be better integrated into all curricula including co-op reflection.

Envisioning actions and impact

After drafting initial revisions to the student and employer evaluations based on a broader approach to student learning assessment, interviews were conducted with participating academic units and other key stakeholders to solicit feedback.

continued overleaf

Case study 8.6 University and programme learning assessment: Using cooperative education evaluation data *continued*

Based on collected feedback, the centre developed a two-part evaluation structure for both students and employers. Core evaluations that encompassed the assessment of student learning priorities were developed for both students and employers. Then, each college and/or school was provided with the opportunity to include a subset of questions specific to their students, which was developed in conjunction with professional accreditation requirements and/or programme outcomes. An electronic reporting tool was developed to improve data delivery and ownership. To improve written reflection, a short reflective analysis was introduced that required students to relate their work experience to a professional personal, or academic goal of their choosing.

Sustainability

Based on the restructuring of the evaluations the centre has improved its relationships with academic stakeholders. It has provided a concrete touchpoint for the evaluation of writing. It has also developed the opportunity for more college-specific feedback which has resulted in stronger accreditation preparation and curriculum development.

Students have had a more explicit opportunity to tie their learning and professional growth to broad categories such as communication and leadership as well as more discipline-specific elements. Through the writing exercise, students have been challenged to articulate what they have gained from each work experience. Furthermore, the analyses have enriched post-employment conversations between students and their advisors, focusing on benefits and implications for future career opportunities.

Key messages

This approach to evaluation of experiential education has allowed the Steinbright Career Development Center to balance the competing needs of institutional and programme assessment. Whilst often these needs intersect, the specificity of professional accreditation can be difficult to integrate in an appropriate manner when working with a wide breadth of majors. With the proper evaluation structure and technical support, offering both has been of great benefit to the university as a whole.

Stephanie Sullivan and Joseph Hawk, Drexel University, Philadelphia, US

Teaching tips: Evaluating enhancements

▶ Any enhancements introduced should be evaluated.
▶ When evaluating a specific enhancement, it is important that staff, students and employers are involved.

ACTIVITY

Thinking about the specific enhancement(s) you wish to make; how will you evaluate your intervention? How will academic staff, students and employers contribute to this evaluation?

SUMMARY

▶ There are wide variations in approaches to WBL and the variety of terms used within this to describe educational and workplace change. For quality enhancement purposes; this means that those involved need to be clear about the nature and purpose of the intended enhancement from the outset.

▶ The case studies illustrate external drivers which emanate from a variety of sources. Whilst each organisation, in different ways, was subject to 'top down' enhancement measures (Table 8.1: Type 3 enhancement), the more prevalent influencers appear to be those of sector, employer and students.

▶ The empowerment of students is a common element amongst the drivers of change in the case studies.

▶ The nature of change and enhancement is iterative, 'messy' and non-linear; it is likely to be incremental rather than whole scale and is reciprocal.

▶ When introducing an enhancement measure outcomes are not always assured, expect the unexpected.

▶ Quality enhancement, especially in a WBL context, is a complex activity. Having no systematic approach to enhancement leads to a degradation in the quality of the learning experience over time.

▶ References

Association for Sandwich Education and Training (2014) *Good Practice Guide for Work-based and Placement Learning in Higher Education.* Sheffield: ASET.

Ball, I. and Manwaring, G. (2010) *Making It Work. A Guidebook Exploring Work-based Learning.* QAA Scotland. Available at http://www.qaa.ac.uk/en/AboutUs/Documents/WBL_Guidelines.pdf accessed August 2014.

Deming, W. E. (1986) *Out of the Crisis.* Cambridge: MIT Press.

Garnett, J. (2008) Recognising and enhancing the quality of university work-based learning programmes, in Garnett, J. and Young, D. (Eds), *Work-based Learning Futures II*, pp. 32–38. Bolton: UVAC.

Higher Education Academy (2014). *Students as Partners Change Programme 2012–13.* York: HEA.

Juran, J. (1970) *Quality Planning and Analysis*. New York: McGraw-Hill.

Lawrence, L. and Corkill, H. (2013) Enhancing the enhancers. Action research as a quality enhancement tool, in Nygaard, C., Courtney, N. and Bartholomew, P. (Eds.), *Quality Enhancement of University Teaching and Learning*, pp. 163–180. Faringdon: Libri Publishing.

Lawson, R., Sanders, G. and Smith, P. (2013) Alternative pedagogies for the professional work-based learner, in Boström, L., Augustsson, G., Evans, C., Cools, E., & Charlesworth, Z.M. (Eds.) (2013). *Building Learning Capacity for Life. Proceedings of the 18th Annual Conference of the Education, Learning, Styles and Individual differences Network (ELSIN)*, pp. 161–174. Billund, Denmark: Mid Sweden University.

Liker, J. K. (2004) *The Toyota Way*. New York: McGraw Hill.

Quality Assurance Agency (2004) *Higher Education Review: A Handbook for QAA Subscribers and Providers with Access to Funding from HEFCE Undergoing Review in 2014–15*. Available at www.qaa.ac.uk/en/Publications/Documents/HER-handbook-14.pdf accessed August 2014.

Quality Assurance Agency (2014) *The UK Quality Code for Higher Education*. Available at www.qaa.ac.uk/assuring-standards-and-quality/the-quality-code accessed August 2014.

Tuning Project (2014) *Quality Enhancement at Programme Level: The Tuning Approach*. Brussels: European Union, Education and Culture DG. Available at www.unideusto.org/tuningeu/quality-enhancement.html accessed August 2014.

▶ Recommended further reading

Council on Higher Education (2011) *Work-integrated Learning: Good Practice Guide*. HE Monitor No. 12. Pretoria, South Africa: Council on Higher Education. Available at http://www.che.ac.za/sites/default/files/publications/Higher_Education_Monitor_12.pdf accessed 14 May 2015.

Gibbs, G. (2010) *Dimensions of Quality*. Available at www.heacademy.ac.uk/sites/default/files/Dimensions_of_Quality.pdf accessed August 2014.

Hawk, J. and Sullivan, S. (2014) *Using Cooperative Education Evaluation Data for University and Program Learning Assessment*. Paper delievered at the WACE International Symposium on Cooperative and Work-integrated Education, Trollhättan, Sweden, 2–4 June 2014. Available at http://www.waceinc.org/uwest2014/proceedings/US/Joseph%20Hawk%20%20-%20US.pdf accessed 14 May 2015.

McEwen, L., Mason O'Connor, K., Williams, C. and Higson, H. (2010) Engaging employers as partners in work-based learning assessment: Proposal for a quality enhancement framework. *Learning and Teaching in Higher Education*. 4 (2), pp. 62–89.

Sattler, P. (2011) *Work-integrated Learning in Ontario's Postsecondary Sector*. Toronto: Higher Education Quality Council of Ontario.

Scott, G. (1999) *Change Matters. Making a Difference in Education and Training*. St Leonards, NSW: Allen & Unwin.

Smith, C. (2012) Evaluating the quality of work-integrated learning curricula: A comprehensive framework. *Higher Education Research & Development*. 31 (2), pp. 247–262.

9 Using social media to enhance work-based learning

Andy Price

IN THIS CHAPTER YOU WILL:

▶ Be introduced to the most popular social media learning tools and platforms

▶ Explore how you might approach the effective use of social media for work-based learning

▶ Consider the importance of 'identity management' for tutors and lecturers engaging with social media in a work-based learning situation

▶ Think about possible barriers to the use of social media in work-based learning

▶ See the relative importance of text, image and video in social media usage

▶ Weigh up the merits of different social media tools and platforms for work-based learning

---

▶ What is social media and how is it used?

Writing about a fast-changing subject like social media is challenging. So whilst this chapter will look at many individual social media technologies and their potential role in work-based learning (WBL), it will also make some general pedagogical conclusions that should continue to be relevant to you. The chapter draws on case studies from higher education (HE) to illustrate the use of these technologies in work-based contexts.

Social media is also often described as Web 2.0, a new iteration of the World Wide Web that has 'interaction' and 'engagement' at its heart. Essentially social media is a mixture of websites and software applications that enable people to create and share content or to engage in social networking. It is a complex, constantly changing ecosystem driven by low barriers of entry and ease of development that mean the next 'big thing' may well be being built in a bedroom down the road from you as you read this! Social media and its associated technologies are rather like a dynamic toolbox, full of useful and exciting apparatus that can enthuse and frustrate an academic in equal measure.

▶ Social media as a learning tool

One of the most persuasive arguments for using social media in work-based learning is that it is already being used enthusiastically by learners, partly because of its pervasive nature across society but also in the case of work-based learners because you become more adept at using social media by actually using it, and these are learners who are already 'learning by doing' in other areas of their lives, including their jobs. So if you engage via Facebook and LinkedIn, for example, you are going where many of your work-based learners already are; you are 'pushing at an open door' and increasing the probability that they will be willing to engage in a way that they are familiar with. It is the 'social' dimension of social media that is the most striking characteristic of it; it fits into many facets of our lives and learning in incredibly subtle ways often complementing, supplementing and enhancing our existing behaviour in a myriad of different ways. The challenge for the WBL tutor is to be able to take a critical enough approach to this in a way that enables them to allow it to make a constructive contribution to learning and teaching. There are six examples of social media and two examples of social tools in the top ten of the *Top 100 Tools for Learning 2014*, the annual survey of learning tools conducted by the Centre for Learning and Performance Technologies (Hart, 2014) (Table 9.1).

Although social media technologies have not been specifically developed, tested or provided by higher education institutions (HEIs) as part of institutional learning and teaching strategies for learners, they are now significant parts of the learning environment that academic staff

Table 9.1 Top 100 tools for learning 2014

1	Twitter	Social media
2	Google Docs/Drive	Social tool
3	YouTube	Social media
4	PowerPoint	Desktop
5	Google Search	Online
6	WordPress	Social media
7	Dropbox	Social tool
8	Evernote	Social media
9	Facebook	Social media
10	LinkedIn	Social media

Source: Centre for Learning and Performance Technologies (C4LPT)

and work-based learners find themselves members of. Social media tools (from Table 9.1) that you may use in your teaching include the following.

Twitter

Twitter is a microblogging and online social network that enables users to send short (140 character) messages, otherwise known as 'Tweets'. Whilst users can send direct messages to each other, Twitter is a largely open service with no privacy controls. For work-based learners, Twitter can facilitate access to other individuals and institutions who have active Twitter accounts. This can be very valuable in terms of access to contemporary knowledge of their activities, thoughts and positions. Also learners and educators in work-based situations can utilise the # (hashtag) feature to create unique discussion tags, for example, #ourproject, for tweets that facilitate quick and easy discussion and enhance networking opportunities, particularly around real-time events, as the input is live and totally up to date. For example, if work-based learners had been asked to watch an online video about a particular sector or subject area, a twitter discussion following the viewing via a specific # (hashtag) would be one effective way to utilise the technology. The following Case study 9.1 outlines the benefits of using Twitter as part of your pedagogy:

Case study 9.1 Building communities of learning: Using Twitter

Most tools aimed at building online communities of learning, including those within virtual learning environments (VLEs), require learners to make deliberate efforts to use them. In contrast, Twitter is widely used away from academic life, and this encouraged me to experiment with it as a user-friendly learning technology within and outside the classroom.

I created hashtags for three of my modules and used Twitter to provide opportunities for continuous, two-way learner feedback and support, promoting engagement within and between classes and encouraging self-led, peer-supported learning.

Uses and benefits within the classroom

▶ *Virtual hand raising* – few students were raising their hand in large group sessions; allowing them to tweet in class offered them a channel to ask questions, which I read whilst they worked on tasks and responded to later in the session.
▶ *Facilitates discussion and collaboration* – group teaching requires interaction but maintaining whole-group-level engagement can be difficult. Asking students to work in small groups, and tweet the points from their discussion which are then displayed on a live Twitter wall (such as www.twitterfall.com), alleviates

continued overleaf

Case study 9.1 Building communities of learning: Using Twitter
continued

this problem, whilst encouraging individuals to make connections between their own thinking, experiences, ideas and those of others. The Twitter stream reduces the need for oral feedback, whilst providing a record of points raised.

Uses and benefits outside the classroom

▶ *Sharing links and resources* – posting links, such as news articles, helps learners to contextualise and see the relevance of topics. Because Twitter can be accessed any time – at work, on a bus, in a waiting room – engagement is more frequent. External input is possible with Twitter, so academics from other institutions, and individuals from the workplace, can contribute.

▶ *Support and reassurance* – encouraging learners to Tweet questions, rather than emailing their tutors brings a number of benefits:

- All of the cohorts can see the questions and responses, unlike a closed email exchange.
- Learners can answer each other's questions, shifting the focus from the tutor as the main source of knowledge.
- The short nature of Tweets (140 characters maximum) means students ask questions as they arise, rather than saving up lengthy emails.
- Short messages encourage a dialogue-based approach to answering questions, rather than the tutor providing a full, long answer with no avenue to assess understanding.
- Using Twitter has significantly reduced my time spent answering queries, but students perceive that my availability has increased and that my support is timelier.

Gary C. Wood, Enterprise Learning Development Officer, University of Sheffield

Google Docs

Google provides a wide range of free social tools, such as Google Docs, Google Sheets and Google Slides, which offer effective ways for work-based learners to collaborate and to be accessible online from any laptop, PC or mobile. These are examples of word processing, spreadsheet and presentation applications. For work-based learners working collaboratively in multiple locations this offers an excellent solution to many productivity issues. Google Hangouts is an instant messaging and video conferencing platform that is part of Google+. Work-based learners may also value Google Scholar, a web search engine that indexes a huge amount of scholarly literature in one place, hence saving them time but also allowing them to search from wherever they are. Google Scholar claims to index the majority of peer-reviewed online journals from Europe and America, as well as books and other non-peer-reviewed journals, and it was estimated to contain

150 million documents in 2014. You may wish to talk to your institutional academic librarian as to the interrelationship between Google Scholar and your institutional collection, particularly online resources.

YouTube

YouTube is the world's largest video-sharing website with an incredibly wide-ranging content covering all topics and sectors; it is becoming a serious competitor to conventional broadcasting channels and offers a significant amount of educationally useful material suitable for your work-based learners and particularly attractive for certain learning preferences. The uploading process is very simple, and as a tutor you may decide to download course content onto YouTube, such as short lectures, information giving sessions and filmed practical demonstrations. YouTube is also a useful vehicle for work-based learners to upload their own self-produced video content about their practice. By linking your YouTube channel to Google+ you can make videos 'private' to selected viewers only. Users of Office 2010 are now able to save PowerPoint presentations as .MWV video files that can be uploaded to YouTube as video; this offers a further way to share traditional learning materials, enhanced by adding a narrative track to the PowerPoint presentation.

WordPress

WordPress is the Internet's most popular free blogging tool; it is a sophisticated content management system (CMS) with features that facilitate many varied user requirements. WordPress exists as WordPress.org and Wordpress.com. WordPress.com has web hosting built in and includes many of the most popular features. It is the easiest way to get started but has limitations. WordPress.org allows you to install your own version of WordPress on a server and design a site with exactly the functionality that you need.

WordPress uses 'themes' for its aesthetic design (many of which are free) and plug-ins (also free) for its interactive features and functionality. Managing a WordPress site is quite simple and the built-in 'dashboard' is an easy-to-use feature. One of the great strengths of WordPress for WBL is its ability to integrate other social tools such as Facebook, Twitter and YouTube, to both disseminate content from WordPress sites onto these platforms and also aggregate content which originated on them. WordPress sites make excellent collaborative environments for work-based learners as they facilitate significant multimedia production.

The following Case study 9.2 illustrates the adoption of social media tools for pedagogy within a BA in professional practice, including blogging:

Case study 9.2 Flexible approaches using social media for communication and networking: BA Professional Practice in Arts (BAPP Arts)

The students on this part-time work-based programme are establishing arts professionals who base their studies on workplace practice. Many work in a freelance capacity in multiple work environments (paid and unpaid) or as sole traders. Established in 2007, 40 students graduated from the programme in 2013–2014.

The BAPP Arts curriculum incorporates the principles of inquiry-based learning with the dynamics of online peer reflection using social media platforms. This blended learning approach acknowledges that students who are professionals in their own right use technologies freely available in their various social and workplace contexts. Learners are asked to start a publicly accessible blog that they continue throughout their studies.

Flexible learning that engages with Web 2.0 to develop online peer interaction provides a useful link to collective online communities of practice and relevant 'digital habitats' (Wenger et al., 2009). The professional practice focus of the course encourages students to look at their own particular context and consider audiences across their arts-related practice. User generated content provides a valuable open-access resource for learners, as well as providing extracts that can be used as supporting evidence for assessment.

Besides establishing public forums for their work, private documentation and journals are used by the students to support insider research (Costley et al., 2010) that is confidential. Students make choices about work experiences and learn how to ethically record learning situations relevant to their university studies. The analysis of workplace phenomena is an iterative process and one that is considered in a final critical review of the inquiry.

The introduction of the 'professional artefact' has enhanced the capacity of learners to share the inquiry with colleagues beyond the BAPP Arts network and allows them to present their 'findings' to a professional audience in a more meaningful way, including audiovisual and visual outputs. An oral presentation is given to peers in person or by Skype and explains the learning undertaken. Presentations or summaries are posted back on the 'live' blogs to bring closure to the learning journey and demonstrate to those new to the programme a sense of what is possible.

Paula Nottingham, Middlesex University

Traditionally, performing arts students do not study research techniques that would be found in, say, a social science degree, but this online approach encourages them to explore and critique current alternative models, methods and theories in their subject discipline and to document their findings as part of their degree. This promotes research awareness and gives them relevant skills for their future careers.

Dropbox

Dropbox (like Google Drive) is a 'cloud' service – a free virtual hard drive where you store and share documents, images, videos and databases. Although not strictly social media the ability to share digital assets is useful in disparate WBL situations and particularly effective for sharing large amounts of documents, for example collaborative project work, which may otherwise clog up users' email inboxes. Dropbox is particularly usable because when an account is created, a new hard drive icon appears on your PC or laptop, where you can store and arrange files in the usual fashion. These files can also be accessed via any web browser and from any PCs or laptops you and your students own (including ones at work). There is also an app facilitating access from mobile devices and automatic synchronisation, meaning that changes to files are simultaneously available from any devices on which users link to the account. Furthermore, links to files (URLs) that you have created in Dropbox can be shared via email, Facebook, Twitter and so on with your students.

Evernote

Evernote is a flexible, multi-platform suite of applications designed for note taking, archiving and curating. A 'note' in Evernote might be a piece of text, part of a web page, a full web page, an image, a voice recording and so on, and these 'notes' can also have files attached. You can then tag, edit and annotate notes, organise them into folders, and export them as 'notebooks'. This is useful for work-based learners who are often compiling information from multiple sources. The basic version of Evernote will let you give permission to someone else to view your notebooks, but you need to upgrade to 'premium' to be allowed to collaboratively edit them, a facility which could be very useful for engagement between student/tutor and student/work colleague.

Facebook

Facebook is a very relevant tool for work-based learners due to its wide user base and ease of use. Once you have created an account with Facebook and a profile as a 'person', you are then able to create unlimited private (or closed) groups that learners can access; as administrator of a group you choose who joins. Any posts to this private group will only appear in the news feeds of the members of the work-based learner group. A Facebook group can easily operate as a virtual noticeboard with discussion space and timelines of learners' activities. Younger learners are particularly willing to seek help and support via Facebook, probably more so than they would in more formal situations. Images, photos, PDFs and videos can all be posted on Facebook as well as links to files in other locations such as Dropbox.

LinkedIn

LinkedIn is presently the dominant professional social networking platform. It has a significant following in the business community due to its ability to easily connect individuals via professional interests, for example, place of work, profession, professional groups, graduating HEI and so on. LinkedIn also allows the creation of interest groups with over one million of these, largely focusing on professional and career interests. For work-based learners LinkedIn provides an important tool with regard to learning, employability and career planning.

The following Case study 9.3 gives some examples of how employed learners can effectively use social media tools as pedagogic vehicles:

Case study 9.3 Expedient use of social media in WBL: Hyper Island

Hyper Island is a Swedish company specialising in work-based education through digital communications; their pedagogical philosophy is firmly rooted in experiential, problem-based learning.

Social media is used to develop a sharing culture between learners and between learners and teachers. Experience within the programme shows that such a sharing culture develops where there is a well-established set of cohort relationships, and staff and students collaborate effectively *prior* to the use of social media.

Hyper Island's pedagogical approach is predicated on developing a strong collaborative culture that in turn enables social media strategies to flourish. In terms of ownership, academic staff, company staff, and students all engage in collaboration and interaction on a level playing field, with control residing between them.

It is not an extension of the typical staff/student hierarchy often enforced through the classroom, and is even replicable using a VLE, if only used as an information and instruction repository.

Success is based on social media being an extension of the collaborative learning community. The first cohort (2011) employed a 'closed' Facebook group to share information and ideas or ask for assistance on work in progress. This group still continues to share information and assist each other with professional projects, demonstrating a true community of practice. Twitter and Instagram are used by each cohort, employing hashtags that identify the cohort and general hashtags relating to the institution (for example, #hyperislanduk).

continued overleaf

> **Case study 9.3 Expedient use of social media in WBL: Hyper Island** *continued*
>
> Usage of these platforms varies across time, with one being more prevalent than others at different points. Presently, Instagram is being predominantly utilised as a blogging tool where learners and teachers discuss work through a combination of still images, text or short videos that capture the learning and progress across the programme. Fundamentally, these tools represent the activity of learners and enable communication (they are 'social media' after all, rather than tools for curriculum content).
>
> One major difference these tools have brought to the classroom is that mobile phones are used during teaching and learning to photograph peers and teachers and share the moment's experiences, learning and reflecting in action.
>
> **Warren Harrison, Principal Lecturer, Teesside University**

Work-based learners' expectations are framed by both their previous educational and personal (including workplace) experiences. The current rich social media world is one that they will have high personal and educational expectations of; one only has to consider the increasing importance put upon the provision of free WIFI, or that many mobile phone contracts now come with free, unlimited Internet access, to realise that access to and use of social media is almost at utility level for a large percentage of the learning population.

Some thought should be given, however, to older work-based learners who may be unfamiliar with social media technologies, and strategies to enable them to master them at a sufficient level will need to be considered. Thankfully, the very nature of social media is such that 'learning by doing' lies at its very heart, and work-based learners already appreciate the power and effectiveness of learning by doing. Practical boot camps or introductory sessions can be based on the actual learning that the work-based learners will engage in, and pairing inexperienced learners with experienced buddies or mentors is a proven way of allowing them to build the necessary confidence and competency .

At its simplest, social media provides a replacement for existing practices, with an enhanced digital form. Social media platforms, like Facebook, Dropbox and Google Docs, can be used by work-based learners as the repositories for digital versions of formerly printed material. In terms of ease of access by the work-based learner (particularly at a distance), there is value in this, which should not be underestimated, especially as work-based learners are often putting together what can become quite large and complex portfolios which evidence their learning (more in Chapter 5). Similarly with communications: emails, tweets and posts can be very effective in 'broadcasting' news and information, simply creating a digital noticeboard. A pedagogical approach to WBL that does no more than this is missing opportunities for a 'participatory culture' to develop (Jenkins, 2006). This would be short sighted, especially when the transdisciplinary nature of much WBL is taken into account (see Chapter 1).

Social media is a multidimensional concept; as Moss and Bromley (2015) point out, it has four main functions: communication, collaboration, networking and sharing, key factors in effective blended learning. Kaplan and Haenlein (2010) have created a classification scheme using the functionality of six different types of social media:

▶ Collaborative projects (Wikipedia)
▶ Blogs and microblogs (Twitter)
▶ Content communities (YouTube)
▶ Social networking sites (Facebook)
▶ Virtual game worlds (World of Warcraft)
▶ Virtual social worlds (Second Life)

What is the potential of using virtual worlds and virtual gaming in your pedagogical strategies? Facebook's recent purchase of the creator of 3D virtual reality glasses, Oculus VR, for $2 billion suggests that there is a social future for these technologies, not least because they offer exciting possibilities around virtual experiential work-based learning which could be particularly useful in offering traditional students virtual workplace experience, as well as helping WBL students to develop. Can suitably useable media creation tools be developed to lower entry barriers for fledgeling content creators like yourself? Social media offers the work-based learner new, innovative and exciting ways to collaborate and co-produce with tutors. If WBL is seen as a 'social process', then using social media is a natural extension of it (Smith and Smith, 2015). The challenge for you is to weave in the appropriate social media tools to enhance the WBL experience for your students.

▶ Using social media in WBL

When compared to a traditional transmission model of learning, social media provides direct virtual contact with the work-based learner and a high confidence level in the quality of the information and knowledge being provided. For a diverse and disparate group of learners in a variety of work-based situations this can be a very powerful way to organise student learning. From a more humanist perspective social media allows you to progressively build and develop relationships with individual work-based learners, increasing the effectiveness of the WBL arrangements. A constructivist approach benefits from the ability to facilitate peer-to-peer relationships and learning as well as the opportunity to create clear frameworks and structures that students can learn within. A high level of involvement with work-based learners can be facilitated and progressively reduced as the work-based learners gain autonomy. Social media platforms provide valuable tools for you to gain insight into your learners' progress as well as offering excellent opportunities for the development and growth of virtual 'communities of practice' (Smith and Smith, 2015).

You can develop 'expansive learning' for groups or organisations as work-based learners begin to reflect upon and develop and change their professional practices above and beyond any specific learning (Ions and Sutcliffe, 2015). The social platforms you initiate can therefore become sustainable vehicles for ongoing lifelong learning. The overarching themes are around communication, collaboration, networking and sharing as identified by Moss and Bromley (2015). To use social media within a specific pedagogical strategy you will need to plan how different forms of it can be used and integrated (see the case studies for some good examples of this). You also need to actively 'nurture' new online groups to enable them to achieve sustainability, at which point you become the 'moderator' helping them remain as focused and purposeful 'public spheres' in the Habbermasian sense. Nurturing can consist of simple confidence-raising activities such as encouraging them to post and comment on Facebook pages, join simple Twitter discussions or set up Google alerts for personal hobbies or pastimes.

▶ Virtual learning environments (VLEs)

When considering the pedagogical use of social media for WBL it is important to understand the functionality provided by your HEI's virtual learning environment (VLE). Many features of VLEs are social and can be thought of as 'proprietary' social media; a chat with your institution's technology learning adviser is a good starting point. Social media tools also provide excellent scope for work-based learners to engage in research activity, as these students are often primarily based off campus as well as usually being new to academic research and writing. Minocha and Petre (2012) provide a comprehensive overview of the subject. The following Case study 9.4 explains how one tutor harnessed their HEI's VLE to good effect:

Case study 9.4 Improving academic writing skills: Using your institution's VLE

A tutor of a skills module for work-based learners was struggling to engage the learners with any academic reading material. In an effort to solve this he decided to tap into the social capacity of the institution's VLE.

The learners were familiar with using other functions of the VLE so the tutor decided to utilise its inbuilt blogging tool to enhance their writing and research skills and asked them to write a weekly review of an article from the set reading.

Strategies were deployed to build skills and confidence whilst enhancing the learning experience:

1. The reading was provided as PDF files via the VLE to enable ease of access for the learners; the tutor prepared all the articles at the beginning of the course and used a 'progressive release' feature in the VLE to auto-publish them at set times each week.
2. The material got progressively more sophisticated and demanding as the module progressed; this was clearly explained to the learners in terms of challenges they would face as they progressed through the reading.
3. The opportunity to post the blog review was time limited to a set period every week.

A number of interesting results occurred, only some of which were expected: the engagement with the written material was greatly improved; tracking the readers via the VLE's analytical tool was easy and very helpful; and final grades in the module certainly exceeded previous years.

But what was most interesting was the 'freedom' that the work-based learners demonstrated in writing about their ideas in the blog reviews, something the tutor had never witnessed in seminar groups. It was clear that a significant number of participants were far happier and more comfortable communicating in writing, via social media, than verbally in a conventional social situation. The tutor gained a valuable insight into learning preferences and learner progress, which was previously unavailable.

Also, the formative feedback given on writing style each week, via comments on their blog reviews, proved very effective and clearly had a positive impact on the work-based learners' understanding of their approach to writing, research and furthermore what was required of them in real workplace situations.

▶ Barriers and challenges

Social media changes fast, you will need to stay engaged to both understand the capabilities of different types of social media and keep up to date with what your work-based students actually use. One of the most consistently useful sources of information about social media is the online magazine Mashable (a leading source for news, information and resources for the Connected Generation) – http://mashable.com/social-media/. Their short, practical, incisive articles cover almost every aspect of social media usage and development.

ACTIVITY

▷ Find out what social media your work-based learners are actually using.
▷ Clarify before a course begins what social tools your learners use, what social platforms they inhabit, and what their social media habits actually are – you could devise a questionnaire.
▷ Ensure the social tools are flexible and nimble enough to adapt; if necessary change your delivery to suit the situation that you discover

---

▷ Identity management

Your personal, individual social media identity may not be the one you wish to convey in a professional educational context. You need a clear strategy as to how you will manage your social and educational worlds in terms of your professional identity. So whilst you may use Facebook groups to develop discursive space with learners, these may well not be people that you would necessarily wish to have as 'friends' of your personal Facebook page; it is important to reflect on this issue and how you will manage it. Some academics take the view that Twitter is a public sphere better engaged in at a professional level because the type of debate that is entered into there is more relevant to their academic identity, whilst Facebook is a more social environment that lends itself to friendships and a social identity. You will also need to discuss this with your work-based learners who will need to maintain varying degrees of separation between their work, education and personal personas.

ACTIVITY

▷ Ask your academic colleagues how they manage their different online identities and what issues they have faced.
▷ Investigate the privacy settings in each social media tool you use.
▷ Ask yourself, 'How do I wish to be perceived by … [different groups of online users]'?
▷ Decide upon a strategy for each social media tool that you intend to use.
▷ Share the information you gather about digital identity management with your work-based learners to help them understand how boundaries easily become blurred in this area.

▷ Institutional policy

Most HEIs now have institutional policies on the use of social media by academics, and it is important to familiarise yourself with your individual HEI's stance. In general, these try to balance facilitating academics with the constructive use of social media whilst protecting the reputation of the institution from unintentional and malicious activity. They usually emphasise the importance of professional identity, as mentioned earlier, which only reinforces the reasons for considering this issue. Most social media platforms, such as Facebook, also have well-developed guidelines for acceptable behaviour, and it is a good idea to familiarise yourself with these, not least as you may have to deal with some unacceptable behaviour on social media, and having a firm basis for doing so is very helpful. The Facebook community standards guidelines can be found here https://www.facebook.com/communitystandards.

▶ Employer constraints

If you are involved in WBL delivered on site in a place of work you will need to familiarise yourself with any constraints employers may have on their use of social media. Issues can range from companies' desktop PCs simply not having installed appropriate software, such as Flash plug-ins, through to the complete blocking of social media sites by company firewalls, presenting significant problems for a learner. Some employers have negative views of employees using social media, so care should be taken to communicate the benefits of this from an educational perspective as part of a WBL strategy. Some employers will react positively to requests to change an ICT learning environment; others are more problematic, and diplomacy is key when investigating the ground rules.

ACTIVITY

▶ Investigate early in the development of your WBL programme what the learner's employer's policies are as to employees using social media.
▶ Explain clearly the learning benefits of their employees having access to social media platforms.
▶ Give organisations as much time as possible to make any changes required.

▶ Using images and video

Work-based learners will have to be very sure about information and images that they are allowed to use from work within their HEI assignments. Similarly, if you are preparing learning materials for online usage, and considering how images, graphics, video content and animation can be integrated into them, you need to be sure that you are allowed to use the images you select. A very good source of copyright-free images (available under a Creative Commons license) can be found on Flickr. The webpage https://www.flickr.com/creativecommons/ explains the various levels of usage of different types of image on the platform. Google's Advanced Image Search http://www.google.co.uk/advanced_image_search also allows the user to find 'free to use or share' images via a 'usage right' filter at the bottom of the page. More information about Creative Commons and how to use copyright-free material is available at http://www.creativecommons.org.uk/

▶ Mobile and apps

The ubiquitous nature of mobile phones means that work-based learners now have round-the-clock access to social media tools and platforms. This access is usually via free apps produced by social media publishers. Whilst this creates greater flexibility in terms of access, it also presents new 'usability' problems due to factors such as small screen size. If you decide to use social media as a learning tool, it is important that you consider how a work-based user navigates the material that you publish. What may appear perfectly acceptable on a desktop or laptop PC may be very difficult to deal with on a mobile phone or small mobile device. It is good practice to check that any learning materials published are accessible on whatever device the learner may use. It is an issue of accessibility that can easily be overlooked and one that is especially pertinent for work-based learners who are often off campus and perhaps travelling at some distance to different branches of their organisation to fulfil their job role.

You may wish to develop your own app to support your work-based learners and there are many free online tools to allow the beginner to do this, as they tend to use graphical interfaces that require no programming or coding knowledge and are relatively easy to master. Your work-based learners may have the interest and capability to develop their own apps, and this is something you might like to encourage. Most apps developed have to be distributed by either the Apple iTunes store or the Google Play store, and a small cost is involved. You should check with your central learning and development department to see if your HEI has an existing relationship that allows apps to be published.

Blogging platforms such as WordPress also have the ability to make self-published websites easily mobile compatible. One very easy solution is for you to create a WordPress blog and use a free WordPress mobile plug-in, effectively offering the best of both worlds with the availability of a desktop website and a native mobile version.

A good starting point to develop your own app is '10 Excellent Platforms for Building Mobile Apps' on Mashable (http://mashable.com/2013/12/03/build-mobile-apps/). Advice on setting up a WordPress blog can be found here http://learn.wordpress.com/.

▶ Writing for social media

A useful writing strategy from journalism involves the 'inverted pyramid' story structure where effectively the whole story is in the first paragraph, headline or title, and subsequent paragraphs can be edited from the bottom of the article without radically changing the meaning of the story or information. This means a reader can get the sense of what is being written about very quickly and then choose whether to invest the time in reading the rest of it. A powerful headline or first paragraph is an important way to help the reader or learner to engage with the material. Similarly, social media users are becoming familiar with the concept of 'click bait'. This is headlines or snippets of news that are so compelling that they successfully drive huge amounts of traffic to the original story. This illustrates the importance of engaging a reader or learner as quickly as possible in the material presented to them. George Orwell's advice on how to write remains very relevant even in social media: use short words, use short sentences, use an active voice and if a word can be cut, cut it.

People respond very happily on social media to a 'call to action' at the end of a post or tweet. So if you want work-based learners to do something – for example, 'email me now', 'tell me what you think', 'visit this website' and so on – tell them in the final sentence that you need them to do it. This will have far greater impact than assuming they understand they need to do it or referring to it somewhere else in the post or text.

▶ Search engine optimisation

If you or your learners write content for social media platforms that you would like others to find then you need to be aware of the key words you are using, especially in your title and, if you have one, your abstract. Online readers find content by using search engines, such as Google, where they will type in a limited number of words; the words they think sum up their search. So if you are writing about 'pedagogy', for example, make sure that word is in your title.

Social media undoubtedly offers a fantastic array of learning opportunities. This chapter has tried to summarise the major ones, but others are being developed all the time. Case study 9.5 illustrates one lecturer's ongoing experiments in a quest to provide innovative learning opportunities to learners:

Case study 9.5 Using social media in teaching: The need for pedagogical goals

To enhance the learning and teaching experience of work-based learners I have used:

▶ Wikis, to co-create lecture notes as a formative and then summative assessment
▶ real-time synchronous collaboration with Hackpad
▶ Tumblr blog for sharing quotes and links
▶ WordPress blogs for reflective and analytical assignments
▶ Twitter for news gathering and building personal profiles
▶ Storify to engage with content curation
▶ Pinterest to create visual collections
▶ Facebook as a group communication tool and for simulating workflow

Some of these interventions have been incredibly successful, others an equally spectacular failure. The most important aspect for any usage is to have a clear pedagogical goal in mind and to share this with the rest of the group. If things don't go as planned, acknowledge and learn from this. Openness in this way not only embodies the medium, it also helps ensure participants embrace the activity.

What motivates engagement? Collaborative wikis have been most successful when used as a summative assessment. Facebook can simulate workflow but is a more formative undertaking, with benefits realised through enhanced working practices.

It might be tempting to make use of social media in WBL scenarios to capitalise on the pre-existing commitment participants have towards any one platform (for example, already use it at work) and the ease with which interconnectivity should arise as a consequence. Be cautious about this for three reasons:

1. Pedagogical goals need to be the driving factor, not an afterthought.
2. Whilst some may consider students as 'digital natives', in my experience their usage of online platforms is almost universally uncritical and narrowly focused. This gives rise to new opportunities for teaching critical media literacy through the use of social media, but don't assume anyone's familiarity with any platform; even the Facebook privacy settings appear a mystery to most.
3. Establish clear boundaries between private and public, between personal life and work setting.

For me, Twitter is an entirely public space whilst Facebook is a mixture of the two. Rather than having separate accounts for work and personal networks, I make extensive use of 'friends lists' to differentiate how I share content. Similarly, I engage actively with students on Facebook but only in defined groups connected with specific topics, classes or activities.

My one final tip for using social media for WBL? Observe the conventions, but don't forget to be yourself.

Einar Thorsen, Senior Lecturer, Bournemouth University

SUMMARY

▶ Social media has successfully diffused into wider society and is used in a multitude of ways in most people's day-to-day life.

▶ Its effective use within WBL should be a natural consideration when developing learning strategies.

▶ Its ability to complement and enhance different pedagogical approaches is powerful and the opportunity to enhance the work-based learner's experience should not be overlooked.

▶ Social media has significant pedagogical benefits for WBL, and using a mixture of different social media in a WBL situation can be very effective and increasingly expected as standard.

▶ Technological development is, however, rapid and you therefore need to monitor both the development of new social media and its actual use by work-based learners to keep your learning approach relevant.

▶ References

Costley, C., Elliot, G. and Gibbs, P. (2010) *Doing Work-based Research Approaches to Enquiry for Insider-Researcher.* London: Sage Publications Ltd.

Hart, J. (2014) *Top 100 Tools for Learning 2014*: *Results of the 8th Annual Survey of Learning Tools.* Available at http://c4lpt.co.uk/top100tools/ accessed 14 October 2014.

Ions, K. and Sutcliffe, N. (2015) Developing yourself, developing your organisation, in Helyer, R. (Ed.), *The Work-based Learning Student Handbook*, 2nd Edn, pp. 51–70. London: Palgrave.

Kaplan, A. M. and Haenlein, M. (2010) Users of the world, unite! The challenges and opportunities of social media. *Business Horizons.* 53 (1), pp. 59–68.

Jenkins, H. (2006) *Convergence Culture: Where Old and New Media Collide.* New York and London: New York University Press.

Minocha, S. and Petre, M. (2012) *Vitae Innovate Handbook of Social Media for Researchers and Supervisors.* Open University and Vitae. Available at https://www.vitae.ac.uk/vitae-publications/reports/innovate-open-university-social-media-handbook-vitae-2012.pdf accessed 14 October 2014.

Moss, C. and Bromley, M. (2015) What can social media (SoMe) do for me?, in Helyer, R. (Ed.), *The Work-based Learning Student Handbook*, 2nd Edn, pp. 162–183. London: Palgrave.

Smith, S. and Smith, L. (2015) Social learning: Supporting yourself and your peers, in Helyer, R. (Ed.), *The Work-based Learning Student Handbook*, 2nd Edn, pp. 184–204. London: Palgrave.

Wenger, E., White, N. and Smith, J. D. (2009) *Digital Habitas Stewarding Technology for Communities,* Portland, USA: CPSquare.

▶ Recommended further reading

Barnes, N. G. and Lescault, A. M. (2012) Social media adoption soars as higher-ed experiments and reevaluates its use of new communications tools. Available at http://www.umassd.edu/cmr/studiesandresearch/socialmediaadoptionsoars accessed 14 October 2014.

Benson, V. and Morgan, S. (Eds) (2014) *Cutting-edge Technologies and Social Media Use in Higher Education*. Hershey, PA: IGI Global. doi: 10.4018/978-1-4666-5174-6.

Cao, Y., Ajjan, H. and Hong, P. (2013) Using social media applications for educational outcomes in college teaching: A structural equation analysis. *British Journal of Educational Technology*. 44 (4), pp. 581–593.

Dalgarno, B., Kennedy, G. and Merritt, A. (2014) *Curriculum Models for the 21st Century in Connecting Student Learning at University with Professional Practice Using Rich Media in Practice-Based Curricula* (pp. 213–233). New York: Springer.

Greenhow, C. and Gleason, B. (2012) Twitteracy: Tweeting as a new literacy practice. *The Education Forum*. 45 (2), pp. 223–245.

Levine, A. and Dean, D. (2012) *Generation on a Tightrope: A Portrait of Today's College Student*. San Francisco: Jossey-Bass.

Liyanage, L., Strachan, R., Penlington, R. and Casselden, B. (2013) Design of educational systems for work-based learning (WBL): The learner experience. *Higher Education, Skills and Work-based Learning*. 3 (1), pp. 51–61.

Long, L. K. and Meglich, P. A. (2013) Preparing students to collaborate in the virtual work world. *Higher Education, Skills and Work-based Learning*. 3 (1), pp. 6–16.

Rios-Aguilar, C., González Canché, M. S., Deil-Amen, R. and Davis III, C. H. F. (2012) *The Role of Social Media in Community Colleges*. University of Arizona and Claremont Graduate University. Available at https://gettingconnected.arizona.edu/?q=Role_of_Social_Media, accessed 01 July 2015.

10 Learning in the workplace globally

Ruth Helyer and Jenny Fleming

IN THIS CHAPTER YOU WILL:

▶ Consider the different terminologies surrounding learning which comes from work and work activity

▶ Look at the meaning of the term 'work-based learning' and where this overlaps and intersects with other learning activities

▶ Examine international terminology

▶ Be offered some definitions around HE initiatives using experiential learning

▶ Be able to explore the blurred boundaries between different routes to 'learning by doing'

▶ What is crucial to work-based learning?

The majority of this book focuses on tutoring work-based learners, using the term **work-based learning (WBL)** as it is recognised in UK higher education – learning which occurs through actually carrying out job roles and tasks and the accompanying critical thinking, analysis and reflective practice that goes with this: 'learning that is acquired in the midst of action and dedicated to the task in hand' (Raelin, 1997, pp. 563–564); 'learning that is situated in the workplace or arises directly out of workplace concerns' (Lester and Costley, 2010, p. 562); and 'learning [which] takes place in the same context as which it is applied' (Lave and Wenger, 1991, p. 40). What is crucial to WBL is the relationship between experience, what happened because of this experience and the individual then reflecting critically upon this phenomenon (Dewey, 1916).

Work-based learners are not always full-time employees; learning can occur during part-time, voluntary and self-employed work. Those who do not have a job can also reap the benefits of WBL by undertaking work placements or internships (see Chapter 13); what is learnt experientially through these opportunities aids the translation of academic theory into practice, via real activities, or project work, which is assessed. WBL is largely unplanned, but this does not mean it cannot be planned, or at least the conditions created to foster it. Much that is learnt in the workplace (as in life) is not at higher education (HE) level and that which is may never be ratified by any higher education institution (HEI). However, that which does become associated with HE is found in flexible, different kinds of programmes, often individually negotiated (see Chapter 4), with titles such as 'Work-Based Studies Degree', 'Negotiated Learning Programme' and 'Professional Studies (or Practice) Route'. These may well include lectures, workshops, tutorials and other recognisable educational strategies; however, there is a strong possibility that the student is required to rarely, if ever, attend the campus, there is often little predetermined curriculum content and the student is allowed (and helped) to design their own content, creating a tailored totally appropriate route for them and their employer/sector, based upon what practitioners are actually undertaking in professional practice. This is in sharp contrast to the more traditional academic programmes where subject disciplines dictate what is in the curriculum.

WBL, as it occurs in the workplace, is not usually assessed or accredited, unless it is presented to an HEI; however, much has the potential to be via the recognition of prior learning (RPL) process (see Chapter 5). The majority of WBL in HEIs concentrates on what students have learnt, are learning and will learn, at work; however, WBL is also considered as a field of scholarship in itself, which interrogates how WBL occurs, thus elevating the subject into a more theoretical and scholarly area of study. WBL always starts with the worker learning in the workplace; many of the other workplace scenarios described in this chapter start with the HEI and its existing students. Eyler (2009) sums up this difference:

> Experiential education, which takes students into the community, helps students both to bridge classroom study and life in the world and to transform inert knowledge into knowledge-in-use. It rests on theories of experiential learning, a process whereby the learner interacts with the world and integrates new learning into old constructs.
>
> (Eyler, 2009, p. 24)

In this description the first kind of student would be a placement student and the second kind would be a work-based learner. Kolb's description of experiential learning as, 'a process whereby knowledge is created through the transformation of experience' (Kolb, 1984, p. 38) reiterates two things: experiential learning does just happen, but it also requires drawing out and facilitating. The idea that a process is involved is what drives the notion that it will still occur in contrived situations (such as work placements) and still bring all the benefits of new learning, development and innovation along with it.

There are differences in the terminology used for learning through work across the globe, and this chapter offers some definitions of similar and overlapping terms as well as some case studies focusing on real-life scenarios to bring context and elucidation, as often these terms are confusingly conflated and treated as falsely interchangeable. Although there are practical, pedagogical and even philosophical differences between these initiatives there are also powerful commonalities, such as:

▶ The fostering of real-life work skills
▶ The creation of autonomous learners
▶ The development of reflective practitioners
▶ The valuing of cutting-edge practice and innovation
▶ The acknowledgement that knowledge is created and used elsewhere, other than in the classroom.

Work-integrated learning (WIL) is a term used (especially in the US, Canada, Australia and New Zealand) to describe planned educational approaches where HEI-based academic learning is deliberately integrated with practical learning at work. A key feature of WIL is that the HEI is responsible for the curriculum and can be seen to 'drive' the initiative; they send the students out to the companies. When compared to WBL, as defined above and throughout this book, you will notice that the major difference is that work-based learners are employed students who find their own way to HE to progress learning that is happening anyway. So WIL is very much driven by the HEI, with WBL being very much driven by the learner. WIL is an 'umbrella' term, encompassing a wide range of models including **practicums, cooperative education, internships, sandwich courses, fieldwork,** and **service learning** (see Helyer and Fleming, 2015, for fuller descriptions of these interventions). Within the different models and frameworks of WIL, the intentions and structure of the placement experience vary.

Practicum is used interchangeably with other terms to refer to experiences actively providing opportunities for the application of theory to practice. In **professional practicums**, the purpose of the workplace experience is to provide an induction of the student into a designated profession. Professions that use this model include medicine (De Beer, 2011), nursing (Grealish and Stunder, 2011), engineering (Todd and Lay, 2011) and teacher education (Cooper and Taylor, 2011). The workplace provides a context for making links between theory and practice and the development of skills and competencies relevant to the specific profession. Completion of a specific number of practice hours is a requirement for registration in certain professions (such as nursing and engineering). It is common for joint teaching appointments to be made between the workplace (such as a hospital) and the HEI so that staff can be involved with learning and teaching in both learning environments.

Cooperative education, often known as 'Co-op', involves integrating academic studies with the learning that occurs through the experience of work. The integration of the learning environments of both the HEI and the workplace is one of the defining features of cooperative education. Co-op is founded upon the development of a collaborative partnership through which mutually beneficial outcomes can be achieved for the student, the host organisation and the HEI (Fleming and Hickey, 2013). A critical component of cooperative education is that the workplace experience is directly relevant and dovetailed into the student's degree or programme of study. The learning outcomes are negotiated through a learning contract or agreement (Chapter 4) that is agreed on by all three parties. Learning is facilitated through encouraging and supporting students to reflect on their experiences. Regardless of the nature of the cooperative education programme, it is crucial that, 'the work component is "authentic" and "integrated" and that co-op […] is a *curriculum model*, not added on' (Coll and Eames, 2004, p. 273, emphasis in original).

Co-op programmes are prevalent in the US, Canada, Australia and New Zealand, and whilst the fundamental principles are common to all cooperative education programmes, there are variances in the structure, length of placement and modes of supervision; these might be discipline, institute or country specific. Many cooperative education programmes in Canada and the US have alternating semesters on campus and within industry over a four- to six-year timeframe (Fenster and Parks, 2008). The rationale for multiple shorter blocks is linked with the progression and integration of on-campus learning. Initial placements early in a degree programme often limit the student experience to observation only and a lower level of contribution within an organisation. However, after a first placement there is evidence that not only are students more motivated to learn in the classroom (Burchell et al., 2000; Weisz, 2000) but also students may decide that a particular sector or subject is not the career direction for them (Van Gyn, 1996). Students are able to set new learning goals for each placement and improve practice through reflection on previous experiences.

Some cooperative education programmes and other models of WIL consist of part-time **work placements**, usually of one to three days per week within one organisation, extending over a semester or a year. This structure is used within many sport programmes (Fleming and Ferkins, 2005) and is common in teacher education programmes, especially early childhood studies (Ryan et al., 1996). The concurrent model is considered to provide an ideal opportunity for integrating what is being learnt in the workplace with the theory being learnt at an HEI, as the students' immediate experiences can be used within class and vice versa. As students are in regular contact with academic staff there are more opportunities for discussion and reflection. However, the disadvantages of this format are often related to a conflict between student learning and the needs of the organisation to have the student 'around all the time'. Conversely, in some smaller organisations there is an advantage of only having a student two days per week, and in that time appropriate learning activities can be made available and the student is not just 'filling in time'. Students may also be able to see the range of activities within the organisation occurring across a longer time-frame (for example, through a whole season of competition) that they may not be exposed to if the required hours were more consolidated. The following Case study 10.1 illustrates a co-op programme in action and points out the centrality of reflective skills to WIL:

Case study 10.1 Cooperative education: Bachelor of Sport and Recreation (BSR)

The cooperative education programme within the Bachelor of Sport and Recreation at Auckland University of Technology (AUT) involves students undertaking 350 hours of placement within one sport and recreation organisation generally two days per week during the final year of their degree.

Central to the success of the programme is the support provided by both workplace and academic supervisors. Workplace supervisors are expected to create an environment that supports 'learning', not just working. Negotiating and planning authentic activities that provide access to both procedural and dispositional knowledge, along with feedback and guidance, are seen as key roles of the workplace supervisor. It is also through meaningful dialogue, social interactions and developing relationships with workplace colleagues that students can begin to understand what it means to be a professional in the sport and recreation industry.

In the BSR cooperative education programme, the part-time placement structure allows for the academic supervisor to play an integral role in the learning process. Academic supervisors are lecturers who teach within the BSR and the supervision role is included as part of their teaching duties.

Students are expected to meet their academic supervisor on a regular basis (ideally every two weeks) and are required to post an entry into an online journal weekly. The student's ability to critically reflect on their experiences is seen as a

continued overleaf

Case study 10.1 Cooperative education: Bachelor of Sport and Recreation (BSR) *continued*

key influence on learning that can be gained through cooperative education. The academic supervisor has a key role in facilitating the development of reflective practice as students often struggle with the reflective process.

Academic supervisors can assist the students to engage in reflection through encouraging them to share their experiences in one-on-one meetings and asking them questions that challenge them to think more critically. Through giving feedback on the online journals academic supervisors are able to help develop reflective writing. Supervisors are able to help students identify the learning that is gained from the experience and assist them to integrate this learning with what they have learnt from the university environment, which is fundamental to the philosophy of cooperative education.

The supervision process is not without challenges and requires a good relationship to be developed between student and supervisor. One-to-one supervision can be considered time intensive, and some academics have moved to small group meetings to address workload issues. However, there is still a strong ongoing commitment that academic supervision is a valued and integral part of the cooperative education experience.

WIL is also used in the form of extended single placements, usually towards the end of a degree programme. There are various names for these initiatives, for example, internships, thick sandwiches and so on. In the UK it is common for students to undertake a one-year-long placement between years three and four of a degree and increasingly common for graduate internship schemes to offer work experience upon completion of a degree. Generally the intention of an **internship** is the development of skills and competencies associated with the discipline or profession. However, there are different interpretations of the requirements for an experience to be considered an internship and a lack of formally accepted guidelines. There are also variations in how these extended single placements are assessed and acknowledged, and whilst an internship may once have been seen as a very precise entry route into a specified profession the term has now become much more widely used due to global unemployment and a highly competitive graduate jobs market.

The usefulness of extended single placements is often connected to a student's need to see a project through to completion, participate in a full range of organisational experiences or allow for a 'consolidated' experience; however this can be driven by administrative as well as educational motives. One driver for the length of the placement is whether it is paid or unpaid; if the placement is unpaid, then the students will probably be required to undertake the placement during term time only, typically for four days per week to allow time for paid employment. Paid placements may not have the same restrictions placed on them, giving students a longer placement experience. Increasingly placements and internships are becoming valued as a means to develop a wide range of generic and transferable workplace skills through learning at work, rather than emphasising one particular sector or job role. This is perhaps part of the growing realisation that the requirements of work are changing rapidly and will continue to change (see Chapter 11).

Many models of short *work placement* experiences exist. **Fieldwork** is similar to practicums and is undertaken as short periods of time in the 'field', or 'real world', as opposed to the classroom. Often fieldwork involves observations but may include some participation in the activities of the organisation. Fieldwork is normally linked with the academic programme in the HEI, contributing explicitly to coursework requirements. **Work placement** experiences might be distributed throughout a programme, sometimes referred to as a *'thin sandwich'*.

Service learning, where students engage in activities that benefit the community, often falls under the umbrella of WIL. These programmes are designed to develop an appreciation of civic responsibility whilst enabling students to develop skills that will enhance their employability in the broadest sense. Service learning is normally granted credit within an academic programme of study. The following case study illustrates how students can develop the skills needed to thrive in the workplace (also expected of a graduate) through service learning placements (Case study 10.2):

Case study 10.2 Developing graduate capabilities through service learning: The PACE (Professional and Community Engagement) programme

The PACE (Professional and Community Engagement) programme at Macquarie University offers students the opportunity to develop graduate capabilities, such as social responsibility, global citizenship and work readiness, through diverse placements including service learning. Service learning aims for a mutually beneficial and potentially transformative educational experience whereby students apply their academic knowledge and skills to meet their learning outcomes, whilst also addressing or supporting identified community needs.

PACE units are generally third-year level and are available in most degree programmes across all four faculties at Macquarie: arts, business, human sciences and science. Host organisations come from corporate businesses, government, and institutions and NGOs in local, regional (rural and remote) and international settings. Activities are carefully planned and can include lab work, community

continued overleaf

Case study 10.2 Developing graduate capabilities through service learning: The PACE (Professional and Community Engagement) programme *continued*

videoing, resource development, project research and evaluation, case management, app development and museum curating, to name a few. Hosts provide the necessary infrastructure and supervision to support student learning and achieve the desired outcomes.

The following provides a snapshot of a PACE activity (see http://students .mq.edu.au/opportunities/professional_and_community_engagement/ pace_stories/wesley_mission/).

A group of three psychology students undertook a PACE activity at the Wesley Mission's Aunties and Uncles programme. In 12 weeks the students compiled an evaluation form to look at the effectiveness of the pilot programme, 'Boys and Men', which supports boys aged between 7 and 13 from the Central Coast and Sydney region of New South Wales.

With the students' help, Wesley Mission was able to evaluate how the children and primary carers found the project, taking into account the environmental, demographic and relational needs of those involved. As a result of the evaluation, Wesley Mission was able to apply for more funding, expand the programme and substantially increase the network of children who can benefit from it.

'I never considered social welfare as a possible career avenue. PACE has opened up my eyes not only to where I can take my psychology degree in social welfare terms, but it's really opened up some career opportunities' (Student).

Our partners are equally excited about the mutual benefit PACE offers:

'I am delighted that the PACE programme has partnered with us,' said Wesley Mission's CEO, Rev Dr Keith Garner. 'PACE is one of the ways we have been able to see the programme as a resource and I hope we've been able to resource young people too in their experiences and their opportunities. PACE is a programme to be recommended.'

Dr Kathryn McLachlan, Macquarie University, Australia

▶ **Learning at work – other models**

In contrast to most models of WIL, which are led by the HEI, in an **apprenticeship**, the workplace supervisor has the primary role of modelling, observing and guiding the student, and the HEI plays a lesser role. The purpose of the workplace experience is for the student to master relevant practices of the occupational group (Lee, 2012). Higher and degree apprenticeships are at HE level, and in the UK they operate in a way not unlike other models of work-integrated learning, with a strong focus on combining 'on the job' instruction with education in formal settings. The following Case study 10.3 gives an overview of higher and degree apprenticeships in the UK and clarifies their clear connections to HE-level learning which is happening within the workplace:

Case study 10.3 Apprenticeship reforms: Higher apprenticeship and degree apprenticeship in England

Apprenticeship is currently being reformed in England. The objectives of the reforms are: to ensure apprenticeships are employer driven, where employers design apprenticeships and have more control over funding; to simplify the system; and to improve quality through rigorous testing and grading.

The UK government defines apprenticeship as follows:

> *An apprenticeship is a job, in a skilled occupation, that requires substantial and sustained training, leading to the achievement of an apprenticeship standard and the development of transferable skills to progress careers.*

Apprenticeship standards are developed by employers working with professional bodies – where appropriate – and clearly and concisely describe the skills, knowledge and behaviours required to undertake a specific occupation. Where relevant, apprenticeship standards meet professional registration and licence-to-practice requirements. Apprenticeship standards are developed as part of a national (England) process, and only one standard is developed for an occupation.

Once developed, apprenticeship standards are assigned a level. As of March 2015, 44 of the standards approved and published were higher apprenticeship standards (encompassing Levels 4–7), representing 34 per cent of the total. To date, apprenticeship standards have been developed for a range of higher-level occupations including solicitor, professional accountant, manufacturing engineer, dental technician and construction technician. Further apprenticeship standards are currently being developed in a range of occupational areas.

An apprenticeship that also includes achievement of a full bachelor's or master's degree can be referred to as a degree apprenticeship. Degree apprenticeships were announced in November 2014 and will be available for delivery (from September 2015) in the digital and software field, automotive engineering, banking relationship management and construction. Other degree apprenticeships are in the process of development. The model which the UK government thinks will be preferred by many sectors involves employers, universities and professional bodies working together to design a fully integrated degree programme specifically aimed at apprentices to develop, test and accredit academic learning and on-the-job training.

Adrian Anderson, UVAC

Major learning at work can be instigated by the completion of **work-based projects** (see Chapter 2, also Workman and Nottingham, 2015). These projects are focused on daily work activities, are relevant to work practices and update knowledge by solving real problems and providing innovative solutions. They transform a workplace activity into deep learning by adding an academic approach to real-time work projects, thereby con-tributing new knowledge, capability, skills and learning to the workplace. Within WBL programmes the work-based projects which become part of the student's award are usually pieces of work that the student would have carried out at work anyway: naturally occurring work. The added academic rigour and format brings extra value to them, transforming them into an assessable format as well as saving the student time. More traditional students also undertake work-based projects, but as these students may only experience the workplace via their placement opportunity the project may be slightly more contrived, or a described scenario or case study, designed to give them experience.

Action learning (chapters 4, 6 and 11, and also Smith and Smith, 2015) can be used within many workplace learning projects; it is built upon a collaborative approach, where participants identify issues, examine them, create an action plan, take action and reflect on that action. Action learning is multifarious and can vary greatly according to the context in which it is applied and the different approaches of those who initiate it. Action learning can be described as a subset of action research. However, there exists a distinction between the two in relation to the utilisation and extension of theory. Action learning focuses on localised learning and does not require the extension of new knowledge in a theoretical sense. Action learning can provide a bridge between individual and organisational learning and is about creating change for an organisation as well as self-development of the individual, so is an ideal tool for applying an individual's WBL to a broader audience. Action learning may involve the formation of a community of practice, of shared work, knowledge, ways of knowing and a situation where new social meanings and realities are collectively constructed. Action learning complements the sociocultural theories associated with many models of WIL. The following Case study 10.4 explores action learning projects and the useful role they can have within an HE programme:

Case study 10.4 WIL: Enhancing WIL through action-learning projects

Incorporating an action-learning project into a Bachelor of Sport and Recreation cooperative education programme (mentioned in Case study 10.1) provides the student with a problem-solving tool that specifically seeks to integrate theory and practice and create positive change for the organisation hosting their work experience placement.

Learning not only involves the integration of current work knowledge and practice but alternative options identified through reviewing relevant literature and available theory. Engaging an action-learning approach facilitates reflection, and this combined with an emphasis on collaboration encourages the students and the industry personnel to actively engage in the learning process.

continued overleaf

Case study 10.4 WIL: Enhancing WIL through action-learning projects *continued*

The action-learning approach utilised for projects consists of four phases:

Phase one – The student in collaboration with both industry and academic supervisors identifies an issue or problem within the context of the organisation where they are undertaking their placement.

Phase two – The student then develops a proposal for the intervention or action. This involves reviewing and reflecting on current practice, examining theory learnt at the HEI, reviewing literature as well as talking to and asking questions of industry personnel and gaining feedback from academic and industry supervisors.

Phase three – The intervention or action is then undertaken and the length of this phase is dependent on the nature of the action or intervention. This phase may include the use of 'mini cycles' where the student will reflect, review, evaluate, modify and redesign the intervention or action. The final step in the process is the evaluation of the intervention and an extensive critical reflection on the overall experience.

Phase four – In this final phase, a detailed report of the project (including reflection on the learning experience) is then submitted for assessment.

Examples of recent projects that have used the action-learning approach include:

▶ A new physical activity programme for a community group
▶ Improving the nutrition of adolescent athletes in a sports institute
▶ An event planning kit for a sports organisation
▶ Improving sport training programmes in schools

Learning is enhanced by the students' recognition that they have a stake and can contribute to the process, having some responsibility for the outcomes. Action learning as a method of inquiry offers a tool that allows students to act as change agents within the workplace setting, which can provide lasting benefits for their learning as well as creating change for the organisation.

▶ Terminology confusions around WIL

Rowe et al. (2012), in their review of terminology, argue that WIL does not fit within neat compartments and this contributes to the difficulty in establishing a consistent typology. It is common that even within one HEI, terms are not necessarily used consistently and the same term is interpreted differently. Meanwhile, Usher (2012) argues against trying to define WIL and comments that 'to define WIL is to attempt to account for the infinite number of learning forms and contexts, which ultimately only renders the definition itself meaningless for practical purposes' (p. 11).

Defining terminology has consequences broader than the confusion caused for some practitioners by a lack of consistency. In Australia in

2005 the Federal government made policy changes to the Common-wealth Grants Scheme. Under the new policies funding is provided to programmes where HEIs guide the learning experience in the workplace, whereas there is no funding to support programmes that are based solely on work experience. Dilemmas are created, 'when the same WIL experiences are called by different names and when different experiences are called by the same name' (Patrick et al., 2008, p. 10). Quality assurance and reporting of activities institutionally and nationally feel the impact of this, prompting calls for a clearer, shared terminology (Peach and Gamble, 2011).

Different terminology can affect the way in which both senior management and academic staff within HEIs choose to engage with WIL. Terminology that includes learning or education may have an advantage in increasing engagement and legitimising the activities within an academic programme. A number of studies report that the success of workplace-based programmes is dependent on good 'buy-in' from management and academic staff, and this comes from their acknowledgement that the experience is focused on learning and development – not simply undertaking work activities for commercial reasons (Chapter 1; Matson and Matson, 1995; Martin, 1998; McCurdy and Zegwaard, 2009).

▶ Connections

The various initiatives and phenomena discussed above share similar principles, most importantly the belief that students benefit from the combination of practical work experience and education relevant to each one. This works in both directions; that is, work-based learners bring their learning from experience at work and in life to an HEI when they decided to formalise and progress this learning, whereas students on more traditional courses are sent out into the workplace from their course setting. Because WBL is primarily about learning from the experience of work and work concerns, (real-time problem solving, responding to real-work issues and so on), its overlaps with the above global initiatives seem obvious. All are concerned with the primacy of learning that occurs where the work activities are happening and the associations with situated learning.

Learning from doing might happen with other work colleagues, resulting in social learning (Chapter 11; Smith and Smith, 2015). It may happen individually or come from other life scenarios outside of work, perhaps aligned to hobbies, personal activities or voluntary and community undertakings. WBL is frequently referred to as 'informal', which it is, in the sense that it is not constrained by formally labelled learning locations, for example, universities, colleges and classrooms; it is instead formed by experience (some of this experience might have included training). It is not informal in the sense of casual, easy or inconsequential, and although 'non-traditional', it is just a different model, not a lesser one.

The commonality crossing the categories of learning discussed above is that the learning underpinning them originates from work, and is of direct relevance to workers in their work environment, and that furthermore student, HEI and employer all stand to mutually accrue the benefits of learning, development and innovation from the relationship. Boud, Solomon and Symes described WBL as, 'a class of university programs that bring [sic] together HEIs and work organisations to create new learning opportunities in workplaces' (Boud et al., 2001, p. 4), and this does broadly encompass most of what is discussed here. There are differences in approach, sometimes major differences, for example, whether or not the student is already employed. Furthermore there are differences within sectors and different kinds of companies involved in the learning process. There are also differences between countries, around, for example, levels of workplace learning (European Centre for the Development of Vocational Training, 2014).

▶ Employability

All HE learning initiatives focusing on or involving the workplace have been receiving increased attention due to the growing focus on graduate employability against a backdrop of increasing numbers of graduates, an ageing workforce globally and rising youth unemployment. Whilst there is diversity in the models described in this chapter, they all are founded upon the desire for mutually beneficial outcomes for the stakeholders. For students, the benefits can be academic and personal development as well as career or employment related. For workplaces the benefits can be created through increased efficiency by gaining extra resources to undertake projects and other activities, the screening of potential new employees, generation of fresh ideas and positive interactions with higher education institutions. The HEI gains closer ties with industry and increased reputation for their graduates. Clearly any of the models of learning in the workplace mentioned in this section are strongly positioned as distinct and valuable activities within a higher education curriculum.

SUMMARY

▶ To develop practice-based skills students need to be exposed to the demands of the real workplace.

▶ Many work-based initiatives from HEIs have overlaps and similar aims – without being exactly the same.

▶ Transformative learning experiences involve a combination of learning from undertaking practice (with its potential to produce new knowledge and theory) and building on accepted knowledge and theory.

▶ Dealing with work-based learners has the potential to make HEIs create much better 'professional' programmes.

▶ Not all work automatically creates learning; some is dull and repetitive.

▶ Traditional courses are increasingly including practice: self-managed and simulated elements for students – valuing what work-based learners have been bringing to their HE programmes all along.

▶ References

Boud, D., Solomon, N. and Symes, C. (2001) New practices for new times, in Boud, D. and Solomon, N. (Eds), *Work-based Learning: A New Higher Education.* Buckingham, UK: Open University Press.

Burchell, N., Hodges, D. and Rainsbury, L. (2000) What competencies do business graduates require? Perspectives of New Zealand stakeholders. *Journal of Cooperative Education.* 35 (2–3), pp. 11–19.

Coll, R. K. and Eames, C. (2004) Current issues in cooperative education, in Coll, R. K. and Eames, C. (Eds), *International Handbook for Cooperative Education: An International Perspective of the Theory, Research and Practice of Work-integrated Learning* (pp. 271–282). Boston: World Association for Cooperative Education.

Cooper, B. and Taylor, N. (2011) Cooperative and work-integrated education in teacher education, in Coll, R. K. and Zegwaard, K. E. (Eds), *International Handbook for Cooperative and Work-integrated Education: International Perspectives of Theory, Research and Practice* (pp. 207–217). Lowell, MA: World Association for Cooperative Education.

De Beer, W. (2011) Cooperative and work-integrated education in medicine, in Coll, R. K. and Zegwaard, K. E. (Eds), *International Handbook for Cooperative and Work-integrated Education: International Perspectives of Theory, Research and Practice,* 2nd Edn, (pp. 151–156). Lowell, MA: World Association for Cooperative Education.

Dewey, J. (1916) *Democracy and Education: An Introduction to the Philosophy of Education.* New York: The Free Press.

European Centre for the Development of Vocational Training (2014) *Terminology of European Education and Training Policy,* 2nd Edn, Avaiable at http://www.cedefop.europa.

eu/en/publications-and resources/publications/terminology-european-education-and-training-policy-0 accessed 23 November 2014.

Eyler, J. (2009) The power of experiential education. *Liberal Education*. 95 (4), pp. 24–131.

Fenster, M. and Parks, D. (2008) Does alternating and parallel programmatic structure make a difference in student outcomes? *Journal of Cooperative Education and Internships*. 42 (1), pp. 33–40.

Fleming, J. and Ferkins, L. (2005) Cooperative education in sport: Building our knowledge base. *Journal of Hospitality, Leisure, Sport & Tourism Education*. 4 (1), 41–47. doi: 10.3794/johlste.41.82.

Fleming, J. and Hickey, C. (2013) Exploring cooperative education partnerships: A case study in sport tertiary education. *Asia-Pacific Journal of Cooperative Education*. 14 (3), pp. 209–221.

Grealish, L. and Stunder, S. (2011) Cooperative and work-integrated education in nursing, in Coll, R. K. and Zegwaard, K. E. (Eds), *International Handbook for Cooperative and Work-integrated Education: International Perspectives of Theory, Research and Practice* (pp. 165–172). Lowell, MA: World Association for Cooperative Education.

Helyer, R. and Fleming, J. (2015) Work-based learning terminologies, in Helyer, R. (Ed.), *The Work-based Learning Student Handbook*, 2nd Edn, pp. 278–287. London: Palgrave.

Kolb, D. (1984) *Experiential Learning: Experience as the Source of Learning and Development*. London: Prentice Hall.

Lave, J. and Wenger, E. (1991) *Situated Learning: Legitimate Peripheral Participation*. Cambridge: Cambridge University Press.

Lee, D. (2012) Apprenticeships in England: An overview of current issues. *Higher Education, Skills and Work-based Learning*. 2 (3), pp 225–239.

Lester, S. and Costley, C. (2010) Work-based learning at higher education level: Value, practice, critique. *Studies in Higher Education*. 54 (5), pp. 561–575.

Martin, E. (1998) Conceptions of workplace university education. *Higher Education Research and Development*. 17 (2), 191–205. doi: 10.1080/0729436980170205.

Matson, L. and Matson, R. (1995) Changing times in higher education: An empirical look at cooperative education and liberal arts faculty. *Journal of Cooperative Education*. 31 (1), pp. 13–24.

McCurdy, S. and Zegwaard, K. E. (2009) Faculty voices: What faculty think about work-integrated learning. *Journal of Cooperative Education and Internship*. 43 (1), pp. 36–53.

Patrick, C. J., Peach, D., Pocknee, C., Webb, F., Fletcher, M. and Pretto, G. (2008) *The WIL (Work Integrated Learning) Report: A National Scoping Study*. Brisbane, Australia: Queensland University of Technology. Available at http://eprints.qut .edu.au/44065/ accessed 18 May 2015.

Peach, D. and Gamble. (2011) Scoping work-integrated learning purposes, practices and issues, in Billett, S. and Henderson, A. (Eds), *Developing Learning Professionals, Professional and Practice-based Learning* (pp. 169–186). Dordrecht, Netherlands: Springer.

Raelin, J. A., (1997) A model of work-based learning. *Organization Science*. 8 (6), pp. 563–578.

Rowe, A., Winchester-Seeto, T. and Mackaway, J. (2012) *That's Not Really WIL! – Building a Typology of WIL and Related Activities*. Paper delivered at the ACEN National Conference, Geelong, Australia 29 October-2 November 2012. Available at http://acen.edu.au/2012conference/proceedings/ accessed 18 May 2015.

Ryan, G., Toohey, S. and Hughes, C. (1996) The purpose, value and structure of the placement in higher education: A literature review. *Higher Education Research and Development*. 31 (3), 355–377. doi: 10.1007/BF00128437.

Smith, S. and Smith, L. (2015) Social learning: Supporting yourself and your peers, in Helyer, R. (Ed.), *The Work-based Learning Student Handbook*, 2nd Edn, pp. 184–204. London: Palgrave.

Todd, A. and Lay, M. (2011) Cooperative and work-integrated education in engineering, in Coll, R. K. and Zegwaard, K. E. (Eds), *International Handbook for Cooperative and Work-integrated Education: International Perspectives of Theory, Research and Practice* (pp. 111–121). Lowell, MA: World Association for Cooperative Education.

Usher, A. (2012) Measuring work-integrated learning: The development of the meta-competency test. *Journal of Cooperative Education and Internships*. 46 (1), pp. 5–15.

Van Gyn, G. H. (1996) Reflective practice: The needs of professions and the promise of cooperative education. *Journal of Cooperative Education*. 31 (2), 103–131.

Weisz, M. (2000) Developing a measure of student attributes. *Journal of Cooperative Education*. 35 (2/3), pp. 33–40.

Workman, B. and Nottingham, P. (2015) Work-based projects, in Helyer, R. (Ed.), *The Work-based Learning Student Handbook*, 2nd Edn, pp. 253–277. London: Palgrave.

▶ Recommended further reading

Brooks, R. and Kay, J. (2014) Enhancing employability through placements in higher education. *Higher Education Skills and Work-based Learning*. 4 (3) pp. 209–300.

Gardner, P. and Bartkus, K. R. (2014) What's in a name? A reference guide to work-education experiences, *Asia-Pacific Journal of Cooperative Education*. 15 (1), pp. 37–54.

11 Learning to learn

Ruth Helyer and Andy Price

IN THIS CHAPTER YOU WILL:

▶ Think about the ways that work-based learning (as already described in preceding chapters) and developing employability skills for more traditional students might intersect

▶ Investigate what the term 'employability skills' covers in higher education

▶ Consider ways to help all students to develop these skills

▶ Be introduced to the importance of analytical reflection

▶ Explore ways to help your students to foster an entrepreneurial mind-set

▶ Discover ways in which your students can both substantiate and express their skills as they become lifelong learners and embrace continuing professional development (CPD)

▶ Graduates – traditional and work based

In recent years higher education institutions (HEIs) have begun to pay increasing attention to the employability of their graduates. This is due to the combination of several factors, including an extremely competitive jobs market, a global recession and many more people choosing higher education (HE) (UK participation figures increased from 12 per cent of the population in 1979 to 43 per cent in 2013 (Bolton, 2014)). Recent increases in tuition fees mean that students become more like customers; they expect to obtain a graduate job, and HEIs are judged on how successful their graduates are in securing such jobs. However, many employers globally still claim that they struggle to find the talented individuals they aspire to employ:

> The paradox is profound: On the one hand, 40 million workers in the industrialized world are unemployed ... Yet executives and managers tasked with hiring new workers often say they are unable to find the right people with the proper skills to fill their vacancies.
>
> (Oxford Economics, 2012)

Work-based learning (WBL) students are already employed; however, they still wish to progress in the workplace, perhaps through promotion or applying to other companies or even different sectors. To do this successfully they must realise that they need to continue learning and developing, enhancing their existing skills and acquiring new ones, 'having the skills, attitudes and belief necessary to win a job, succeed in that role, and move on to an even more fulfilling role in the future' (Adecco, 2012, p. 40). They may already realise how much they have learnt through doing their job and the power of continuing lifelong learning; they have probably enrolled with an HEI not only to validate this learning with a qualification but also to further build upon it and progress. Taking responsibility for their own learning and development in this way is crucial in such a fast-moving and competitive world.

▶ Where does learning happen?

There are powerful connections between the different areas in which learning occurs, and all students should be encouraged to proactively maximise the overlap in their learning experiences, rather than viewing them as disparate and unconnected or, even worse, just allowing them to happen. The emphasis on different areas will differ from one student to the next, but a full-time traditional student might well be learning as much about crucial workplace skills from their part-time job as a full-time employee is from theirs, and both need to be aware of the need to actively think about and analyse this learning, rather than letting it 'wash over' them. Metacognition, or literally thinking about thinking, is a useful practice for all learners to adopt and can be introduced through simple tasks such as planning how to approach a learning task, checking own understanding and appraising own progress towards the learning task's conclusion. Encouraging metacognition in your students is a useful step towards them taking responsibility for their own learning and development and, as lifelong learners, realising that learning opportunities are all around them.

The following diagram (Figure 11.1) shows that the major areas of influence on learning – work, life and formal study opportunities – all overlap and interconnect with each other, and it is often within these overlaps that the most powerful learning occurs.

Case study 11.1, on p. 209, illustrates how the overlapping areas of students' learning experience are important by outlining some details about the profile of 'an engineer' and sharing what one HEI has put in place to try and make sure that their students develop transferable, generic graduate

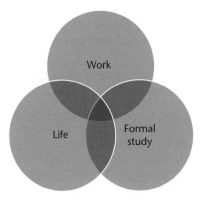

Figure 11.1   Where areas of learning via experience overlap

skills alongside subject- and sector-specific skills. The case study reiterates that the overlapping areas of the above figure are vitally important and should not be consigned to separate consideration.

Case study 11.1 Developing student learning beyond knowledge acquisition: Transferable skills for engineers

Engineers demonstrate the way that learning is brought together from all areas of life, the academic, the workplace and the personal and human experience; they create our physical world by making things that work and making things work better in a complex world.

Engineers are doers, illustrating experiential learning – learning by doing. They seek out problems and visualise and 'engineer' creative solutions and improvements; they make decisions between the conflicting demands of costs and benefits in their drive to produce something of value. They take into account the multiple dimensions of real life.

In common with all students engineering graduates require transferable, generic skills alongside their subject-specific skills, if they are to thrive in the workplace and in life. Enterprising and entrepreneurial graduates are a vital resource for the UK's future and well-being, as has been well documented in publications from the Dearing Report (National Committee of Inquiry into Higher Education, 1997) to *An Education System Fit for an Entrepreneur* (All-Party Parliamentary Group for Micro Businesses, 2014).

Tryggvason and Apelian (2012), in their *Shaping Our World – Engineering Education for the 21st Century*, suggest that engineering is best understood in relation to other disciplines and show that engineers create our physical world, but the authors fail to point out the clear need for enterprising/entrepreneurial individual(s) needed to generate value out of the products created by any of the disciplines.

continued overleaf

Case study 11.1 Developing student learning beyond knowledge acquisition: Transferable skills for engineers *continued*

The Doctoral Training Centre for Advanced Metallics at the University of Sheffield has devised a programme to facilitate the teaching of transferable skills. This intervention is a Diploma in Personal and Professional Skills. Furthermore the skills are embedded into the students' consciousness by practice. A problem-based learning experience is developed via an exercise taking two weeks. Students, in groups, tackle 'real-life' problems in an SME (small- and medium-sized enterprises). In its second year, students, staff and industrial partners have all claimed to have felt the benefits.

What has made this work?

▶ The reality of the task
▶ The tight time limits imposed
▶ The responsibility on students to function and deliver as part of a group of 'professional' consultants
▶ The necessity to employ skills towards generating and proposing solutions
▶ Students practising transferable skills
▶ Students impressing potential employers

This has been a successful programme which highlights the importance of ongoing collaboration between academia and industry.

Plato Kapranos, University of Sheffield

▶ What are employability skills?

Definitions of employability skills differ, from job-seeking skills such as interview techniques and producing an effective CV, to generic skills such as communication, teamwork and leadership skills. Yorke and Knight summarise them as, 'a set of achievements, understanding and personal attributes that make individuals more likely to gain employment and be successful in their chosen occupation' (Yorke and Knight, 2007, p. 158). Some graduate professions demand very specific skills, and all require a combination of generic and explicit skills, expertise and knowledge. The world of work is evolving; those seeking to work, remain employed, be promoted or enjoy successful self-employment need to develop a further layer to their transferable and generic abilities. Skills such as resilience and adaptability are crucial because jobs and markets change quickly. Indeed, some will never find employment in 'their chosen occupation' (Yorke and Knight, 2007, p. 158). Instead, they must be capable of changing their focus and consciously applying their talents to new and differing roles and challenges. HEIs promote their graduates as problem solvers and analytical and autonomous thinkers, and graduates now more than ever need to use these skills to facilitate their own careers and enhance the workplace.

▶ Making implicit learning explicit

Another commonality across both work-based and more traditional students is that much learning in life is implicit. This is why work-based learners need to be guided through a self-audit when they commence their HE programme of study (see Chapters 2, 4 and 5). The experience of working develops skills and knowledge within the worker that they may take for granted; study at HE level too, offers opportunities to students to learn more than just the course content. It is useful to encourage your students to track and record this skills development, as not only will this serve as a useful record for themselves and encouragement to keep developing, it also offers evidence for future interviews and job applications. By noting examples of how and where learning took place your students will be well placed to confidently describe their skills and expertise to prospective employers and colleagues. Using something like the grid below initiates the development of a mind-set to track and evidence skills acquisition; it is not unlike the format some use to record and plan their CPD development and represents an area where HE and the workplace can learn from each other (Table 11.1).

▶ Reflective analysis for skills development

One of the most important skills for your students (work-based and others) as they learn and develop is active reflection. It is only by reflecting on events that they will make sense of them; learners must take the time to reflect on what they are learning through their experiences in order to utilise, build upon and progress that learning. By reflecting effectively on their learning your students will see opportunities that otherwise might be missed as well as be able to articulate and evidence their other skills, knowledge and expertise.

Reflection begins almost as soon as we are born and influences how we view ourselves and define our identities and profile. We look back,

Table 11.1 The skills grid

Skill	What?	Where and when?	How?	Evidence	Location	What next?
Teamwork	Work together to solve problem **Often covers many skills – for example technology, communication, leadership, creative**	Group work assessment Mech. Eng class May 2016 **Can be diverse and ongoing**	By taking on roles Sharing Discussing Giving joint presentation responding to questions and feedback Reflecting on work role and previous projects **Activities Research Written material**	1) Copy of minutes and actions from team meetings 2) Copy of presentation – PP slides 3) Copy of handout 4) Video of presentation 5) Blog that began due to discussion 6) Report from line manager re use of new product idea **Quality over quantity Key things that prove learning happened (Usually include change)**	On USB stick or CD-ROM Printed examples in file On mobile phone Online please provide a link – **Precise, meaningful records**	Currently undertaking advanced PP course Have written up the presentation between us taking feedback into account Have been reading and researching problem solving **Learning never ends – students need to be encouraged to take responsibility and to keep planning and recording**

Source: Based on Helyer and Kay (2015)

and hopefully avoid repeating mistakes, what Schön (1983;1987) famously labelled 'reflecting on action'; but reflection goes beyond looking back to include the present; 'reflection in action is where we may reflect in the midst of action without interrupting it. Our thinking serves to reshape what we are doing while we are doing it' (Schön, 1987, p. 26). One of the main reasons for encouraging your students to hone their reflective skills is the fact that reflective skills facilitate an intelligent and informed analysis of how all other skills are developing. Therefore, purposeful reflection facilitates ongoing personal and professional learning and develops learner practitioners who are capable of demonstrating their progression towards HE learning outcomes and standards.

▶ Sharing reflection

Sharing information and knowledge gained from reflecting on experience improves practice, and collaborating around new knowledge leads to change as well as personal and organisational development (Ions and Sutcliffe, 2015). However, sharing requires open-mindedness and a willingness to listen to others and to act upon criticism (Dewey, 1933), but it is normal that your students may feel vulnerable exposing themselves in this way. You should try to overcome this by encouraging groups and networks to form amongst fellow workers/students who can support each other in a non-judgemental way and encourage input. See the Teaching Tips.

Teaching tips

Peer support in the reflection process is important:

- ▶ Support can be achieved via networks, buddying or mentoring.
- ▶ Pairs should be chosen by expertise and experience.
- ▶ Ex-WBL students make good mentors for new WBL students.
- ▶ Some WBL students may prefer a mentor from work.
- ▶ It allows students to discuss their anxieties honestly and safely.
- ▶ Learning often occurs socially with other people; analytical reflection usually happens alone.
- ▶ Arranging for your students to share its outcomes brings it to life with extra facets of meaning, level and application.
- ▶ Action learning sets (Revans, 2011) and communities of practice (CoP) (Wenger, 1998) are proven (non-judgemental) methods of 'learner to learner' support.

▶ Reflecting through action learning

Action learning is a social form of learning whereby participants come together to work on issues and share learning, helping each other to learn through reflection by asking open questions and, crucially, not offering one another advice (Smith, 2009; Smith and Smith, 2015). The sets operate as communities of practice; the joint enterprise is to address real business issues through open questions and dialogue. The following Case study 11.2 illustrates the benefits of action learning:

Case study 11.2 Using action learning: A higher-level leadership programme

A group of owner-managers of small- and medium-sized businesses enrolled at their local university as students on Leading Growth, a ten-month leadership programme. They are work-based learners, undertaking study alongside their professional activities and using their workplace as a context to put into practice what they learn. The programme involves:

- ▶ Think tanks
- ▶ Coaching
- ▶ Action learning
- ▶ Visiting other companies
- ▶ Reflective consolidation sessions
- ▶ Developing a trusted peer network

Self-reflection is facilitated through learning logs and reflective diaries. Leading Growth is underpinned with a participative pedagogy; this means that learning is viewed as a social construction that takes place between people. Participants can, in effect, teach themselves and then share this learning with their work teams to encourage a culture of leadership and self-perpetuating development. The work-based learners view each other as peers with relevant experience.

The action learning sets meet as groups of six, plus a facilitator, to interrogate a work-related issue. They meet six times over the course of the Leading Growth programme.

The work-based learners have come to trust their fellow students:

'There genuinely isn't that pressure between people here [to trade], so rare, so unique to find a forum where people can just bring themselves, and not the businesses, to learn, that is incredibly invaluable.' – Student A

The students do not know all the details of each other's issues, but they share problems and concerns that resonate from their own workplace. This can help them to think about a problem or a situation objectively, encouraging them to stand back and create time to think about how to seek a resolution.

'I step back and let my team have the space to answer the question for themselves. Previously I would have jumped straight in with my idea of a solution.' – Student B

continued overleaf

Case study 11.2 Using action learning: A higher-level leadership programme *continued*

Students have commented that the skills they are learning are transferable to home and other scenarios:

'It is working in the work place, but I also now find myself reflecting and helping my children and coming out with some quite profound inspiring statement, it really works!' – Student C

The work-based learners comment that they feel liberated and have made real changes in the workplace as a result of the peer learning, reflective practice and open questioning techniques.

Sue Smith, Teesside University and Laurie Smith, Teesside University

▷ Theory and reality can meet in reflective practice

To be useful to WBL students, analytical reflection should not be considered as theoretical; it should combine theory with real-world experiences and learning, to create a synergy between a practitioner's experiences, feelings and emotions, and their activities and achievements (Brockbank and McGill, 1998). The catalyst created when intellect, feelings and working practices come together can produce an ongoing process for your students where it is second nature for thinking, acting, questioning and collaborating to work together and create multifaceted, smart responses and therefore superior results to what would have been achieved with a one-dimensional response (remember Figure 11.1, in which the overlapping areas where learning occurs are illustrated).

When WBL students use the RPL (recognition of prior learning) process to claim academic credit for past learning (Chapter 5), having developed skills of reflection will assist them, and you, as tutor, enormously. You can refine your assessment tools to help with this, using and grading; some of the following will develop your students' reflective skills:

▷ reflective essays
▷ a series of short narrative statements
▷ reports
▷ journals
▷ logs
▷ diaries
▷ blogs
▷ portfolios and so on

Information on building skills of reflection can be included in your student handbooks, as part of your induction days, by allowing access to your past students' successful reflective work and through offering sessions which contain information about, and support around, learning theories and styles, metacognition, self-analysis of strengths and weaknesses, and the writing of personal statements and future plans. These activities help to create practitioners who continuously reflect, plan and develop, routinely revisiting the manner in which activities are conducted, rather than assuming that the 'old way is the best'.

▶ Is reflection circular?

If you start to read about reflection in academic work and work-based practice you will find that it is commonly illustrated in a circular format, of activity or event – reflect, then act again, refine activity and so on. However, in real life reflection is more iterative and messy than a neat circle suggests, because being genuinely reflective takes time and will invariably be more difficult, even painful, than anticipated. As tutor you must facilitate and guide, and your students will learn to trust you. Looking backwards, forwards and sideways, whilst trying to make connections with what is happening right now, can feel fragmented and disjointed, but reassure your students that this is normal. Genuine, analytical reflection draws upon knowledge lying deep within (tacit knowledge), which is often taken for granted and not explicitly acknowledged. Students often know, and are

---

Teaching tips

In order to help build reflective, self-aware practitioners you, as tutor, need to:

- ▶ Have good listening skills – respond with prompts and encouragement rather than instructions.
- ▶ Realise that work-based students know their own workplace – don't force your own ideas, plans and priorities on them.
- ▶ Accept that this is not a traditional tutor–student relationship, where the teacher is the holder of all the knowledge.
- ▶ Have the skills to tease out what is important – students will reveal aspects of their job, thoughts and ideas.
- ▶ Have an ability to provoke students into thinking, analysing, looking back and being critical, whilst you support, encourage and guide rather than tell.
- ▶ Be willing to learn a lot – WBL students are often highly skilled within their own workplace.
- ▶ Have knowledge of theory – which you share, use and interrogate in order to transform and enliven it – whilst accepting that new theories develop all the time.

continued overleaf

Teaching tips *continued*

▶ Have an ability to show the power of combining expertise, experiences and knowledge of theory, in an attempt to fill the gap between theory and practice (Schön, 1987).
▶ Accept that the traditional notion of knowledge as being finite and capable of being owned or held by one party and passed on to another is increasingly challenged.

---

good at, much more than they realise, which is why it is important to introduce them to the idea of metacognition.

Remind your WBL students (and your students who are experiencing the workplace through placements and internships) that the activities they are undertaking through work and the learning process are entwined, and because of this they should reflect strategically on what they have learnt through past experiences, not just through current study but more generally along their life path. This will encourage them to become lifelong learners who appreciate the power of learning and can establish where they are – in terms of career, personal development and learning, which is crucial for planning and progression. Remind your students to acknowledge what they have learnt so that they have a base on which to build their next stage of development, rather than starting from nothing.

ACTIVITY

Reflection

To help your students to reflect analytically, get them to follow these steps:

▷ Think of a time when an experience and its outcomes have had an effect on their actions
▷ What happened? – event, activity, incident, experience
▷ Consequence? – result, outcome, product
▷ Thoughts – feelings, reactions, impressions
▷ Be proactive – contemplate, think, deliberate
▷ Interrogate – analyse, question, consider the thoughts/feelings of other parties
▷ Evaluate:
▷ The details – what, why, when, how, where and who?
▷ Which skills helped them to succeed?
▷ Which skills areas felt lacking?
▷ Did they 'think on their feet' ('in action') and amend things as they went along?
▷ Or did all their analysis come at the end ('on action')?
▷ Looking to the future – develop: strategies, approaches, tactics
▷ Would they do exactly the same next time?

Based on Helyer and Kay (2015)

Activities like those above are designed to encourage students to think critically about their past actions within the context of what is happening in the present and what may happen in the future. This encourages a reflective response to events, which in turn paves the way for future continuous professional and personal development. Growing a continuous ethos of reflection means that an individual begins to automatically challenge and question why tasks were undertaken in a certain way, rather than just focusing on the mechanics of how they were carried out. This dynamic, enquiring mind-set will aid their ongoing development and furthermore enhance their entrepreneurial propensity.

▶ Fostering an entrepreneurial mind-set in your students

When work-based learners begin to reflect strategically, the context and rationale for their learning becomes more significant; their thinking moves from the short-term operational to the mid-and long-term strategic. Career planning becomes more overt, and their understating of the business context within which their organisation operates becomes more important. New softer managerial skills and abilities become more important as does the ability to innovate and add new value to the organisation. This is now widely understood as moving to an enterprising or entrepreneurial position as a work-based learner. The Department for Business, Innovation and Skills (2013), the All-Party Parliamentary Group for Micro Businesses (2014) and The European Commission (2012) have all called upon HE to develop entrepreneurial skills and attitudes in students and graduates as part of their role in underpinning an innovative and dynamic economy.

Most often this is approached through the idea of developing an entrepreneurial mind-set in learners. This can be differentiated from an 'employee mind-set' (the dominant model of graduate employment in the 20th century) in several key ways:

Teaching tips

An entrepreneurial mind is one where learners:

- ▶ Develop the ability to recognise opportunities
- ▶ Are skilled at evaluating opportunities
- ▶ Can marshal the resources necessary for the task
- ▶ Can inspire and lead others
- ▶ Have the determination to drive an idea forward regardless of the setbacks

continued overleaf

> **Teaching tips** *continued*
>
> They also harness significant conceptual thinking, problem solving, reflection and metacognitive activity at graduate level and practise personal skills and attributes perhaps not called upon in conventional programmes of study.

If you are concerned about your students' employability, and their progression at work if already employed, then working towards developing an entrepreneurial mind-set will offer both the potential of job creation through business start-up and self-employment and greater success in the jobs market and workplace through the acquisition of important skills desired by employers. The development of entrepreneurial and intrapreneurial skills and attitudes go 'hand in hand' and reflect on many changes in the graduate labour market that lead increasingly to portfolio careers, virtual organisations, project-based work and self-initiated client-focused activity. They are also an important constituent of a change to work practices within organisations, where the commercial imperatives of any activity or project are now expected to be understood by all employees in a way that was previously not necessary. WBL often has a commercial context that may be either an implicit or explicit factor in the learning but brings an important dimension to it. Equally WBL may increasingly be taking place in situations initiated by learners as 'entrepreneurial' solutions to organisational problems. One further point to consider is that 'new ideas' that solve organisational problems are not simply the domain of the private sector. The public and third sectors need entrepreneurial innovation if they are to thrive and survive. So WBL through entrepreneurial practices is increasingly becoming desirable in all sectors of the economy; maybe one of the challenges is to nurture an understanding and appreciation of this phenomenon in learners and their employers to build entrepreneurial capital in organisations. Case study 11.3 on p. 221 illustrates this.

▶ Developing business literacy

A perennial complaint from employers is that graduates are not 'business ready'. The CBI (2009), the British Chambers of Commerce (Cullinane, 2014) and research from YouGov (Harris, 2013), all identify 'lack of business preparedness' as a serious problem. Employers expect graduates to 'hit the ground running' and make a positive contribution to the company as quickly as possible. One dimension of this is familiarity with broad business culture – the norms, behaviours and language of the commercial (and increasingly non-commercial) world. Although many WBL students are already in employment they still need to be aware of rapid developments in the workplace, requiring an almost constant upskilling, and for unemployed full-time students this is to some degree being tackled by the growth of work placements in degree courses. However, where these opportunities do not exist, HEIs need to look for learning situations where students can encounter, practise and experience a functional 'business literacy'; this does not mean replicate the content of business and management degrees across all programmes, but rather make it possible for students to learn about the core components of business culture from enterprise projects and social enterprise initiatives. Simple things like budgets, plans, meetings, negotiations, customers and so on, all come to life when they are real, tangible parts of a lived experience. The acquisition of a basic 'business literacy' should be a key part of any entrepreneurial activity undertaken by learners regardless of their programme of study. They should also be approached contextually and, where possible, should be nuanced with regard to the subject area involved. For example, the business literacy needed by an engineering graduate may be significantly different to that needed by a fashion graduate, although there will also be key transferable and generic skills that they will both need. Many HEIs engage their work-based learning students as mentors for their more traditional students and report that working together develops skills in both partners such as critical thinking, confidence, creativity and adaptability as well as helping them to become articulate and aspirational.

▶ Experiential learning and developing entrepreneurial capacity

For you as a tutor the pedagogical solution to the challenge of enabling learners to develop an entrepreneurial mind-set lies in experiential, student-led learning through work-based situations that allow all the stages of the entrepreneurial mind-set model to be explored and reflected on in an iterative and holistic way. One of the best ways to learn about entrepreneurship is through entrepreneurship: by providing a clear framework of opportunity identification, analysis, logistical organisation, leadership and determination, you will be able to facilitate the high-level reflective, metacognitive activity in your learners that is expected of HE graduates. Work-based situations that develop an entrepreneurial mind-set need to be authentic if they are to work. The learner who has the opportunity to do this in real time as part of their employment will gain much; other learners, perhaps those enrolled on full-time university and college courses, have three alternatives: within the curriculum, co-curricular and extra-curricular. All of these have limitations and are somewhat prescribed by the culture of the institution in which they occur. Student-led entrepreneurial activities are implicitly workbased and are a form of experiential learning where 'ideas are turned into action'. For many non-practice-based programmes they may provide the only ways that students can engage in authentic student-led collaborative learning. The following Case study 11.3 shows how students without employment were able to build their workplace skills and, much more, by setting up and running a food cooperative:

Case study 11.3 The benefits of extra-curricular activity: Student Food Co-op

A member of academic staff secured a small grant from the unlimited social enterprise zones to work with students to develop an on-campus student-managed food cooperative. This was to be an educationally purposeful extra-curricular activity.

The founders had a number of motivations including student welfare, student nutrition, access to ethical and fair trade products plus the economics of the initiative. It was agreed that a cooperative model would be the most suitable with students and staff joining the co-op for a nominal fee that would entitle them to buy goods at little more than cost price. As a social enterprise, the social benefits would be to the members and any surplus would be reinvested in the co-op.

The students created a plan including:

▶ Gathering as much information as possible to secure a sustainable future for the initiative
▶ Visiting other university food co-ops and a very well-established cooperative food wholesaler
▶ Putting an organisational structure in place
▶ Allocating responsibilities to individuals
▶ Producing a schedule for preliminary trading

The group wanted to create a high profile and be visible to other students so they approached the students union for permission to trade in their building. This was granted and a very positive relationship formed.

Even at this stage it was clear that the project required students to take on new responsibilities around areas like financial planning, logistics, organisation and promotion, as well as teamworking and leadership. The member of academic staff who had initially secured the small grant provided significant support but was always clear that the students would ultimately run the initiative and be responsible for its sustainability.

The food co-op now trades weekly on campus, has over 200 members and was recently shortlisted for an environmental award. Many students involved have commented on how this social entrepreneurship has developed them as people and made them more confident, assertive, effective, and able to lead as well as work more successfully in groups.

Many of the students commented that although working on the co-op was away from the classroom, an added benefit was that the tasks that they had to deal with actually made them better prepared for academic challenges.

▶ The role of extra-curricular activity

Many authorities (Pascarella and Terenzini, 2005; Kuh et al., 2008; Bryson, 2014) have identified the positive role that 'educationally purposeful' extra-curricular activities, such as student enterprise activities, have on student engagement, educational attainment and employment prospects. Students who use the time outside the classroom on campus to be involved in activities that engage with peers learn new things and face challenges, and are demonstrably more 'engaged' with their educational community. Their sense of identity as belonging and being valued is built and reinforced as they develop their personal skills and increase their social capital (Thomas, 2002). These developments help them to deal with any problems and issues arising from their programme of study and will also provide the framework of lifelong relationships which will impact on every aspect of their life, particularly their careers. Try to actively support your students to engage with 'educationally purposeful' extra-curricular activities, as students from non-traditional backgrounds are often unfamiliar with the benefits that such activities can bring them and can judge them negatively as frivolous and distracting.

There is considerable current interest in how 'social enterprises' or businesses with social goals can fill the gaps increasingly left as the state withdraws from many areas of social provision; social enterprises are usually understood as non-profit-making businesses that have social goals and reinvest any surplus in the business rather than distribute it to shareholders. Charities and local council-run services are increasingly converting to social enterprise models as effective ways to maintain their service provision. Plus many conventional businesses are very public about their contribution as responsible citizens as part of the corporate social responsibility (CSR). Work-based learners may well already be working in social enterprises or have the production of social goals as part of their responsibilities.

What might be a suitable enterprise activity for your students? It should be borne in mind that social value is as important as financial value in many situations and that running a social enterprise delivers all of the learning benefits of a conventional enterprise as well as the added benefit of being socially useful. The global student organisation Enactus helps students to form teams in individual HEIs, who then devise and deliver social projects via business principles which empower beneficiaries to co-develop sustainable solutions to their problems. The very act of running an Enactus social programme is intrinsically a WBL situation. It is experiential, active and emergent, requiring the participants to problemsolve, reflect and continuously improve as they learn how to deliver their goals. This is therefore a very good route via which traditional students can experience experiential learning and self-development but equally so for more conventional work-based learners who are looking to develop new skills (for example, leadership) that they are unable to access in their existing situation. Indeed some work-based learners may well be employees in a social enterprise or even running their own social enterprise. This form of WBL produces high value outputs that a wide range of global employers see as highly attractive in employees. Developing an entrepreneurial mind-set in a social context clearly produces the new softer managerial skills and abilities mentioned earlier. The following Case study 11.4 demonstrates this:

Case study 11.4 Engaging students through social enterprise: Enactus and HEFCE UnLtd

Within HE, social enterprise is increasingly coming to the fore as an important method of engaging students with enterprising activities but with the additional bonus of delivering social or environmental outcomes. Globally Enactus has for over 25 years nurtured a growing international community of student social entrepreneurs. In recent years in the UK HEFCE and UnLtd have worked together to stimulate social entrepreneurship in the HE sector.

The Enactus model is for universities, or Enactus teams consisting of students, staff and business advisers, who then identify social or environmental problems that can be tackled through enterprising action and business principles. The aim is to empower communities to develop sustainable solutions to their problems whilst allowing the participants to face the challenges and setbacks associated with real-world situations.

Enactus is supported by a wide range of significant global companies who take a keen interest in the success of the individual Enactus teams. Each year the teams compete in regional and national competitions where they must prove the impact of their social programmes; the winners of each national competition go through to a global final. The individual projects are judged on what is called a triple bottom line – profits, people, planet – and are evaluated on their relevant economic, social and environmental impacts.

The HEFCE UnLtd partnership in the UK is an attempt to create a culture of social entrepreneurship across the HE sector. Beginning with a pilot in 2009, it now supports a programme of work with £2 million invested from the Higher Education Innovation Fund and 18 university partners. This is part of the UnLtd SEE Change, Social Entrepreneurship Education initiative that aims to support HE institutes to become hubs supporting social entrepreneurs beyond their staff and students, championing social inclusion and economic development in their communities https://unltd.org.uk/hefce/.

This basic 'knowledge transfer' model allows learners to lead and own a social project that commits to deliver real outcomes through the team working and learning in a structured and collaborative fashion. Enactus has significant support amongst many 'Blue Chip' employers who recognise that the values it develops in participants (initiative, entrepreneurship, leadership and so on) are exactly what they require in graduate recruits.

The above chapter shows how much is to be gained by offering work-based experiences to all of your students and, wherever possible, trying to let your cohorts of work-based and traditional students mix. Traditional students now may well become your work-based leaners of the future when they come back to you as employed postgraduates, imbued with enthusiasm for lifelong learning and CPD and being aware of learning and undertaking learning in a deliberate way.

SUMMARY

▶ All students benefit from workplace experience and those without real work need to be given the opportunity to engage with work experience though placements, internships or similar.

▶ A well-developed graduate will have many of the skills valued by employers. Often help is needed in drawing out and articulating these skills; especially useful are activities which build reflective practice.

▶ There are now many more employed students attending HEIs and more could be done to maximise their undoubted work-based skills, not only to both empower and further develop the students but also to utilise them as excellent peer mentors for their fellow students who may not have their workplace experience.

▶ The 21st century employment marketplace is competitive and evolving; individuals need to take responsibility for their own learning and be helped to understand the power of being a lifelong learner.

▶ Due to the rapidly changing nature of the workplace your students need to be encouraged to emphasise transferable skills alongside their degree-/subject-/sector-specific ones. It is vital to be adaptable, resilient and creative and hopefully your institution's enterprise education will help them to achieve this.

▶ References

Adecco (2012) *Unlocking Britain's Potential.* Available at http://www.unlockingbritainspotential.co.uk/ download/index.php accessed 2 August 2014.

All-Party Parliamentary Group for Micro Businesses (2014) *An Education System Fit for an Entrepreneur:Fifth Report by the All-Party Group for Micro Businesses.* London: TSO Available at http://www.enterprise.ac.uk/index.php/component/rsfiles/view?path=Reports%2FFinal+Report+-+An+Education+System+Fit+for+an+Entrepreneur.pdf accessed 14 May 2015.

Bolton, Paul (2015) *Participation in Higher Education.* Commons Briefing Papers No. SN02630. Available at www.parliament.uk/briefing-papers/sn02630.pdf accessed 14 May 2015.

Brockbank, A. and McGill, I. (1998) *Facilitating Reflective Learning in Higher Education*. Buckingham: Society for Research in Higher Education and Open University Press.

Bryson, C. (2014) *Understanding and Developing Student Engagement*. Abingdon: Routledge.

CBI and Universities UK (2009) *Future Fit: Preparing Graduates for the World of Work*. London: CBI. Available at http://www.cbi.org.uk/media/1121435/cbi_uuk_future_fit.pdf accessed 14 May 2015.

Cullinane, Sophie (2014) Employers are 'struggling' to find 'work-ready' graduates, but are graduates really to blame? *The Debrief*. 12 September 2014. Available at http://www.thedebrief.co.uk/news/real-life/employers-are-struggling-to-find-work-ready-graduates-but-are-graduates-really-to-blame-20140911996   accessed 14 May 2015.

Dearing Report see National Committee of Enquiry into Higher Education.

Department for Business, Innovation and Skills (2013) *Enterprise Education Impact in Higher Education and Further Education: Final Report*. Available at https://www.gov.uk/government/uploads/system/uploads/attachment_data/file/208715/bis-13-904-enterprise-education-impact-in-higher-education-and-further-education.pdf accessed 14 May 2014.

Dewey, J. (1933) *How We Think: A Restatement of the Relation of Reflective Thinking to the Educative Process*. Massachusetts: DC Heath and Company.

European Commission (2012) *Effects and Impact of Entrepreneurship Programmes in Higher Education*. Available at http://ec.europa.eu/enterprise/newsroom/cf/_get-document.cfm?doc_id=7428 accessed 14 May 2015.

Harris, Sarah (2013) Half of employers say graduates are 'not up to the job': Findings fuel fears that universities fail to equip students with life skills. Daily Mail. 12 September 2013. Available at http://www.dailymail.co.uk/news/article-2419431/Half-employers-say-graduates-job-Findings-fuel-fears-universities-fail-equip-students-life-skills.html accessed 14 May 2015.

Ions, K. and Sutcliffe, N. (2015) Developing yourself, developing your organisation, in Helyer, R. (Ed.), *The Work-based Learning Student Handbook*, 2nd Edn, pp. 51–70. London: Palgrave.

Kuh, G., Cruce, T., Shoup, R. and Kinzie, J. (2008) Unmasking the effects of student engagement on first-year college grades and persistence. *The Journal of Higher Education*. 79 (5), pp. 540–563.

National Committee of Inquiry into Higher Education (1997) Higher Education in the Learning Society.London: HMSO.

Oxford Economics (2012) *Global Talent 2021*. Oxford: Oxford Economics. Available at: https://www.oxfordeconomics.com/Media/Default/Thought%20Leadership/global-talent-2021.pdf accessed 14 May 2015.

Pascarella, E. T. and Terenzini, P. T. (2005) *How College Affects Students: A Third Decade of Research*, vol. 2. San Francisco: Jossey-Bass.

Revans, R. (2011) *ABC of Action Learning*. Surrey: Gower Publishing Ltd.

Schön, D. A. (1983) *The Reflective Practitioner: How Professionals Think in Action*. New York: Basic Books.

Schön, D. A. (1987) *Educating the Reflective Practitioner*. San Francisco: Jossey-Bass.

Smith, L. (2009) Experiences of action learning in two SME business support programmes. *Action Learning: Research and Practice*. 6 (3), pp. 335–341.

Smith, S. and Smith, L. (2015) Social learning: Supporting yourself and your peers, in Helyer, R. (Ed.), *The Work-based Learning Student Handbook*, 2nd Edn, pp. 184–204. London: Palgrave.

Thomas, L. (2002) *Building Social Capital to Improve Student Success.* Exeter: BERA.

Tryggvason, G. and Apelian, D. (Eds) (2012) *Shaping Our World: Engineering Education for the 21st Century.* Hoboken: John Wiley & Sons.

Wenger, E. (1998) *Communities of Practice: Learning, Meaning, and Identity.* Cambridge: Cambridge University Press.

Yorke, M. and Knight, P. (2007) Evidence-informed pedagogy and the enhancement of student employability. *Teaching in Higher Education.* 12 (2), pp. 157–170.

▶ Recommended further reading

Gibbs, G. (1998) *Learning by Doing: A Guide to Teaching and Learning Methods.* London: Further Education Unit.

Helyer, R. (2007) What is employability?: Reflecting on the postmodern challenges of work-based learning. *Journal of Employability in the Humanities.* Available at http://tees.openrepository.com/tees/bitstream/10149/113951/2/113951.pdf accessed 14 May 2015.

Helyer, R. and Kay, J. (2015) Building capabilities for your future, in Helyer, R. (Ed.), *The Work-based Learning Student Handbook*, 2nd Edn, pp. 31–50. London: Palgrave.

Helyer, R. and Lee, D. (2012) The 21st century multiple generation workforce: Overlaps and differences but also challenges and benefits. *Education + Training.* 54 (7), pp. 545–578.

Helyer, R. and Lee, D. (2014) The role of work experience in the future employability of higher education graduates. *Higher Education Quarterly.* 68 (3), pp. 348–372.

High Fliers Research Ltd (2014) *The Graduate Market in 2014.* Available at http://www.highfliers.co.uk/download/GMReport14.pdf accessed 14 May 2015.

Houses of Parliament, Parliamentary Office for Science and Technology (2011) An ageing workforce. *Postnote . 391 (October).* Available at http://www.parliament.uk/pagefiles/504/postpn391_Ageing-Workforce.pdf accessed 14 May 2015.

Lucas, B., Hanson, J. and Claxton, G. (2014) *Thinking Like an Engineer: Implications for the Education System.* London: Royal Academy of Engineering.

Office for National Statistics (2013) *Graduates in the Labour Market.* Available at http://www.ons.gov.uk/ons/rel/lmac/graduates-in-the-labour-market/2013/rpt---graduates-in-the-uk-labour-market-2013.html accessed 14 May 2015.

Owens, J. and Tibby, M. (Eds) (2014) *Enhancing Employability Through Enterprise Education: Examples of Good Practice in Higher Education.* York: HEA.

Perrin, D. and Helyer, R. (2015) Make your learning count: Recognition of prior learning (RPL), in Helyer, R. (Ed.), *The Work-based Learning Student Handbook*, 2nd Edn, pp. 96-119. London: Palgrave.

Quality Assurance Agency (2012) *Enterprise and Entrepreneurship Education: Guidance for UK Higher Education Providers.* Available at http://www.qaa.ac.uk/en/Publications/Documents/enterprise-entrepreneurship-guidance.pdf accessed 14 May 2015.

Siebert, S. and Costley, C. (2013) Conflicting values in reflection on professional practice. *Higher Education Skills and Work-based Learning.* 3 (3), pp. 156–167.

12 A transcultural dance: Enriching work-based learning facilitation

Tony Wall and Ly Tran

IN THIS CHAPTER YOU WILL:

▶ Examine what it might mean to be an international work-based learner

▶ Appreciate the vibrant array of different perspectives international work-based learners offer, which can be rich learning assets

▶ See a pedagogic model for work-based learning contexts where both you and your work-based learners gain new ways of thinking and acting

▶ Share strategies for integrating diverse examples and cases, connect to and validate diverse experiences and prior knowledge and accommodate diverse work-based learner needs

▶ Look at strategies which enable and sustain a learning environment across cultural boundaries conducive to work-based learning success

▶ Being 'international'

The internationalisation agenda continues to stimulate debate within higher education (HE) (Shaw, 2014) and is of relevance to work-based learning (WBL) courses, including attracting full-time and distance students from overseas, sending domestic students abroad on work placements and study, off-shore delivery through establishing overseas campuses or other transnational partnerships and joint education programmes, staff mobility and internationalisation of the curriculum. As a tutor who is facilitating work-based learners you may well be dealing with students from around the globe; it is important to consider your work-based learners' cultural situation. Try the activity below to put this into context:

ACTIVITY

▶ Imagine that you are a tutor on a WBL course at a higher education institution (HEI) in the UK. In your opinion, which of these work-based learners are likely to be an international work-based learner? Tick if you think they are international.

A ❑ A serial entrepreneur in Brisbane, Australia
B ❑ An educational manager in Dubai
C ❑ A director living/working in London (born in Thailand)
D ❑ A marketing manager living/working in London (born in China)

▶ Thinking about the international students you have identified above, what is the single most defining feature of an international work-based learner?

Student A is an international WBL student; Student B is classed as a domestic WBL student because he has property and permanent residence in the UK; Student C is classed as a domestic WBL student because she has right to remain in the UK and Student D is classed as an international WBL student because she does not have permanent residency in the UK. These answers seem counter intuitive to what we might typically understand by the term 'international', but these real examples serve to illustrate that the term 'international' is often an administrative label universities use to abide with the complex immigration regulations of a specific country. Immigration status and place of residence are not pedagogic issues and cannot tell us about the needs of individual learners. Students may have similar academic writing needs, or be new to concepts of WBL and reflective practice, despite being classed differently.

▶ Models of WBL facilitation

There are two models of WBL facilitation when working with such learners:

▶ A homogenous deficit model – where 'international students' are a supposed homogenous group who are 'problems to be fixed'.
▶ A transcultural asset model – where there is a diverse group of work-based learners, each bringing learning assets such as cultural experiences and perspectives to the learning experience.

Anglophone HEIs have tended to approach international students as 'problems to be solved' and stereotyped them as 'passive, rote learners, lacking in critical thinking and independent learning skills and prone to plagiarism' (Ryan, 2011, p. 637), and this is symptomatic of a deficit model of students. However, a number of research studies (Rienties et al., 2012; Green and Farazmand, 2013) demonstrate that international students can actually 'outperform' domestic students. Furthermore *'the Asian learner'* and *'the Chinese learner'*, with a supposed 'propensity for rote learning', are myths (Marambe et al., 2012; Run and Richardson, 2012).

Similarly within the specific context of work-based or experiential learning pedagogies such as inquiry-based learning (IBL), Bache and Hayton (2012, p. 421) found that there were 'wide ranging expectations and past experiences amongst international students, and differing levels of adaptation to, and enthusiasm for, an IBL approach'. A key message here is made by Fritz, Chin and DeMarinis (2008, p. 244), who argue that 'international students with culturally diverse needs should not be considered as one homogenous group'. In other words, it is not so much the approaches to learning that are culturally determined, but rather there is a 'variety of contextual factors that affect these students' capacity to adapt' (Run and Richardson, 2012, p. 313). This ability to adapt is core to a strand of research into student success in distance learning which is pertinent in the context of WBL courses (Subotzky and Prinsloo, 2011; Baxter, 2012; Gebhard, 2012).

As a tutor you may feel you have minimal influence on HEI systems; however, you do have a central role in orchestrating many of the contextual factors that influence the work-based learner's adaptivity, alongside other learning resources within the HEI. There is an array of practical tips requiring minimal effort and involvement that can be immediately applied in your daily practice to ideas that will take more time and energy to implement fully. Under the deficit model, enabling adaptivity has been about teaching the student a superior way to think or write; tutors might send their work-based learners with English as a second, or other, language to writing classes or give them additional support materials on the use of critical reflection in WBL. The pedagogic issue in taking this approach is that it can ignore a work-based learner's current localised knowledge and understandings and marginalises those who do not share a common grounding in a Western context. In turn, this can affect learner (and tutor) motivation, engagement and academic achievement, as shown in the real example below (Case study 12.1). It positions an international work-based learner as someone who is in a Western HEI to learn about the 'superior' Western ways of doing things:

Case study 12.1 Clarifying expectations: Enabling personal writing styles to shine and grow?

Chen is a learner in Taiwan studying on a WBL master's programme related to education. Chen was an experienced learner and had enjoyed academic success in her undergraduate studies. She felt very confident in her academic writing and had always enjoyed her academic studies.

As part of her programme, Chen was able to send her work to her tutor for formative feedback. Though she was enjoying her course, she was not so happy when she received tutor feedback on one of her first essays.

To Chen's surprise, the tutor had criticised her work and many of the comments were related to her style of writing. One of the most perplexing for Chen was the comment relating to how her introduction was not 'clear or direct enough'.

From the tutor's perspective, she was expecting Chen to state her argument and then explain how she would achieve it, in a fashion similar to '*It is argued that ... The first section discusses ... the second section discusses...*'

However, Chen valued a style that raised more curiosity in the reader and arrived at the argument at the *end* of the piece of writing. She liked to do this by opening the essay with a poignant metaphor, ancient citation or a question. She particularly liked the proverb '*Tell me, I'll forget. Show me, I'll remember. Involve me, I'll understand*'.

For Chen, such literary tactics act as a beautiful artistic frame which sets up the rest of the essay, which then can be followed by a detailed discussion around a number of points and then concluded with a statement of the argument at the end.

The comments were especially upsetting for Chen because she had developed and refined her writing style over many years, and she valued such a creative literary style that involved the reader; furthermore, these were tactics that had previously delivered academic success.

As she progressed on her course, Chen adjusted her writing style to align more with what the tutor wanted, because she wanted to achieve the best she could. However, not allowing her to develop and refine her own style did affect Chen's motivation and engagement in her course.

An alternative model of WBL facilitation is based on valuing the diversity of perspectives that are brought to a learning experience by the work-based learner – the diverse asset model. Here, adaptivity might be interpreted as a mutual or collaborative enterprise where both the tutor and the work-based learner alike find and develop new ways of thinking or writing which emerge from the interaction; it becomes a genuine educational experience for both (Ryan, 2011). Enabling opportunities for work-based learners to share their current localised knowledge and understandings helps to position them as active co-constructors of knowledge and boost their agency, and therefore motivation to engage. The resources within both models may well be very similar, but the purpose and even *attitude of engagement* is different; the first is for the purposes of *replication* (the deficit model), whereas the latter is for the purposes of *co-development* (the asset model). A real example of how a tutor adopted an attitude of curiosity rather than accusation and reprimand is illustrated below (Case study 12.2). This 'asset-based' pedagogy challenges much conventional practice in teaching but shifts the grounds on which both tutor and work-based learner can engage educationally – moving towards being 'Fellow Travellers' on a mutual journey of discovery (Trahar, 2010):

Case study 12.2 How to write: A case in coping with diversity in writing practices

Juan was an experienced WBL tutor. He had lived and worked abroad but was relatively new to facilitating learning with work-based learners across the globe.

Academic writing is an important set of skills to Juan, and although he recognises they take time to develop, he remembers an incident that made him re-evaluate his teaching practices.

At one point in time he was facilitating a work-based learner in the Middle East, Noureen. He had engaged in multiple Skype tutorials about a draft of Noureen's work-based project report but was then shocked when he looked closer; he found that the text in the draft was mostly copied from Internet sources and books.

However, though his automatic reaction was to reprimand Noureen for her academic malpractice (plagiarism), he was also curious as to how she had gone about developing her draft. He decided to speak to Noureen and ask her about her academic writing practices.

He was surprised to find that Noureen had developed her own way of creating her assignments through the medium of English: she would first scan key literatures and copy large chunks of text and place them in an order that made sense to her.

She would then integrate and synthesise the material into her own words, and it would be through this process she would learn how concepts linked or, more precisely, compared and contrasted. After various iterations of amending the piece, she would then submit a piece that was her own work.

Using a more empathetic and positive frame, without accusations or reprimand, Juan constructed his feedback to Noureen. In it, he was able to emphasise how important it was that the work was her own words and also explain additional ways to link analytical points.

To Juan's surprise, Noureen did actually produce an acceptable final version. Through this incident, Juan realised that there is the potential for formative feedback to interrupt well-established writing processes and that there may well be different writing practices with which he is unfamiliar, especially when the learner's first language is not English.

As a result of this insight, Juan is making his formative assessment strategy more flexible to respond to the needs of all of his work-based learners and allowing each student to decide what they want to share with him at the formative stage.

Activity

Developing practical ways to help culturally diverse work-based learners
Think of a time you found a work-based learner behaving differently from what you expected or instructed:

▶ What was your reaction?
▶ How might this have influenced how the work-based learner felt or engaged?
▶ What might have been the outcome if you had reacted differently?
▶ What responses might you experiment with next time if this happened again?

The rest of this chapter focuses on practical 'asset-based' strategies that can be used with work-based learners.

▶ A transcultural dance: A metaphor for mutual adaptivity

The productive metaphor, *a transcultural dance*, can guide how you facilitate work-based learners and emphasises this mutual learning journey. Facilitation as a transcultural dance positions you and work-based learner(s) in situations which both respond and adapt to each other in a learning environment – a *pedagogic* dance that requires sensitivity to each other's needs, preferences and experiences, which cross cultural boundaries. Just like learning any new dance, it takes time, energy and effort from both you and your work-based learners; you might step out of sync, or accidentally step on each other, but it is the *adaptivity* to learn the intricacies which drives the learning (of both and all) forward. Adaptivity is about you finding creative ways of facilitating learning which positively enable work-based learners to use their own cultural background, knowledge and values, but which also mean they are enabled to meet the requirements of the specific WBL course on which they are studying – just like Juan above (Case study 12.2). In this way, adaptivity includes:

▶ Interacting in ways which operate from the work-based learner's existing understanding of how their work (or their wider world) functions from their own current cultural context
▶ Using this as a springboard to understanding new and alternative ways of seeing the world of work

▶ Enabling the learner to navigate between existing and alternative cultural practices and the assessment requirements of the specific WBL course on which the learner is registered (or in other words, creatively adapt to the new learning opportunity).

There are different strategies for you to engage in a transcultural dance, some requiring less challenge than others (Tran, 2012):

▶ **Integrating** examples and cases from different cultural settings within a learning experience, so that work-based learners can make sense of learning points through different contexts and situations

▶ **Connecting** to the diverse experiences of work-based learners and validating them, so that each work-based learner can relate to the learning points being made and feel that they can make a valuable contribution to that situation

▶ **Accommodating** the needs of a diverse work-based learner base, so that each work-based learner with their own cultural background and experience can engage with the learning situation

▶ **Reciprocating** the learning of alternative cultural perspectives, so that there is a growing learning experience for you and your work-based learners, one where the subtle differences between work and academic practices are identified, explored and adapted (where possible) (Figure 12.1)

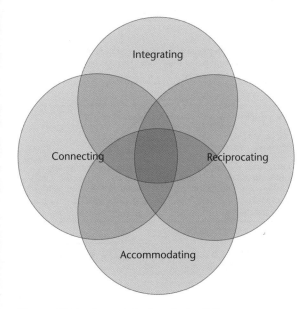

Figure 12.1   Four strategies of adaptivity

Integrating

One of the easiest and quickest strategies to encourage adaptivity is to include examples and cases from different cultural contexts. This might involve you undertaking research about work practices in different cultural settings or involving work-based learners in such investigations (possibly linking this to research skills development activities). Overlaying this with one of the many theoretical frameworks about organisational culture (Table 12.1) can provide insight into how a work-based learner might plan out a work-based project, whom to involve, whom not to involve, which formal procedures or processes to follow and so on. The table below presents a specific example of a model (by Flores et al., 2012) and uses it to identify dimensions of work-based project design that the work-based learner will need to consider within their specific working context:

Table 12.1 A framework to aid project design

Participative decision making
In designing a work-based project, a work-based learner might reflect on the extent to which their team/department/organisation allows its staff to: • *Share their views on what the problems are* • *Share information and ideas about solutions* • *Share the implementation of solutions* • *Share the evaluation of results* This would give insight into who should be involved in a work-based project; for example, if a managing director typically makes all the decisions, it is important to involve him/her in the design of the project.
Openness
Within different workplaces, there are differing levels as to the acceptability of staff: • *Consulting with others inside and outside the organisation* • *Sharing information within others inside and outside the organisation* Being sensitive to this cultural information will help the work-based learner decide how easy certain internal information might be to obtain (or whether some might be inaccessible). It will also tell the work-based learner how much consultation might be needed for the recommendations from the project to be accepted and therefore implemented (for example, from no consultation through to extensive consultation).
Learning orientation
In becoming aware of this aspect of organisational culture, the work-based learner may identify the extent to which their team/department/organisation: • *Encourages people to learn new things at work* • *Encourages people to learn without fear of mistakes* • *Has processes to evaluate and improve results at work* <div align="right">*continued overleaf*</div>

Table 12.1 A framework to aid project design *continued*

The organisational processes that are required in a culture with a high fear of mistakes are typically different from ones which encourage learning through trial and error (and mistake). In finding out about this aspect of culture, the work-based learner will identify any important processes to follow or find out they have a high level of freedom in their approach (and therefore have to express their own creativity).

Transformational leadership

The behaviour of leaders in a team/department/organisation helps the work-based learner identify the extent to which leaders:

- *Communicate a clear sense of strategic direction of where the team, department or organisation is going*
- *Encourage people to learn and develop new skills*
- *Encourage new ideas and innovative problem solving*

This might help identify whether (or not) the work-based learner involves the leader(s) in the design of the project, for example, in terms of getting wider support. In relatively low transformational leadership cultures, for example, the scope and size of the project might not be as far ranging as a project in a high transformational culture.

Source: Based on Flores et al. (2012)

Teaching tips: Integrating

To integrate this work into your own practice it is important that you:

▶ Find out about different work practices from multiple cultural settings and integrate these examples in relevant discussions.
▶ Design learning activities to encourage work-based learners to investigate and analyse different work practices across cultural contexts.
▶ Utilise online discussion boards and blogs to initiate and develop examples for your future usage.
▶ Use cases and examples of work-based projects across cultures and encourage learners to reflect on the cultural factors when designing a work-based project.

Activity

Taking the above points into consideration think about the following questions:

▶ How might a manager approach improving the performance of a single team member?
▶ How might a member of staff give feedback to a colleague?
▶ How industry- or role-specific tasks are completed. How might a nurse speak to a patient? How are accounts processed?
▶ How people might prefer to learn at work?
▶ How people might prefer to reflect and analyse at work?
▶ Who should be involved to ensure the project is allowed to happen?
▶ Who should be involved in the project to ensure it makes an impact afterwards?
▶ What processes should be used to involve these people?

Connecting

Connecting is about becoming aware of the specific prior experiences of individual work-based learners within the learning experience and validating that prior experience as a useful learning asset. Valuing the work-based learner and their history makes them feel like a valued member of the learning community and enriches the learning experience with cross-cultural examples and cases. You can design learning activities in such a way that you become systematically aware of a wide range of information: practices across cultural contexts, preferred study patterns, preferred academic writing practices and so on. Asking the work-based learner to reflect on the organisational culture of their own working context can also help elucidate design features of WBL projects, but it is important to withhold judgement and appreciate that things may work differently in different contexts. Consistently connecting and validating in this way takes practice, and more effort than integrating, but provides much more information and a stronger rapport to facilitate engagement. Case study 12.3 below illustrates how this can be done when working with work-based learners from diverse cultural backgrounds:

Case study 12.3 Tapping into student motivation: A case in connecting

Andrew teaches hospitality management, and at the centre of his teaching is his endeavour to help international work-based learners see the intimate link between their courage to engage in cross-border education in a foreign language and their potential capacity to transform their own learning and develop life-enhancing skills.

Through discussion with his international work-based learners, Andrew engages them in critical self-reflection and self-discovery of their strength and determination to undertake an international education and the implications for learning on his course. Andrew uses the following strategies:

▶ Raising work-based learners' self-awareness of their own abilities to change and boosting their confidence during tuition time (and outside of it where possible) by:
  • Making time to convey admiration for the learner's courage to undertake cross-cultural education (for example, '*I admire your courage to study on this course here in Australia*')
  • Identifying small examples of when learners have shown a capacity to work outside of their comfort zone (for example, '*I think you handled that situation very well...*' or '*I can see you are working well in that group*')
  • Encouraging learners to self-reflect on their 'hidden' transcultural strengths (for example, '*You seem to know about how to deal with a group – how might that be useful in a career in the human resources department of a tourist organisation?*')

continued overleaf

Case study 12.3 Tapping into student motivation: A case in connecting *continued*

▶ Increasing the awareness of individual work-based learner professional interests and career expectations during tuition time by setting tasks for them to research the work roles or careers they are seeking to progress to.

▶ Making explicit connections between the learning content and work-based learners' work interests where relevant. For example, if the work-based learners are learning about motivation theory and you know that some of them are interested in progressing their careers in human resources, then ask questions or set tasks that require them to explain how that theory may help them make decisions in that role.

▶ Being sensitive to work-based learners' facial expressions (for example, on video conferencing equipment) that may indicate their uncertainty about new concepts; for example, a frown, or a twitch in an eyebrow might indicate uncertainty (the learner may not directly ask you to clarify).

▶ Explaining information in multiple forms, including through practical demonstrations and visual aids such as pictures and drawings, and involving work-based learners in drawing a picture to illustrate the learning concept.

ACTIVITY – CONNECTING

1. Design learning activities to enable your work-based learners to share their existing knowledge around academic practices as well as professional work practices relevant to your course. For example, find ways to encourage your learners to reflect on how they currently approach their academic writing and how this can be applied to the course. Some generic questions provide an opportunity for you to discover their prior knowledge without making assumptions or generalisations:

   ▶ How did you decide what to focus on?
   ▶ How did you decide what to read?
   ▶ How many published sources did you read?
   ▶ What did you read that was given to you by your teachers?
   ▶ How did you plan your writing?
   ▶ How did you decide what to comment upon?

2. Find ways to validate or appreciate academic or work practices with which you are not familiar, without judgement or criticism. This can be a springboard to suggest how things might be different (for example, '*It is interesting for me to learn this is how it works in your organisation … How might this be different in…?*')

3. Find ways to validate or appreciate the positive intentions and efforts of individual work-based learners (for example, '*I know you have put a lot of effort into this … I can see you have tried to…*')

4. Encourage learners to reflect on the features of the organisational culture (Table 12.1) in which they work and use this information to design work-based projects. Withhold judgement (for example, '*That is interesting … That is different from the way it is done in…*'), but encourage the learner to consider how it might be different in different settings ('*How might this be different in a context where…?*')

Accommodating

Another strategy for adaptivity is becoming aware of the specific learning needs of your WBL students and accommodating these needs. Quizzes or reflective diagnostics are useful in stimulating discussion about these needs. Accommodating might involve ensuring that your expectations of thinking, writing and acting are as explicit and as clear as possible and are consistently communicated in a variety of ways during the learning experience. For example, reflective writing and how to engage with a WBL tutor may be unfamiliar to all learners and will need modelling through examples and practice. International learners will use a variety of sources to find out the requirements of their course, including asking their tutors and other learning support staff, seeking guidance on the course site and seeking sample assessments (Tran, 2008). The Case study 12.4 below illustrates some ways to get to know your international work-based leaners better:

Case study 12.4 Getting to know individual needs: A case in not generalising

Susan is an experienced WBL tutor and has been teaching in China over the last few years. She has learnt over time that the learning needs of Chinese learners tend to be generalised by institutions.

Included in some of these generalisations have been claims that Chinese learners are prone to rote learning, are competent and confident at mathematics, and so on. However, Susan has found this way of thinking to be very problematic in practice and contrary to her experience.

Her own approach is based on investing time in getting to know learners on an individual basis through the design of one-to-one and small group interactions wherever possible.

Specifically, she finds that taking this individualised approach aids in building a detailed knowledge of the following:

▶ What the individual learner's strengths are, or what they feel competent and comfortable in doing (for example, they may feel confident in writing about their professional area)
▶ Areas where they might need additional support (for example, linking analytical points or paragraphs together)
▶ Potential cultural norms that might be hindering the learner's engagement in her particular style of tutoring (for example, some learners may not feel they should contribute in a small group setting)

For Susan, this more personalised approach provides an informal opportunity to create a safer space for her as a tutor to engage more meaningfully with her learners. More precisely, Susan thinks that being able to express and share

continued overleaf

Case study 12.4 Getting to know individual needs: A case in not generalising *continued*

humour with her work-based learners is an important part of this, which in turn helps her to build rapport and establish trust.

In cultures where 'not losing face' is important, this approach provides a mutually supportive space for the work-based learner and their tutor to relax and discuss things more openly and, in turn, engage more fully within the learning situation.

Overall, this pedagogic set of practices avoids generalising about an individual work-based learner's strengths when it comes to studying and learning (for example, the stereotypical strength of interpreting or analysing statistics), as well as learning areas that need development (for example, citing or critical reflection).

At its heart, Susan's approach acknowledges that individual work-based learners often bring different sets of prior educational experiences and skills to their courses, all of which are useful learning assets for the WBL tutor.

Sandra Hopkins, Lecturer in Management, Henan Province, China

Beyond initial diagnostic efforts, you can also involve key pedagogic tactics to help communicate key concepts to work-based learners from diverse backgrounds. Case study 12.5 shows how adaptivity can help you as a tutor to better understand differing cultural perspectives:

Case study 12.5 Helping the work-based learner to know their cultural perspectives: A case in continuing adaptivity

Having been involved in teaching for four years in Melbourne, Ana Rosa feels passionate about the transcultural interaction to which she is exposed in her international classes. Born in England and migrating to Australia, she has some transcultural experience in living and working abroad, which greatly assists with her teaching.

For her, continuing adaptivity has been at the heart of her pedagogic journey in teaching and in accommodating the transcultural needs of international work-based learners.

Specially, she adopts these key strategies in her teaching practices:

▶ Raise self-awareness of cultural communication norms by creating tasks that encourage discussion and interaction in groups (for example, a team or group work activity on or offline). This experience can then be used as a focal point to begin to openly discuss some of the possible norms influencing the experience.

▶ Use plain language (rather than slang) to explain WBL concepts, but avoid talking in childish language as this can be regarded as disrespectful; this might involve some experimentation with your work-based learners.

continued overleaf

> **Case study 12.5 Helping the work-based learner to know their cultural perspectives: A case in continuing adaptivity** *continued*
>
> ▷ Use topic-based quizzes at the beginning of the teaching period to gain understanding of each work-based learner's learning needs. There are multiple instruments available, and they can also be the starting point for additional discussion around the validity and usefulness of the concept of 'learning styles' (depending on academic level).
>
> ▷ Explore how to adapt teaching methods in relation to different learning needs (see the Tips box below for examples), such as integrating more experiential activities or more writing development activities; again this might involve experimentation and calibration with your work-based learners.
>
> ▷ Design and deliver ice-breaking activities for work-based learners to experience intercultural situations:
> • These might be a team or group working activity which can be delivered face to face or online (for example, one of many team building activities).
> • Allow the international work-based learner to respond in their native language and ask domestic learners to guess the meaning; this stimulates debate about words, body language and interpreting the behaviour of others.
> • Encourage domestic work-based learners to imagine themselves to be speaking another language and be in another country (for example, use images and sounds of a busy street in India or China); this stimulates a different level of empathy and allows work-based learners to experience responding in a different setting.

Work-based learners may not be aware of what they need to aid their academic success at the start of a programme, especially if they are returning to education. Research into student identity and academic success is useful here to help you develop other strategies for accommodating needs. Key themes that have been linked to academic success include:

▷ Spending enough, regular time on their studies. This has been found to predict academic grade (Mo and Zhao, 2011; Ren and Hagedorn, 2012), alongside how much time learners spend on a course site (Sun and Rueda, 2012). Busy work-based learners need to balance work, home and study (Selwyn, 2011; Baxter, 2012; Sun and Rueda, 2012), and the two aspects here are: first, making regular time available for studies, so that it becomes part of life, and, second, that this is enough time (Park and Choi, 2009; Subotzky and Prinsloo, 2011; Baxter, 2012; Gebhard, 2012).

▷ Having a strong and supportive personal learning resource network. This is another predictor of student success (Park and Choi, 2009; Subotzky and Prinsloo, 2011; Baxter, 2012; Gebhard, 2012) and is linked to the first point: work-based learners will often depend on their network in order to fulfil all of their responsibilities (or at least attempt to).

▶ Taking a self-reflective and self-leadership approach to their studies. Apart from using reflection within their WBL studies, taking a reflective approach to their performance as a student also influences success (Subotzky and Prinsloo, 2011; Gebhard, 2012). This includes being able to motivate themselves throughout their studies (Masjuan and Troiano, 2009; Baxter, 2012) as well as being able to believe they can succeed (Subotzky and Prinsloo, 2011; Sun and Rueda, 2012). Encouraging this reflective approach during formal tuition and course evaluation is one useful way to systematise learners' reflections about whether they are spending enough regular time on their studies and have put in place an appropriate personal learning resource network.

Teaching tips

Accommodating

1. Use quizzes/diagnostics at the start of a WBL course to identify learning needs (the Kolb/Honey and Mumford Learning Styles Inventory, Visual-Auditory-Kinaesthetic preferences, PICO (Personal Intercultural Change Orientation)).

2. Be explicit about:

   ▶ The ways of thinking you wish to promote on your work-based course (the use and application of theory, use of multiple texts or perspectives, evaluation of theory and the evaluation of the learner's own (or other people's) thinking and behaviour)

   ▶ The core focus of learning and assessed tasks and the expectations associated with engaging with them (are you expecting the work-based learner to reflect on an experience, review theory, both, or something else?)

3. Consider ways of integrating academic writing development within course design, including the design of shorter assessment pieces and formative feedback.

4. Present information in different formats so the work-based learners have the opportunity to interpret from different and multiple angles (for example, literal/metaphoric, written/spoken/visual).

5. Select a range of books for different reading abilities and make it clear which books are useful starting points (that is, springboards to make sense of other texts).

6. Encourage learners to become aware of and build their own personal learning networks and make it easy to find contacts in all documentation. Also see tasks in Wall and Tran (2015).

continued overleaf

Teaching tips *continued*

7. Encourage work-based learners to be clear about the strongest reasons for why they are studying. Validate these in and outside of formal tuition (for example, '*I admire your confidence and ambition in studying in a different culture*').

8. Encourage learners to reflect on their performance in their studies – specifically, ask learners to reflect on their own strengths and the extent to which they think they are spending enough regular time on their studies.

9. Be mindful of stereotypical views of international students. You may decide to prepare your work-based learner to deal with these (for example, a 'polite responses' fact sheet) or you might want to institute changes outside of your work-based programme (for example, requesting alternative wording in university information).

10. Space out tuition and assessment periods to enable learners to be able to digest and process any new information.

Reciprocating

Reciprocating can be the most challenging strand of the adaptivity process as it focuses on becoming open to learning multiple perspectives beyond your own familiarity and experience. The work-based learner will acquire new perspectives from you, and you as tutor will also learn alternative ways of knowing, reflecting and writing. You will have to navigate between and amongst cultural contexts you come into contact with and the requirements of the course you are delivering and assessing. This might involve revisiting some basic assumptions about the academic practices you are seeking to develop with your work-based learners, for example questioning the flexibility of the assessment brief. The ultimate in reciprocating must be becoming a work-based learner yourself; see the Case study (12.6) below:

Case study 12.6 When the WBL *tutor* becomes the international work-based *learner*: A case in reciprocating

Melissa teaches law in Sydney, Australia. She is from an Anglo-European background and is very conscious of building a mutual learning environment. Melissa stresses that one of the key pedagogical principles underpinning her practice is to validate and build on the work-based learner's cultural knowledge, experiences and understandings of professional practices in their home contexts.

Here, she places emphasis on integrating international and domestic work-based learners in teaching contexts: when learning activities are designed in a way

continued overleaf

Case study 12.6 When the WBL *tutor* becomes the international work-based *learner*: A case in reciprocating *continued*

A case in reciprocating continued that enables international work-based learners to actively share their knowledge and experiences, they often feel more motivated to learn and reflect on what is connected and meaningful to them.

Yet Melissa also demonstrates that developing culturally inclusive practices involves climbing her own learning curve about cultural practices in other countries and raising work-based learners' awareness of the diverse and alternative practices shaped by different national contexts.

To facilitate this, she actively learns about examples of disciplinary work-based practices in different countries through the media, including newspapers and the multicultural television channel, SBS (Special Broadcasting Service). In other words, she reciprocated and repositioned herself as an 'international learner'. She says:

> I try to read widely the papers. I like to know the national leaders. I try to refer to the history of the country as best I can … A news junky. I watch SBS news and find information out all the time. Just when it comes up, I'm a great believer in using examples. And if I can say, well, in China you do it this way, but here we do it this way. And I always try to say, it's like Road A and Road B getting to town, we'll both get there but we'll go a different way and try and make it simple like that. And then if the work-based learners are interested, they ask more questions, that kind of thing and we can take it from there.

In so doing, Melissa engages not only herself but all her work-based learners in transnational knowledge connection and helps everyone develop global awareness. Her positive culturally inclusive approach makes international work-based learners feel valued because they are given the opportunity to share their cultural knowledge and play a role in contributing to the enrichment of the learning situation.

Teaching tips

Reciprocating

1. Enable work-based learners to develop different and creative ways to express their understandings of the strengths and limitations of theories or of particular courses of action in reflection.
2. Enable work-based learners to express and build their arguments in different ways but in ways which still achieve the learning outcomes of the course.
3. Enable the development of different writing styles through example essays or excerpts and by giving constructive feedback through the 'feedback sandwich' (positive points – development points related to learning outcomes – positive points again).
4. Reflect on your own expectations and practices of assessment and consider how it might be possible to expand the ways work-based learners might achieve the required outcomes in different ways.

The teaching tips in this chapter can help to enable all work-based learners to join you in an enjoyable transcultural dance, where each individual brings a different set of moves learnt from multiple cultural milieus. The moves may be different from your own, and there can be effort and energy involved in learning new moves in ways that work for both you and your learners. An important starting point is to be willing to operate with the assumption that all work-based learners bring with them a diverse set of learning assets for you to tap into and from which all can benefit.

SUMMARY

▶ Seeking out the 'learning assets' in each of your WBL course interactions has benefits for all involved, including yourself.

▶ Do a self-check on your own practices: where are you connecting, integrating, accommodating and reciprocating?

▶ Consider which of the strategies and tactics outlined in this chapter you can start implementing immediately.

▶ Consider which areas might take more time and thinking about (such as rethinking the fundamental concepts like critical reflection and analysis, or experiential learning more broadly) and start a journey of curiosity.

▶ References

Bache, I. and Hayton, R. (2012) Inquiry-based learning and the international student. *Teaching in Higher Education.* 17 (4), pp. 411–423.

Baxter, J. (2012) Who am I and what keeps me going? Profiling the distance learning student in higher education. *The International Review of Research in Open and Distance Learning.* 13 (4), pp. 107–129.

Flores, L. G., Zheng, W., Rau, D. and Thomas, C. H. (2012) Organizational learning: Subprocess identification, construct validation, and an empirical test of cultural antecedents. *Journal of Management.* 38 (2), pp. 640–667.

Fritz, M. V., Chin, D. and DeMarinis, V. (2008) Stressors, anxiety, acculturation and adjustment among international and North American students. *International Journal of Intercultural Relations.* 32, pp. 244–259.

Gebhard, J. G. (2012) International students' adjustment problems and behaviors. *Journal of International Students.* 2 (2), pp. 184–193.

Green, R. D. and Farazmand, F. A. (2013) Applied project learning outcomes: Differences between United States and international students. *Business Education & Accreditation.* 5 (1), pp. 41–51.

Marambe, K. N., Vermunt, J. D. and Boshuizen, P. A. (2012) A cross-cultural comparison of student learning patterns in higher education. *Higher Education*. 64, pp. 299–316.

Masjuan, J. M. and Troiano, H. (2009) University students' success: A psycho-sociological approach. *Higher Education*. 58, pp. 15–28.

Mo, S. and Zhao, L. (2011) An analysis of student activities and performance in management distance education courses. *International Journal of Education Research*. 6 (1), pp. 86–96.

Park, J. H. and Choi, H. J. (2009) Factors influencing adult learners' decision to drop out or persist in online learning. *Educational Technology & Society*. 12 (4), pp. 207–217.

Ren, J. and Hagedorn, L. S. (2012) International graduate students' academic performance: What are the influencing factors? *Journal of International Students*. 2 (2), pp. 135–143.

Rienties, B., Beausaert, S., Gronert, T., Niemantsverdriet, S. and Kommers, P. (2012) Understanding academic performance of international students: The role of ethnicity, academic and social integration. *Higher Education*. 63, pp. 685–700.

Run, H. and Richardson, T. E. (2012) Perceptions of quality and approaches to studying in higher education: A comparative study of Chinese and British postgraduate students at six British business schools. *Higher Education*. 63, pp. 299–326.

Ryan, J. (2011) Teaching and learning for international students: Towards a transcultural approach. *Teachers and Teaching: Theory and Practice*. 17 (6), pp. 631–648.

Selwyn, N. (2011) Digitally distanced learning: A study of international distance learners' (non)use of technology. *Distance Education*. 32 (1), pp. 85–99.

Shaw, C. (2014) Should academics adapt their teaching for international students? Online Discussion. 25 July 12–2 p.m. Available at http://www.theguardian.com/higher-education-network/2014/jul/22/should-universities-adapt-teaching-support-international-students-live-chat accessed 6 August 2014.

Subotzky, G. and Prinsloo, P. (2011) Turning the tide: A socio-critical model and framework for improving student success in open distance learning at the University of South Africa. *Distance Education*. 32 (2), pp. 177–193.

Sun, J. C. Y. and Rueda, R. (2012) Situational interest, computer self-efficacy and self-regulation: Their impact on student engagement in distance education. *British Journal of Educational Technology*. 43 (2), pp. 191–204.

Trahar, S. (2010) *Developing Cultural Capability in International Higher Education: A Narrative Inquiry*. Abingdon: Routledge.

Tran, L. (2008) Unpacking academic requirements: International students in management and education disciplines. *Higher Education Research & Development*. 27 (3), pp. 245–256.

Tran, L. (2012) Internationalisation of vocational education and training: An adapting curve for teachers and learners. *Journal of Studies in International Education*. 17 (4), pp. 492–507.

Wall, T. and Tran, L. (2015) Learning to become an international work-based learner, in Helyer, R. (Ed.), *The Work-based Learning Student Handbook*, 2nd Edn, pp. 205–226. London: Palgrave.

▶ Recommended further reading

Guardian Education (2014) *International Students*. Available at http://www.theguardian.com/education/internationalstudents accessed 6 August 2014.

Higher Education Academy (2012) *Teaching International Students*. York: HEA. Available at http://www.heacademy.ac.uk/teaching-international-students accessed 9 July 2014.

Lipson, C. (2008) *Succeeding as an International Student in the United States and Canada*. Chicago: Chicago Guides to Academic Life.

Palgrave Study Skills: International Students: Assignments (2014). Macmillan Publishers Ltd. Available at http://www.palgrave.com/studentstudyskills/page/international-students-assignments accessed 18 May 2015

Ryan, J. (Ed.) (2013) *Cross-cultural Teaching and Learning for Home and International Students: Internationalisation of Pedagogy and Curriculum in Higher Education*. Abingdon: Routledge.

Ryan, J. and Louie, K. (2007) False dichotomy?: 'Western' and 'Eastern' concepts of scholarship and learning. *Educational Philosophy and Theory*. 39 (4), pp. 404–417.

Sovic, S. and Blythman, M. (2012) *International Students Negotiating Higher Education: Critical Perspectives*. Abingdon: Routledge.

Tran, L. (2013) *Teaching International Students in Vocational Education: New Pedagogical Approaches*. Camberwell, Australia: Australian Council for Educational Research Press.

Tran, L. (2013) International Student Adaptation to Academic Writing in Higher Education. Newcastle upon Tyne: Cambridge Scholars Publishing.

13 Promoting learning through work-based experience: Mimetic learning in action

Stephen Billett

IN THIS CHAPTER YOU WILL:

▶ See how the findings of projects within an international teaching fellowship (Billett, 2011), demonstrate that pedagogic practices and processes of engagement in higher education settings can be used to support learners to participate in work experiences, before, during and after those experiences

▶ Find ways in which the learning that higher education students gain through work-based experiences might be understood and optimised

▶ Read that much of this learning arises through students' mimetic processes (observation, imitation and practice)

▶ Investigate how support for this learning, and its integration into higher education programmes, will optimise its effect

▶ Be offered illustrations of the augmentation that is provided by enriching students' experiences through tutors' pedagogic practices

▶ Discover ways in which students can engage with what they experience and reconcile what they have learnt across the different settings of educational institutions and workplaces

▶ Engaging students in work-based learning experiences

This book has largely focused on work-based learners as employed students who enrol with an higher education institution (HEI) having already learnt a good deal via their experience of work and life; however, full-time students in HEIs can also learn in and through work-based experiences, and the integration of such learning within programmes of study has now become a common feature of contemporary higher education (HE) provision. Such experiences are central to effective student learning and graduate outcomes, in particular work readiness (Department for Innovation, Universities and Skills, 2008; OECD, 2010). Yet, much of the learning arising through work-based experiences occurs outside of organised teaching experiences: that is, beyond the immediate influence of tutors and educational institutions, and those experiences and the learning arising from them may, or may not, be aligned with what are the intended learning outcomes of the educational programmes. Importantly, this learning is largely initiated, directed and mediated by students themselves through their workplace engagements and activities, rather than being taught (Billett, 2014c). Consequently, it becomes increasingly necessary to consider HE students' roles in learning processes within workplaces and how that learning can be supported and augmented by, but also reconciled with, what is intended to be learnt in their education programmes (Billett, 2014a). Yet, rather than being seen as that is, independent students working and learning alone, this learning process is highly interdependent as students engage and interact with others, artefacts and practices, albeit in ways that are student initiated and directed (Billett, 2014b): there is nothing particularly unusual about this learner-focused process. It is how most learning across individuals' lives occurs (Billett, 2014d). That is, through their engagement in activities and interactions of different kinds in educational institutions, at home, at work or elsewhere. Optimising this learning in work settings and supporting its integration in their programmes of study necessitates consideration of how to prepare and assist students for those activities and interaction: that is, to promote their capacity and readiness for being effective interdependent learners.

Central to this directed, but interdependent, kind of development is that which is learnt through observation, imitation and rehearsal, referred to as mimesis or mimetic learning (Billett, 2014d). Whilst having limitations and shortcomings, this process of learning is foundational to human cognition, knowing and learning and contributes directly to individuals' ongoing development (Lacoboni, 2005) across the life course. Yet, within schooled societies, this process of learning is often downplayed, marginalised or even dismissed as being mere copying (Byrne and Russon, 1998). Yet, quite to the contrary, this learning process engages with and extends a range of human capacities, including higher-order cognitive functions (Barsalou, 2008). Accordingly, it can secure a range of learning outcomes from how to perform occupational tasks through to understandings about the best ways to proceed with work tasks, and from securing basic factual knowledge about occupational concepts through to rich understandings, such as causal links and associations between or amongst things (for example, problem solving or clinical reasoning) and the development of the values and attitudes important to the enactment of occupations.

Drawing on research from a national teaching fellowship project that sought to identify how best to provide and integrate experiences in practice settings across six Australian universities and 20 projects from diverse occupations within them (Billett, 2011), this chapter sets out some bases for students' mimetic learning at work and in HE and also for how you and your students can optimally use work-based learning (WBL) experiences and integrate what is learnt in their HE programmes. Its case progresses, first, by discussing the process of mimetic learning, before drawing upon the project's findings to advance concrete suggestions about how you might support your students to engage with and optimise learning in work settings and integrate that learning into HE courses.

▶ Process of learning through work

Human learning arises through what we experience and how we respond to those experiences. Through this experiencing, changes arise in what we know, can do and value. This change is called learning. As we have experiences all of the time and continually across our lives, we are constantly learning. In doing so, we consider what was experienced in the past and use what we know, can do and value to assist make sense of what we are currently experiencing (Valsiner, 1998). When we have experiences that are totally novel, new learning can arise that extends how we understand things, directs our efforts to make sense of what we have experienced and reconciles it with what we know, can do and value (Valsiner, 2000). When we have experiences that are familiar these serve to reinforce, refine and sustain what we already know, what we can do, and what we have come to value (Billett, 2001).

Of course, beyond these experiences being variously novel or familiar to individuals, different kinds of experiences have distinct legacies, leading to particular kinds of learning outcomes. To develop procedural capacities, achieving particular goals, such as performing work tasks, engagement with procedures to realise those tasks, and opportunities for practising them, can assist in learning to perform them effectively. Similarly, understanding a particular topic may well be best learnt through engaging with texts and activities that assist in identifying and testing propositions (links between concepts). Hence, concepts of mathematics, language, science and health-care might best be developed through engaging with texts of different kinds and with activities that develop, and assist in applying and assessing, knowledge of mathematics, use of language, scientific propositions and issues associated with human physiology and disease. Educational programmes often seek to provide particular kinds of experiences to direct students' engagement with particular forms of knowledge and the learning of it. Noteworthy here is that HE has often been associated with the development of strong conceptual understandings, frequently referred to as 'theory'. So quite intentional experiences are provided to develop and assess those kinds of learning outcomes. Texts, assignments and argumentation within written assignments are often used to develop these kinds of conceptual capacities.

However, rightly or wrongly, HE provisions have been criticised for focusing too much on conceptual development and failing to assist the learning of some kinds of procedural capacities associated with work activities, for instance (Department for Innovation, Universities and Skills, 2008; Universities Australia, 2008). This criticism has led to the claim that both 'theory' and 'practice' are equally valuable although this is not a very informed or helpful line of criticism. When students learn how to engage with texts, write assignments and prepare arguments they are also developing procedural capacities, such as how to read, assess the worth of ideas and express them effectively, for instance. More helpful, is the concern that these kinds of experiences may not lead to the kinds of capacities required for occupational roles beyond graduation: that is, the types of activities and interactions provided in and through HE are not generating the kind of capacities required to make smooth transitions to the occupations for which students are being prepared. Rogoff and Lave (1984) advised that 'activity structures cognition' and the contributions of those activities include the physical and social contexts in which the activities occur as they are part of that experiencing. The following case study illustrates this (Case study 13.1):

Case study 13.1 When education doesn't reflect reality: One student's first experience of the workplace

Stephen completed his course in clothing manufacture in Manchester in the UK during the 1970s. Although having done very well at college, his education experiences had been wholly college based. Hence, he had not come to understand the practices, processes and concepts associated with clothing manufacture where it actually occurred – in a clothing factory. His first experiences in this kind of workplace were therefore very difficult because what he had experienced and learnt did not resemble, and was not applicable to, activities in such workplaces. The point here is that the physical and social contexts provide a manifestation of how work tasks are undertaken, interactions occur and how individuals come to engage. Together, these factors all have impacts on what we know and how we organise that knowledge, and on our ability to use what we know, can do and value, effectively.

This indicates the importance of students having the range of experiences in contexts that resemble or constitute actual authentic instances of the occupations that they are learning about being practised. These experiences assist them to learn what they need to know, can do and value in circumstances beyond what they encounter in their educational programmes and institutions. So there is considerable worth in providing students with workplace experiences associated with their selected occupation. This worth includes accessing the kinds of activities and interactions that will assist them in performing those roles and then identifying how to integrate them into their HE learning (Billett, 2009b). This point emphasises the importance of not just having experiences of the kinds provided by educational institutions or workplaces, but instead, having both kinds of experiences and in ways that are effective in providing some kind of continuity or a planned set of experiences, designed to assist students effectively develop those capacities (Ericsson, 2006). Furthermore, the need for these two different kinds of experiences also suggest that they must be brought together and reconciled by students so the learning arising from each is not viewed as being distinct, but rather united in ways that augment their distinct contributions.

▶ Learning experiences don't always need a tutor

It follows, therefore, that a key element of students' experiences in work settings and their reconciliation and integration is the degree by which they engage with those experiences. Even if it were helpful, you cannot follow your students into workplaces and guide their learning in those settings. Yet there is nothing inherently problematic about a processes of learning not directly mediated by you as tutor, even within educational programmes. We know that much of children's learning, including that of important social and language capacities, arises through their everyday engagement with the social world before they get to school (Sticht, 1987). It is these everyday learning processes that generate capacities that permit school-age children to function and learn in school, albeit through the ability to understand language. However, the schooling experience can build upon what they know to assist them understand rules of grammar and syntax, for instance. Moreover, the vast majority of individuals' learning across their lives beyond schooling – their lifelong learning – occurs in the absence of tutors and others who directly guide that learning (Rogoff and Lave, 1984; Scribner, 1985; 1992; Ingold, 2000). So much of the learning and development associated with adult roles and relationships, sustaining our employability and securing advancement across our working lives, for instance, arises through ongoing everyday learning and is independent from teaching (Billett and Pavlova, 2005). This is true of the WBL discussed in the chapters of this book.

Yet both learning in the absence or presence of tutors or guides is largely founded on mimesis: observation, imitation and practice (Billett, 2014d). This process is likely to be central to students' learning through the experiences in workplace settings and then when engaging in integrating those experiences with what they have learnt through their courses and as directed towards course outcomes. Consequently, prior to considering how both you and your students can support that learning, it is worth outlining what constitutes mimesis and also mimetic learning

▶ Mimesis and mimetic learning

Mimesis comprises the process of observing, imitating and then reproducing what has been observed (Jordan, 1989). This is an important process for securing the kinds of capacities people need for being successful in education and practising occupations, for instance. The knowledge that is required to be learnt to develop those capacities needs in large part to be found beyond individuals because it is generated by the social world and they need to be engaged by it in order to learn (Billett, 2014d). So mimesis is central to how individuals come to learn socially derived knowledge such as that required for occupations. It is a foundational and key process underpinning human cognition and is central to individuals' learning (Baldwin, 1898; Reber, 1989; Marchand, 2008; Jordan, 2011). Jordan (1989) suggests it is the process we use across our lives in childhood socialisation, the acquisition of language and daily living skills, including those required for work and social activities all of which are dependent on the ability to imitate and the motivation to do so. The processes of observation, imitation, introspection and rehearsal are necessary for humans to: (i) understand the context for action, (ii) place themselves in the position of observed actors or in that of understanding the artefact and (iii) generate and reproduce those behaviours, actions and practices with their own bodies (Reber, 1992). So rather than mimesis being seen as uninformed mimicry, it not only requires but promotes higher-order capacities. Moreover, a reliance on direct interpersonal interactions is largely absent in anthropological accounts of how the learning of occupational and other capacities has occurred in circumstances outside of educational institutions (Bunn, 1999; Gowlland, 2011). All of these propositions position mimesis as the commonest of learning processes throughout our lives and also across human history (Billett, 2014d). From this perspective, Bunn (1999) and Marchand (2008) suggest a wide range of procedural, conceptual and dispositional capacities are acquired in this way and largely in the absence of direct interpersonal guidance. Indeed, the locus for and premises of this learning largely reside within learners themselves. So mimetic learning is:

▶ Used here to accommodate a broad set of contributions to this form of learning
▶ Founded upon how humans come to engage with the world beyond them
▶ Focused on how humans respond to experience, enact their cognition and generate representations in memory
▶ About securing and developing what we know, can do and value (inter-psychological or intra-mental capacities within the person)
▶ Premised on, and shaped by, the ongoing and foundational process of individuals' learning (Billett, 2014d)

▶ Tutors' practices to optimise this learning

There are probably two key practices that you can adopt to support your students' mimetic learning in workplace experiences and, furthermore, facilitate the integration of that learning into their programmes. The first relates to the organisation and enactment of the workplace experiences and how they are sequenced, the duration and being clear about the purposes for which students are being provided with these experiences. Given that the term 'curriculum' refers to the 'course to follow' or 'path to progress along', these considerations can be described as curriculum concerns. The second is about how you can enrich students' experiences in practice settings and then bring them together with those in their course work and realise the intended outcomes of their programmes. Here, these are called pedagogic practices as it is these practices that aim to enrich students' learning experiences.

▶ Tutors' curriculum practices

In considering the curriculum, you have two broad roles:

▶ Organising the 'intended curriculum' – what it is intended that the students will learn and what will be provided to facilitate this.
▶ The 'enacted curriculum' – what actually is implemented. When organising students' experience in practice settings, the first consideration is to identify the particular educational purposes these experiences are intended to achieve.

Within HE, there are a range of reasons for providing students with work experiences, which include learning about:

▶ Their selected occupation
▶ Variations of that occupational practice
▶ How to apply what they have learnt in educational settings
▶ The kinds of settings where they will practise
▶ Building the capacities required for effective work
▶ Meeting occupational licensing requirements

You need to be clear about what educational purposes you are aiming to achieve (Billett, 2011) and then attempt to organise the sequencing, duration and kinds of experiences to secure those desired outcomes. There are considerable differences in the kinds of experiences that can help students understand more about their selected occupations, how it is practised across different settings and in developing the procedural capacities to be effective in occupational practice.

Consideration should be given to:

▶ Where these experiences are located within a programme
▶ The length of the practices (from short observation onwards)
▶ The potential to experience a number of different kinds of work settings or several periods of experience in just one or two settings

---

Teaching tips: Effective curriculum practices for supporting mimetic learning

▶ When planning experiences, be clear about their purpose and align the students' experiences with the intended educational outcomes.
▶ Alignment extends to the duration of those experiences and how they are either focused within one workplace or provided across a number of workplaces.
▶ Deliberations about curriculum include whether it is necessary to provide specific kinds of experiences either to redress potential limitations of what is available in the workplace or to address particular students' readiness.
▶ Understanding that readiness is central to knowing the extent to which the students' mimetic learning is likely to be effective.
▶ It may be only when you become familiar with a particular cohort of students and with what they 'know, can do and value, that you can identify the means to select and enact appropriate experiences.
▶ When facilitating the enactment of appropriate experiences for a particular groups of students, in order to best meet the needs and readiness of the particular group, consider the type and most appropriate sequencing of student experiences and how they might be enacted to secure the required kinds of learning outcomes.

Research as part of my national teaching fellowship suggests that students prefer gradual participation in workplaces so that they can progressively engage in activities that are within the scope of their existing development. Therefore, they are benefiting from activities that they are capable of engaging in and learning from and which are not outside of the scope of their readiness for participation and effective learning (Case study 13.2).

Case study 13.2 Making the programme appropriate to learners' needs: Developing and sequencing content to cross cultures

In a social work programme that had a large contingent of international students it was necessary to provide those students with:

▶ Understandings about what constitutes social work
▶ The kinds of societal structures that support disadvantaged people
▶ The kind of societal values underpinning such institutions and their practices (for example, client confidentiality)

An orientation experience was necessary because many students came from countries without social welfare systems, let alone social workers. More broadly, consideration was given to students' confidence, including their readiness: that is, whether they had the base procedural occupational skills to perform effectively in workplaces, should this be part of their experience.

So prior to engaging these procedures in healthcare settings, students on healthcare courses initially learn about and practise these skills (for example, temperature taking, dressings, sutures) in clinical laboratories. However, these kinds of experiences need to be appropriately sequenced into the programme of study (that happens before their practice experiences).

▶ Tutors' pedagogic practice

In terms of pedagogic practices, the findings from the national teaching fellowship project identified those likely to be effective as follows:

▶ Before students engage in workplace experiences
▶ During those experiences
▶ On completion of those experiences

▶ Prior to practice-based experience

Prior to students engaging in workplace experiences it is helpful to orientate students to the requirements for their activities in workplaces, so they are aware of others' expectations. Aligned with this aim is making them aware of the goals that they need to achieve (learning outcomes), and also what is unreasonable for them to be expected to do, the kinds of support available to them and the duty of care that needs to be exercised towards them. Beyond this kind of awareness you also need to prepare your students to be active interdependent learners: that is, making them aware of effective learning practices in workplace settings. For instance, you may remind them of the importance of observations, how they might seek to engage (not too independently and not inactively) and how they might go about interacting in the workplace, for the purposes of participating and learning. Moreover, because workplaces are often contested environments, it may be helpful for them to be prepared to deal with awkward, confrontational and hostile situations before they arise. All of this can assist students to engage in ways that will support their mimetic learning.

Teaching tips: Pedagogic practice PRIOR to practice-based experience

▶ Establish bases for experiences in the practice setting, including developing or identifying capacities (practice-based curriculum, interactions).
▶ Clarify expectations about purposes, support, responsibilities and so on (such as goals for learning).
▶ Inform about purposes, roles and expectations of different parties (for example, advance organisers).
▶ Prepare students as agentic learners (in other words, develop their personal epistemologies – epistemologies are the processes by which humans make sense of what they experience and decide how to go about doing what they do) – including emphasising the importance of observations, interactions and activities, through which they learn.
▶ Develop the procedural capacities required for practice.
▶ Prepare students for contestations (for example, being advised to forget everything learnt during their studies).

▶ During practice-based experience

There are also practices you can use to support student mimetic learning in work settings during their placement, work experience, practicum and so on. These include not only emphasising being active in their work activities and engaging with others, and identifying situations which bring potential learning (meetings, discussions about cases and so on), but also finding ways to engage actively and interact with more experienced practitioners.

> **Teaching tips: Pedagogic practice DURING practice-based experience**
>
> It is helpful for there to be:
>
> ▶ Direct guidance by more experienced practitioners (such as proximal guidance)
> ▶ Sequencing and combinations of activities ('learning curriculum', practice-based curriculum)
> ▶ Active engagement in pedagogically rich work activities or interactions (for example, handovers)
> ▶ Effective peer interactions (such as students learning collaboratively)
> ▶ Active and purposeful engagement by learners in workplace settings

There are pedagogic practices that can only occur once students have completed their workplace experiences. Through sharing their experiences with others, individuals can more easily make comparisons and better understand and benefit from a broader array of learning opportunities. More than just merely bringing students together, it may be necessary for you to facilitate these processes to deliberately draw out similarities and differences and see how their experiences related directly to the kinds of outcomes that are attempting to be achieved through their educational programme. Part of this engagement includes the active reconciliation between what is being taught in HE settings and what is being experienced through workplace experiences and how the two different kinds of experiences can be understood and brought together. There are likely to be contradictions in what is being proposed in both settings and some critique (of what happens in both settings) may well be particularly important here.

Considerations here include the sharing of student experiences to emphasise differences in how occupations are practised and, through this, assisting the development of adaptable understandings about those practices. For instance, the ways in which healthcare provisions in a large metropolitan hospital are often quite different from those in a small rural or regional hospital might be understood through these methods. Specialisation might be prized in the former, while adaptability and a broader range of healthcare capacities would be expected of nurses, doctors and allied health professionals in the latter. Encouraging constructive critical considerations of what is experienced also needs to be encouraged. Rather than accepting what is being proposed in both the educational and practice settings, it is important that students come to critically appraise what they have experienced in both to develop further what they 'know, can do and value' in ways which they can subsequently apply elsewhere. The pedagogic practices you organise are important here because students, whilst having their experiences and engaging with them in the immediacy of practice, may lack the capacity to be objective, critical or even comparative. Hence, you may need to draw out similarities, differences and particular practices associated with specific requirements as these can assist with making explicit links between what the students are learning and the overall goals of their HE programme.

▶ After practice-based experience

Particular pedagogic practices can enrich students' learning experiences and prepare them to be interdependent learners. This educational goal is important for students to subsequently support their engagement and appraise their experiences gained through their placements. The projects within the teaching fellowship identified some practical means by which you might engage pedagogically with your students:

Teaching tips: Pedagogic practice AFTER practice-based experience

▶ Facilitate the sharing and drawing out of experiences (articulating and comparing – commonalities and distinctiveness, for example, canonical and situational requirements for practice).
▶ Explicitly make links to what is taught and learnt in the HEI and what is
  experienced in practice settings.
▶ Emphasise the agentic and selective qualities of learning through practice
  (for example, personal epistemologies).
▶ Generate critical perspectives on work and learning processes in students.

A pedagogic practice that was reported as being potent across the various projects is students engaging in small groups that provide peer support and collaborative interaction through which they can support each other, share experiences and collectively draw upon their range of experiences. These group activities occur outside the workplace itself (except, for instance, when large numbers of nurse or medical or physiotherapy students from big cohorts form these groups in their hospital settings). So consideration should be given to planning the formation of such groups in order to facilitate activities being established prior to students engaging in practice settings. The groups will operate outside of their work experiences and therefore give maximum support and impact.

▶ Students' practices to optimise their learning

Students' active engagement in experiences in practice settings and their reconciliation of this with other experiences in their educational programmes, as outlined earlier, is essential for rich learning to arise. The mimetic processes in which students engage are essentially a product of what they 'know, can do and value', as directed by their interests and energies. Students do not experience curriculum documents per se, but only what is provided for them, therefore, beyond the 'intended' and 'enacted' curriculum is the importance of what the students experience and learn from that experience (Billett, 2014c). Indeed, the pedagogic practices referred to in this chapter are about student engagement, not didactic teaching. Students engage in mimetic learning through their personal epistemologies; these epistemologies are bases from which they come to know about, respond to and value what they encounter, and appreciate the exercise of their efforts in learning about it (Billett, 2009a), albeit mimetically. It follows, therefore, that rather than a focus on teaching, promoting students' learning is most important. It is they who do the learning and you (and their experiences in work settings) merely offer them an invitation to change. Ultimately, it is how students take up that invitation, and in what ways and for what purposes, that shapes change (learning occurs).

Part of your teaching task is to first emphasise the importance of their engagement and direct their participation in workplace-related experiences in ways which secure the best kind of learning outcomes for them. Second, extend that engagement to assisting them to work together and understand the responsibilities of collaboration. Certainly, when students have completed their practicum (Chapter 10), they commonly reported that an essential, almost compulsory, element of their HE experience was for them to have the opportunity to discuss, elaborate on and compare their experiences. Not only does it allow students to share their experiences but also to resolve issues they face, both in terms of their work-and learning-related experiences. Challenges to personal confidence and competence can be addressed by group processes after workplace experiences (Billett, 2011). One of the limitations of mimetic learning is that it is an essentially personal process; having opportunities to engage with others permits an articulation of what has been experienced and a sharing of those experiences. Your intervention may be required to explicitly link what students have learnt mimetically in their courses and workplace experiences, with the overall aims of the course. The interdependence which is an essential part of effective (mimetic) learning can be given particular potency when links and associations, applications and limitations, dispositions and preferences can be made explicit, discussed and aligned with the kinds of learning that students need to secure their preferred occupation upon graduation. The following Case study 13.3 illustrates the important role of peer and colleague support when learning in the workplace:

Case study 13.3 Peer support learning in the workplace: Teamwork, networking and sharing tasks

Students in a public relations programme undertook work placements in not-for-profit organisations and struggled to identify how they would engage the organisations in PR activities because the staff within them lacked understanding about these processes and were reliant upon the students.

The demands of such an activity led some of the students to disassociate themselves with the task and allow others to take an unreasonable amount of the work burden. As a result they were not learning how to work as a team, which was the intent of the experience.

In this case it would have been useful if the tutor had emphasised the importance of students working together, forming supportive groups and arranging interactions with peers to provide a supportive environment through which they could:

▶ Share experiences
▶ Consolidate what they were learning
▶ Act as support when circumstances became difficult for them
▶ Communicate effectively
▶ Articulate their feelings
▶ Find connections, commonalities and differences

▶ Key findings from the teaching fellowship

The key findings from the teaching fellowship for helping with student engagement in work-integrated learning experiences are the following:

▶ Students' interest and readiness to engage in the learning process is central.

▶ Contemporary HE students are 'time jealous'. This goes beyond merely lacking time (being time poor); students described a strategic use of their time, allocating time and energy to what they believed to be a worthwhile and necessary investment.

▶ Many HE students have significant amounts of paid part-time work outside of their study commitments (and some WBL students have full-time jobs).

▶ Many HE students have family and social commitments to fulfil.

▶ Work placements/experiences are often very time consuming and can take students away from securing the paid part-time work they need to pay for food and accommodation and other priorities.

▶ If students perceive that particular workplace experiences are not worthwhile they will either reject or treat superficially their engagement in that task.

▶ Energies are directed towards assessable tasks or those that place students in a particular situation which is important or threatening to them.

▶ Students are concerned about how they balance engagement between the HEI and workplace supervision, which focuses their attention on what they needed to know, do and value.

▶ Students prefer to participate incrementally in work-related activities, in ways that reflect their readiness.

▶ Students prefer to understand the work environment and the kinds of roles involved and ways those roles need to be enacted before being placed in the situation where they have to perform work tasks.

▶ Students prefer performance requirements to be staged (making sense in terms of incremental learning and addressing learner readiness).

▶ Students' readiness to perform and abilities to learn effectively need to be considered in relation to, and to be included as part of, the intended and enacted curriculum and then to be supported by specific pedagogic practices.

SUMMARY

▶ Both placement students and employed work-based learners need to be active learners during their time in workplace settings, whether HEI-organised placements or their own job. This will help them to participate in effective ways in both the work activities and in exercising and promoting their mimetic learning processes.

▶ To aid these processes students need to be informed about workplace learning, convinced of its worthand adequately assisted to realise its potential.

▶ Whilst being essential, and in some ways a separate experience to those that can be provided in HE settings, these experiences are important for the requirements of effective practice and also for preparing students to be able to continue to engage and learn across their working lives.

▶ Effective mimetic learning can assist learners to respond to everyday challenges, opportunities and the need for ongoing learning across their working lives.

▶ References

Baldwin, J. M. (1898) On selective thinking. *The Psychological Review.* 1, pp. 1–24.

Barsalou, L. W. (2008) Grounded cognition. *Annual Review of Psychology.* 59, pp. 617–645.

Billett, S. (2001) Learning through work: Workplace affordances and individual engagement. *Journal of Workplace Learning.* 13 (5), pp. 209–214.

Billett, S. (2009a) Personal epistemologies, work and learning. *Educational Research Review.* 4, pp. 210–219.

Billett, S. (2009b) Realising the educational worth of integrating work experiences in higher education. *Studies in Higher Education.* 34 (7), pp. 827–843.

Billett, S. (2011) *Curriculum and Pedagogic Bases for Effectively Integrating Practice-based Experiences.* Sydney: Australian Learning and Teaching Council.

Billett, S. (2014a) Integrating learning experiences across tertiary education and practice settings: A socio-personal account. *Educational Research Review.* 12 (C), pp. 1–13.

Billett, S. (2014b) Interdependence on the boundaries between working and learning, in Harteis, C., Rausch, A. and Seifried, J. (Eds), *Discourses on Professional Learning: On the Boundary Between Learning and Working* pp. 369–386. Dordrecht, The Netherlands: Springer.

Billett, S. (2014c). Mediating learning at work: Personal mediations of social and brute facts in Harteis, C., Rausch, A. and Seifried, J. (Eds), *Discourses on Professional Learning: On the Boundary Between Learning and Working,* pp. 75–93, . Dordrecht, The Netherlands: Springer.

Billett, S. (2014d) *Mimetic Learning at Work: Learning in the Circumstances of Practice.* Dordrecht, The Nertherlands: Springer.

Billett, S. and Pavlova, M. (2005) Learning through working life: Self and individuals' agentic action. *International Journal of Lifelong Education.* 24 (3), pp. 195–211.

Bunn, S. (1999) The nomad's apprentice: Different kinds of apprenticeship among Kyrgyz nomads in Central Asia, in Ainely, P. and Rainbird, H. (Eds), *Apprenticeship: Towards a New Paradigm of Learning,* pp. 74–85. London: Kogan Page.

Byrne, R. W. and Russon, A. (1998) Learning by imitation: A hierarchical approach. *Behavioral and Brain Science.* 21 (5), pp. 667–721.

Department for Innovation, Universities and Skills (2008) *Higher Education at Work: High Skills: High Value.* Sheffield: Department for Innovation, Universities and Skills.

Ericsson, K. A. (2006) The influence of experience and deliberate practice on the development of superior expert performance, in Ericsson, K. A., Charness, N., Feltowich, P. J. and Hoffmann, R. R. (Eds), *The Cambridge Handbook of Expertise and Expert Performance,* pp. 685–705. Cambridge: Cambridge University Press.

Gowlland, G. (2012) Learning craft skills in China: Apprenticeship and social capital in an aritsan community of practice. *Anthropology and Education Quarterly.* 43 (4), pp. 358–371.

Ingold, T. (2000) *The Perception of the Environment: Essays on Livelihod, Dwelling and Skill.* London: Routledge.

Jordan, B. (1989) Cosmopolitical obstetrics: Some insights from the training of traditional midwives. *Social Science and Medicine.* 28 (9), pp. 925–944.

Jordan, B. (2011) *The Double Helix of Learning: Knowledge Transfer in Traditional and Techno-centric Communities.* California, US: Palo Alto Research Center.

Lacoboni, M. (2005) Neural mechanism of imitation. *Current Opinions in Neurobiology.* 15, pp. 632–637.

Marchand, T. H. J. (2008) Muscles, morals and mind: Craft apprenticeship and the formation of person. *British Journal of Education Studies.* 56 (3), pp. 245–271.

OECD. (2010) *Learning for Jobs.* Paris: OECD.

Reber, A. S. (1989) Implicit learning and tacit knowledge. *Journal of Experimental Psychology.* 118 (3), pp. 219–235.

Reber, A. S. (1992) An evolutionary context for the cognitive unconscious. *Philosophical Psychology.* 5 (1), pp. 33–51.

Rogoff, B., and Lave, J. (Eds) (1984) *Everyday Cognition: Its Development in Social Context.* Cambridge: Harvard University Press.

Scribner, S. (1985) Knowledge at work. *Anthropology and Education Quarterly.* 16, pp. 199–206.

Scribner, S. (1992) Mind in action: A functional approach to thinking. *The Quarterly Newsletter of the Laboratory of Comparative Human Cognition.* 14 (4), pp. 103–110 (Reprint of 1983 lecture).

Sticht, T. J. (1987) *Functional Context Education.* San Diego, CA: Applied Cognitive and Behavioural Science.

Universities Australia (2008) *A National Internship Scheme: Enhancing the Skills and Work-readiness of Australian University Graduates.* Canberra: Universities Australia.

Valsiner, J. (1998) *The Guided Mind: A Sociogenetic Approach to Personality.* Cambridge: Harvard University Press.

Valsiner, J. (2000) *Culture and Human Development.* London: Sage Publications.

▶ Recommended further reading

Flint, K. J. (2011) Deconstructing workplace 'know how' and 'tacit knowledge'. *Higher Education, Skills and Work-based Learning.* 1 (2), pp. 128–146.

Appendix   Ethics and the work-based learner

One of the differences between traditional students and work-based learners is the ethical issues that arise when they are studying. Usually ethical concerns only arise when undertaking research studies and consequently may not be of immediate concern for traditional university students. Increasingly, however, awareness of the implications of studying at work, and even undertaking desk-based projects, even those which do not require primary data, has highlighted some issues that may need to be discussed with learners.

The baseline assumption with an ethical approach to learning and working is that one's own actions should do no harm to others, should not infringe the rights or dignity of others and should seek the common good. However, these may not fully encompass the concerns of others.

The checklist below may help you to develop ways of working with work-based learners that take into account some of these ethical dilemmas. It may be useful to reflect upon this with colleagues and to consider strategies already available to you.

Ethical checklist	Methods and approaches
Encourage learners to reflect on their role: • How might their studies impact on colleagues and family? • What sort of forewarnings might be helpful to discuss with others so that there are no untoward surprises during the course of studies?	*Developing self-awareness of how the individual's behaviour can affect others is a useful approach and could be illustrated using a Mind Map or similar to identify areas of risk.*
Consider whether the dignity, rights or protection of others might be compromised through the proposed learning activities or project plans: • What, if anything, needs to be in place before the learner begins on this activity? • Should someone grant permission? Does the learner's manager know his/her intentions?	*Contemplation of these issues should lead to increased communication between the learner and significant stakeholders.*
• What could be potential ethical dilemmas? • Is there any chance that the learner will be confronted with cases of bad or poor practice or exposed to illegalities? • What contingency plans might be required to protect the learner, the organisation or the university?	*Discuss possible contingency plans with colleagues and learners to prepare them for this rare, but potential difficulty.* *continued overleaf*

Ethical checklist *continued*	Methods and approaches
• Who should be approached to gain permission to access data and information from the workplace? • Is the learner aware of this? • If the data is part of a research project how has the university approved the research approach? • Is it appropriate in relation to the learner's role and position within their organisation?	*See chapters 4, 6, 7 and 8.*
• To what extent might the learners potentially invade others' responsibilities when undertaking their learning?	*Ensure learners appreciate that many colleagues participate and work with them through goodwill, reciprocity and trust, and consequently assumptions made by a learner regarding participation in their learning may be erroneous and even exploitative.*
• Ensure that learners maintain anonymity and confidentiality of colleagues, stakeholders and other participants.	*Any information, photographs or documentation used should have permission from the learner's manager or the individual involved.*

Teaching tips

Discussion groups, online or in person, reviewing some ethical dilemmas, can help to raise the consciousness of work-based learners of the ethical practices that might be considered acceptable or otherwise. Offering an ethical model to aid discussion and analysis may help to provide a structure within which alternative perspectives can be aired. Set some ground rules for the group before starting such conversations, and ensure everyone has a way of being heard and expressing their opinions. You probably will not get consensus on an issue, but you will encourage development of an argument and recognition that individuals see things very differently.

Consider the following:

▷ What could the ethical challenges and dilemmas be for you, the organisations you work with and in, and your work-based learners?
▷ How might a company feel about its future business plan being scrutinised by a relatively junior member of staff?
▷ How might a school react to teaching assistants observing children's behaviour, even if not invasive?
▷ If you were a scientist working with animals, how might you feel sharing a classroom or online discussion with someone who seemed overly interested in what your work involved?
▷ How might you react if your manager was keen to take the credit for your project findings?
▷ What could you do to support your learner who witnessed some poor practice from colleagues when investigating requirements for a new policy document?

Index